Testimoni

GU00857771

The science of Tantra is unique, co
unique still, is a modern book on the a
maintains the original meaning and depth of the practice, yet making
it accessible to our time. Chandi Devi and J. Ram Sivananda's, "From
Om To Orgasm" accomplishes this. The authors have a knack for the
intuitive explanation of Tantric practices, putting them in a light that
all can benefit from -- certainly this book is more than theory. It tells of
the integration of the body and soul, which is the heart of this subject
-- relating our everyday experiences, emotions, and instincts to the
divine creativity within.

The authors thoroughly examine the subject from the traditional
perspective, carefully keeping to the teachings, yet adding fresh zest and
life, making them enjoyable and practical. At the heart of Chandi Devi
and J. Ram's words are joy, life, beauty, and love -- essential attributes
for the Tantric path. Certainly, "From Om To Orgasm" is a must have
for the casual reader, for one who wishes to expand their practice, or
for the serious student. Many blessings to Chandi Devi and J. Ram
Sivananda for this endeavor.

...Bradley Rockow, Vedic Astrologer, http://www.omjyotish.com

"From Om to Orgasm" provides outstanding wisdom for both the
Tantra curious and seasoned Tantrika. It offers philosophy, principles
and practices for both the sincere student and the casual searcher.
Contained in "From Om to Orgasm" are the ancient secrets of Tantra,
masterfully explained for the western mind.

"From Om to Orgasm" is a definitive guide to sacred sexuality
in the 21st century that draws deeply on ancient wisdom, I highly
recommend it to anyone who desires a deeper understanding of Tantra
and those who desire to follow this path as a way to experience more
bliss and spiritual growth. It will absolutely enrich your life beautifully.
Dakini, Daka and traditional mainstream couples alike will greatly
benefit from reading "From Om to Orgasm"

...David the LionHeart, Founder of Bliss Intstitute for Sacred
Sexuality www.blisstantrayoga.com

This book is a regular "everything you ever wanted to know about tantra and forgot to ask"! I don't think most Americans have any idea the depth of the path. Chandi and Siva clearly and concisely inform the reader so you know what you might be getting involved in if you choose a tantric path.

…Maia Berens, Santa Monica, CA, www.whataboutlifecoaching.com

In the fast paced and technologically driven world of today, we are far too involved with running around, working constantly and from everywhere, and trying to meet deadlines. The world of internet, laptops, Blackberries, iPods, iTV and iPhones has increased our social networking and accessibility, but has diminished our sex lives to brief periods of half hearted enjoyment. Yet, you thought you knew everything about love, sex and relationships.

In this book, Chandi Devi and J. Ram bring about a unique and meditative approach to sex. They talk about weaving an enhancing relationship with oneself, the beloved, and ultimately the divine, and about joining of the masculine and feminine energies of Shiva and Shakti. The book gives us a flawless, enlightened and uninhibited path to divine sexual expression and practices. It teaches the magic of improving communication between partners, which helps in healing the mind, body and soul. This sensitive, informative, intelligent and comprehensive book is definitely worth reading. This book is not about 'sex' but an authoritative guide to bliss.

…Sidhartha Pani, MD, Boston, MA

One can't help but benefit from Chandi's well researched, clearly written, and immediately applicable advice on love techniques from antiquity that are as applicable today as they were thousands of years ago. Your life, not just your love life, WILL be better after you read it.

…Dean Romano, author, Lexington, MA

…Outstanding and has full potential to become a classic reference work... recommending it to my students as a must read.

…David

Tantra is usually thought of as "that sex stuff. In fact, it is an entire spiritual tradition, and as such, includes a philosophy of all aspects of life, including sexuality.

Unfortunately, in the West, the focus has usually been only on the sexual aspects. In this book, the authors, drawing from classic and modern sources, personal experience, and a variety of associations by non-tantric traditions, present a much wider view of Tantra than is normally found in books directed towards Westerners. There are a lot of great concepts brought out in this book that are not covered by other popular books.

...LB, reviewer

Your book really was interesting. I think something like this is needed, amongst the overly done sexual aspects of tantra; amongst the simplistic and conceptually barren books on tantra; this book I think sheds some needed light on the core practices, and reveals how the body is instrumental in awakening.

...Bradley Rockow, Vedic Astrologer http://www.omivotish.com

From Om to Orgasm

The Tantra Primer for Living in Bliss

by

Chandi Devi and J. Ram Sivananda

authorHOUSE®

AuthorHouse™
1663 Liberty Drive, Suite 200
Bloomington, IN 47403
www.authorhouse.com
Phone: 1-800-839-8640

First published by AuthorHouse 4/23/2008

ISBN: 978-1-4343-4960-6 (sc)

Printed in the United States of America
Bloomington, Indiana

This book is printed on acid-free paper.

Ganesh

Lord Ganesh, also called Ganapati, is the Remover of Obstacles and the Lord of Wisdom who grants all success to mankind. This elephant-headed God, the son of Shiva and Parvati, has four hands and a big belly. In his hands are a rope to carry us to the Truth, an axe to cut away our ego, and *Prasad* (a sweet delicacy) to reward our spiritual efforts. His fourth hand is always extended in a *mudra* for blessings. His vehicle is a tiny mouse that represents tremendous wisdom, intelligence and presence of mind. We chant his most esteemed mantra, "*Om Gam Ganapataye Namaha*" to invoke his   blessings at the beginning of all auspicious opportunities, such as marriage, a new business or venture, before embarking on a trip, or taking an exam.

//om//

Table of Contents

Part Two: Iccha, The Burning Desire

Part Three: Kriya, Taking Action

Disclaimer

This book is not meant to replace competent medical advice. Anything contained in these pages is not intended to be a diagnosis, prescription, recommendation, or cure for any specific kind of medical, psychological, emotional, sexual, relational or spiritual problem. Any person suffering from venereal disease or any local illness of his or her sexual organs, prostate gland, or any other disorder should consult a medical doctor or other competent professional before practicing any of the methods presented herein. Most of all, we would like to remind the reader to practice safe sex.

To Chad & Erin

Preface

India is the cradle of the human race,
The birthplace of human speech,
The mother of history,
The grandmother of legend,
And the great-grandmother of tradition.
Our most valuable and most constructive materials
In the history of man are treasured up in India only.
...Mark Twain

Access to the Vedas is the greatest privilege this century
may claim over all previous centuries.
...Oppenheimer

A millenium before Europeans were willing
to divest themselves of the Biblical ideal
that the world was a few thousand years,
the Mayans were thinking of millions
and the Hindus billions.
...Carl Sagan

The aim of the doctrine of Hindu philosophy
and of the training in yoga is to transcend
the limits of individualized consciousness.
...Heinrich Zimmer

Throughout history, many of the world's distinguished scientists, philosophers, writers and artists have challenged the dogma of organized religion, exposing it as a vain exhibit of power and control over the masses, while applauding the spiritual wisdom and open-mindedness of the East, particularly in India. Eastern spirituality has always embraced reverence and respect of God's manifestion in other cultures, forms and gender. This lack of condemnation and judgment made a lasting impression upon the lives of history's most eminent men and women.

The teachings of the East place emphasis on the principles of *artha, kama, dharma* and *moksha,* (wealth, desire, ethics, and enlightenment) and on the concept of *karma,* reincarnation, ego, and a loving feminine/masculine Divineness residing within us, rather than a stern, fearful, patriarchal figure who is separate from us.

Tantra is that branch of ancient Hinduism that accepts sex between two people as a microcosm of the creation of the Universe. World religions have suppressed and repressed a natural disposition towards sex, creating a vacuum that manifests as fear, guilt and shame. Thus, we have become separated from our authentic Self, which is love.

Tantra has, unfortunately, received notoriety in the West as a shallow and "easy" yoga for unbridled, undisciplined sex. Tantra is actually a lifetime process that cannot be undertaken without self-discipline, and control over the senses, mind and emotions.

In the beginning, many of us may have an interest in Tantra because we desire to attract a relationship built on sex, intimacy and depth. When we enter into a relationship with another soul we generally start off with such optimism, clarity and enthusiasm. We are full of hope, energy and passion. And then the inevitable happens. We start to take each other for granted, our interest begins to wane, and our old habits creep in. So, we explore ways to bring the life back into our relationship. We try self-help books, seminars, sex therapy and even multiple partners. We look outside of ourselves for relief--but we still feel unfulfilled and empty.

We are willing to try anything. We have heard about an Eastern practice called tantra, but what is it, and how do we start? Is it safe? Is it necessary to switch to another religion? Will it really work?

The authors will attempt to answer these questions--to clarify and identify the components that comprise the traditional practice of Tantra, or more specifically, what is referred to as the left-hand path of *kaula* tantra.

The term *kula,* or *kaula,* (the "family" or "clan"), can also be interpreted as the "cosmic family", where the union of *Shiva* (masculine) consciousness and *Shakti* (feminine) energy, creates the bliss of *kundalini* (life force in the individual, energy)--necessary for personal transformation. On the *kula* path, aspirants seek and find a spiritual purpose in everyday life; hence, this is known as the "path of the householder". Many *pundits* (experts) believe that the left-hand practices of the *kula* path are the most powerful and highest form of spiritual disciplines. The *kula* path is also said to be the fast track to enlightenment.

The tantric path is known as the path of the *vira* (hero or warrior), because of the courage and tenacity required to battle the "inner demons" and insidious temptations that lurk within. The journey towards enlightenment and self-improvement is an arduous task, not to be undertaken by the easily intimidated. Like any worthwhile endeavor (such as getting a degree), it takes discipline, work, and application.

A purposeful understanding of the principles of Tantra allows us to change and find a peaceful and happier existence in life. The wisdom of the ancient sages is as valid today as it was thousands of years ago. The human condition is the same now as it was then. We feel many of the same emotions, suffer from the same fears, and battle with the same inner enemies.

Our presentation of tantra is based on original scriptures, teachings of the masters and our personal experience. This is not a scholarly treatise or a scientific exploration of tantra, but rather, a basic introduction into some of the principles and practices that comprise this discipline.

While several valid tantric traditions are available, it is not our intention to construct a comparative discourse on all these traditions. However, we have included some valuable Buddhist doctrines as it relates to living life to its fullest. It is our intention that this book will act as an impetus for beginning a self-study course of Tantra and meditation--whether it is slanted towards the Hindu, Tibetan or Buddhist traditions, or a combination of all. Basically, all the traditions stress the need for self-discipline, mindfulness, controlling the ego, and respecting others.

We have divided this material into three basic sections:

Part One concentrates on the basic principles of tantra passed on from the sages through scriptures, and oral traditions. In Sanskrit, this "information" is called *jnana* (spiritual wisdom and knowledge). Any ambition we may entertain is fruitless without an adequate knowledge of the subject, so in Part One, we will attempt to present a basic understanding of tantric doctrines.

Part Two focuses on *iccha* (spiritual will or desire). In this section, we present some basic objectives that humans have, such as gaining more love and passion, and overcoming fear and guilt. To attain these objectives, we must be willing to subdue our ego and unbolt a new door of awareness.

Part Three centers on *kriya* (spiritual and effective action). We provide a descriptive approach to greater intimacy, based on *jnana* and *iccha*. We define practices that improve a couple's bodily response and disposition to effectuate greater intimacy and bliss.

At the beginning of each chapter, we have a "Quick Tantra Tip"--an exercise or practice that you can do in five minutes or less. We suggest you allow a minimum of five minutes a day for thirty days to determine if the path of Tantra is compatible with you. Most of these exercises are easy to do and can be done while driving, waiting in line at the post office, in front of the computer or in the doctor's waiting room. You will not need much space, you do not need special clothes, and in most instances, no one will know you are doing anything. There are exercises to do alone or with your beloved. Either way, if the teachings resonate with you and you remain diligent, this practice *will* change your life. Finally, we will summarize each chapter by highlighting a particular challenge for each of you, plus an activity to do as a couple.

Tantra is an all-inclusive practice, where equality exists, regardless of class, race, or gender, and while we have attempted to maintain a neutral gender voice, in some instances, it was necessary to select either a masculine or feminine voice for easier reading.

Throughout this book, we will be using many Sanskrit terms, most of which have no comparable counterpart in English. Sanskrit, said to be the oldest language in the world, is called the language of God, because it has more terms relating to spirituality than any other language. Each *sound* and *letter* (not *word*) has a vibratory energy and meaning on the gross level, spiritual level and suble level. The reader is referred to the glossary toward the end of the book for the most commonly accepted meanings, appreciating the fact that a deeper, more profound definition exists in almost all cases.

We would like to give our deepest thanks to the late James Stout, who gave permission to reproduce some of his writings in part or whole. It is with great respect and gratitude that we share and incorporate portions of his works in this presentation. To Anthony Benson, thank you for the title.

We would also like to thank Swami Muktananda, Bhagawan Nityananda, Bhagwan Shree Rajneesh, Jesus Christ, Einstein, Thoreau, Nietzsche, Mark Twain, Ralph Waldo Emerson, William Blake, Carl Sagan, Plato, Einstein, Thomas Caryle, Oppehnheimer, Jnaneshwar Maharaj, Kabir, Babaji, Bhagavan Ramana Maharshi, Toynbee, Rumi, Swami Sivananda Radha, Alan Watts, Carl Jung, Lord Buddha, Leo Tolstoy, Hazrat Inayat Khan, Sharon Gannon, Napoleon Hill, Joseph Campbell, Aristotle, D.H. Lawrence, Heinrich Zimmer, Emmanuel Kofi Mensah, Dalai Lama, Swami Satyananda Saraswati, Helen Ellerbe, Voltaire, Yang Sheng Yao Chi, William B. Yeats, Golda Meir, Abraham Twerski, Oscar Wilde, Albert Pike, Mahatma Gandhi, Jean de Boufflers, Gustave Flaubert, Percy Bysshe Shelley, Gurdjieff, Alan Watts, and all the greats whose quotes are sown throughout this book.

To the Great Ones for their Sublime Teachings
To our Gurus for their Blessings of Infinite Grace
To the Supreme Mother and Her Consort, Divine Consciousness,
May we always strive towards Perfection and Union with Thee.
Humbly, we bow to your lotus feet.
Namastyaste Namastyaste Namastyaste Namonamah
Hrim Om.

…Chandi Devi Saraswati Kumari
J. Ram Sivananda

Part One

Jnana, The Search For Knowledge

Jnana, or spiritual knowledge, is the understanding of our self, our world, and our relationship to it. The spiritual masters of Islam say that if the soul is not allowed to grow, it can create chronic diseases, degenerative, and emotional diseases. When man forgets this, he damages his soul and is called "insan", which means "he who has forgotten".[1]

The longing to know Divine Truth drives us to seek and gain knowledge about our spiritual connection to other beings and the Universe, because without this, we feel incomplete and are lives seem purposeless and unfulfilled.

It is a blessing to have the longing of our soul, and even more, to have the passion to act upon it. Seeking of this knowledge is one of the three prerequisites to spiritual fulfillment and manifestation of mundane (earthly) desires.

---

[1] Grandmother's Secrets, by Rosina-Fawzia Al-Rawi, Interlink Books, 1999, page 83

Chapter One

The Principles

Tantra focuses on awakening the kundalini shakti (sexual energy or Life Force), and utilizing that energy for rejuvenation, inspiration and fulfillment. This chapter deals with the mental aspects of Tantra according to the ancients. You will be introduced to the knowledge and wisdom of many complementary disciplines that were given to seekers on the path of enlightenment.

The sages gave us specific life skills that are important for us to gain inner peace, live in bliss and have a more abundant life. Having the background and basics, and knowing how and why we do certain techniques are necessary components that need to be mapped in order to find a more successful life, as well as a meaningful connection with your partner.

The couple that understands and applies this knowledge to their lovemaking will build a stronger foundation and a more complete and satisfying relationship that unites them in body, mind and spirit. There is nothing higher than the divine union of two souls becoming One.

Here's a Quick Tantra Tip:

How to instantly convert negative thoughts and emotions to thoughts and emotions that feel good:

Twenty seconds of pure positive focus is all that is needed to change your state. When you are experiencing negative emotions, imagine you are walking on a path. On one side you have all the bad feelings and thoughts and on the opposite side is a beautiful scene, robust with flowers, the beach, or whatever you love and has meaning to you. Negative energy is just "trapped" energy. It is "stuck" there on the slimy side. Talk to it lovingly and invite it to come over to the nice side of the path. Then hold that focus for at least twenty seconds. Negative thoughts are simply *energy* needing to be changed and you can change your state by inviting them to the "nice" side. Just twenty seconds of concentrated thought should bring you relief if you have held the focus. Then, give thanks, smile, enjoy your new state and go on with the rest of the day. This method is also excellent when you want to eliminate old ways of behavior and manifest a new state of being.

Because your feelings are the barometer that measures your state, you can check your state often during the day. You can control your thoughts and emotions rather than have them control you. This really works.

Tantra

> When you make the two into one,
> And when you make the inner like the outer,
> And the outer like the inner,
> And the upper like the lower,
> And when you make male and female
> Into a single one,
> So that the male will not be male
> And the female not be female ...
> Then you shall enter the kingdom.
> ...*Jesus Christ, Gospel of Thomas, 22-4*

The term "tantra" comes from the Sanskrit root for expansion *(tan)* and liberation *(tra)*, therefore tantra is said to be the path of "liberation through expansion". Tantra represents an experiential aspect of the human /divine relationship that intricately weaves a tapestry of ancient principles, techniques, and contemporary practices, taking us from duality to unity.

Many scholars have placed the *Vedas* to 5000 B.C., which would make Tantra the oldest spiritual tradition, dating back to India during the Dravidian civilization (7000-8000 B.C.) where excavations of stone and clay figures of the *lingam* (phallus), and the *yoni* (vagina), have been excavated in the area known today as Pakistan. Archeological evidence indicates that the sexual union of male and female had a deep spiritual connotation, combining the unity of nature (feminine aspect) with consciousness (masculine principle).

Another typical tantric view, held by many scholars and *pundits* (experts), however, is that the Tantras followed the *Vedas*. For our purposes, we can say that tantric practices have their Vedic "equivalent", since both traditions share many of the same practices, deities, mantras, and yantras. Some Vedic texts, such as the *Upanishads,* support the tantric notion of *Kundalini* and chakras, even providing rather explicit sexual rituals.

Which tradition came first is not at issue here, as there remains one truth, which is that Tantra Yoga is a profoundly disciplined tradition that places an enormous emphasis on personal experience. Westerners are attracted to tantra as an integrative and all-inclusive spiritual practice, which makes no distinction between worldly wants and spiritual needs. It differs from other paths in its acceptance and use of all the senses, including sex and emotions, to help humankind evolve spiritually. Tantra encourages us to enjoy more fully the world in which we live, using our body as a vehicle to access other worlds.

Other spiritual traditions warn that desire for material pleasures is in conflict with spiritual aspirations. They favor intellectual learning over spiritual experiences. Human beings, however, have a natural urge to fulfill their desires, and unless these two impulses can be reconciled, we fall prey to guilt, perversion, obsession and hypocrisy. Tantra differs from other traditions in that it takes the whole person--and their worldly desires--into account. Tantriks are the "practical" theologians.

Tantra is a spiritual path for integrating body, mind and spirit as tools for achieving self-realization. It is a system of expansion and awareness where every person is invited to realize his or her full potential.

As a sexual art, tantra is the joining of two souls together in a cocoon of bliss, to reach oneness of spirit. Surrendering the ego is the key to entering this bliss and creating love and awareness.

By expanding our awareness, we learn to distinguish our limited ego nature from our authentic Self. As we begin to realize our own divinity, we can see the divine in our beloved, in all people, in all of life.

Tantra is the science of cosmic principles applied to our physical existence, with spiritual disciplines the crucible that holds it all together. Tantra is the convergence of truth, art and science, intimately accessible to the divinely intoxicated mind of a seeker.

The unmanifest Self, which is hidden, is undecipherable to the unprepared. Yet, behind every manifestation is that very Self. This occult knowledge is not available without preparation on the part of the seeker. Much information on tantra has by necessity remained an occult science, because the mysteries of the Universe are not meant for the masses.

We can identify tantra as a spiritual path requiring strict external moral disciplines and internal moral strength. Tantric thought is that all paths lead to the same goal--liberation and union with God. In tantra, there is no separation of "I" and "God". The concept of sin, guilt and shame is non-existent; hence, "confession" is not a part of this tradition. Tantriks believe God exists everywhere, and that there is nowhere he is not.

Tantra is a system of practices that takes us beyond our limitations--balancing and freeing us from our mental and emotional bondages. Contrary to popular belief, tantra is not a system for self-gratification or ego-driven modes of behavior. It is a spiritual path based on the principles of *Shiva* and *Shaki,* consciousness and energy. It is a high path that validates all religions, respects all teachers, and is all-encompassing.

===

Science is not only compatible with spirituality;
it is a profound source of spirituality.
...Carl Sagan

===

As practitioners, we regulate our own behavior because we accept the concept of *karma* (action and reaction). As we observe our habits and reactions to external influence, we can amend and rectify our actions and thoughts accordingly. We become the witness to our own selves.

When we quiet our mind and go within, we eventually replace our old habits with more positive states of being. Meditation and yogic practices cleanse and eradicate our pain and suffering, and help us release unfruitful patterns (such as the habit of poisoning our body with alcohol, cigarettes, junk food, and bad thoughts). We learn to respect our inner temple, the sanctuary that houses the divine being that was privileged to manifest in this life.

Fooled by ignorance, certain people,
deprived of the tradition,
imagine the nature of Kuladharma
according to their own mind.
If merely by drinking wine, men attained fulfillment,
all addicted to liquor would reach perfection.
If mere partaking of flesh led to the high state,
all carnivores in the world would gain great merit.
If liberation were ensured by sexual intercourse
with a woman,
all creatures would be liberated by female companionship.
...Kularnava Tantra

Unfortunately, tantra has become trivialized as "sexual tantra"; fabrications vitiated by those with addictions, irresponsible vanity and corrupt ideals. Although sexuality is one of the components of tantra, it is by no means the entire essence of tantra. To limit tantra to sex alone is considered an abuse and corruption of the scriptures, for tantrik study requires intense preparation, self-discipline and self-restraint. Without this diligence, we seek the inner sanctuary in vain.

In traditional tantra, preparatory work (through meditation primarily) and initiation by a *Guru* (a qualified teacher) is a prerequisite to the more advance practices, such as *maithun*, physical union. The *Guru,* by necessity, imparts deep "secrets" only to those devotees who are capable of accepting the teachings--that is, they are emotionally fit, mentally aware, physically capable, spiritually awake, and morally conscious.

However, in today's "ego-tantra", a more lenient, democratic system exists, which allows novices and anyone without the proper training and skills, to participate in all its "manufactured" functions, usually for a fee. The texts and scriptures advise that participation in these so-called "tantric" rites by the unenlightened is detrimental and ill-advised. Studying scriptures and the words of a true *Guru,* one who himself has undergone the painstaking process of purification, is the preferred way to benefit from Tantra and any of the other yogas.

Realizing it may be difficult to locate a self-realized *Guru,* a seeker could still benefit from studying with a qualified teacher (see section on the *Guru* Principle), in preparation for the arrival of an enlightened Master. In the meantime, aspirants are encouraged to further accelerate their own progress by gaining as much knowledge as possible on their own by:

1. Reading the words of the sages
2. Having a daily meditation practice
3. Keeping in good company (conscious people)
4. Remaining resolute and committed to the practices

Traditionally, the Tantrik disciple also had to observe strict guidelines, such as:

1. Offering worship, to the deity, to the fire, to the spiritual teacher and to the goddesses
2. Refrain from eating until offering food to the deity
3. Refrain from using the property dedicated to the deity, the *Guru* and goddess
4. Not engaging even for a moment in idle and unavailing pursuits
5. Remaining fixed in the practice of yoga or in that of the mantra

Although modern western culture allows for more lenience, respect is still expected.

Tantra is sought out for various reasons. Some people have a sincere desire for self-realization, and a passion for the teachings. There are those who are genuinely interested in sexual practices as a spiritual communion and are willing to make the necessary effort, and there are others who simply have an adolescent fascination for sex.

Tantra is not to be confused with sex therapy. Although sex therapy is useful in today's society, it is a tool for sexual dysfunctions, and should not be classified under the broad blanket of tantra.

We can draw a clear distinction between classical tantra and "neo-tantra", sometimes referred to as "California Tantra". Many do not actually have the prescribed background to qualify themselves as "tantriks". Some neos have little or no intention of ever doing the intense preparatory work required of them, and perhaps they simply are unaware that the difference between what they believe to be tantra and the actual traditional tantra is staggering.

Many neos separate their practices into four categories. Some follow the white, or austere path. Others participate in weekend red activities, which may include orgies, and open, demonstrative sex with multi partners; still others practice the pink path, which is somewhere between the white and red paths. The pink path focuses on soft-core exercises without any explicit sexuality and little spiritual preparatory work, with some psychology thrown in.

Indeed, this diluted version is fun, safe, and helpful, however, rather than blending these two entities, red and white--to create pink--red and white should remain as two separate entities. Pink consists of half white and half red--diluted and watered down. Red practice, focused on the lower chakras, is by itself unconscious sex, like porn.

White alone (upper chakra focus) is not grounding, unless one has undergone intense *sadhana,* spiritual practices. Without *sadhana* a person could be all in the head (i.e. intellectual) and still have no depth or experiential understanding.

The ideal is to "join" the two opposite polarities, not "blend" them together. We want to keep hot red in the lower chakras, and shimmering white at the upper chakras--simultaneously.

The power is in the joining of opposites, like in *yin/yang*, and *Shiva/Shakti*. The powerful energy manifests when the union of the two opposite polarities dissolve into One. This vibration of two as one is one kind of *mudra* (positioning) that leads to orgasm. When the union happens--not with another person, but with the whole existence, then it is *Mahamudra,* the great orgasm.

Finally, there are those who follow a black path. These practitioners engage in black magic, sorcery, and the macabre. Their language is power over others. Then, there are other cults, such as Wicca, and pagans who engage in sexual activities that they refer to as tantra.

There are some whose activities can only be described as "anti-tantra". One couple makes the outlandish claim that the *guru* precept has been obsolete for centuries, and they claim that their book is the perfect *guru*. On their "high path", they state a married couple must get a legal divorce and remain divorced for at least one year and a day, before they can join their group, whose convenient objective is to swap partners. They believe that they are practicing "freedom" and "non-attachment"--two attributes of the enlightened mind.

However, this is a *very* limited understanding. On a mundane level, we are, of course, free to "do" anything we want, but the "freedom" yogis refer to is freedom from the *limitations* of our ego mind, such as freedom from judgment, anger, hatred, fear, envy, worry, cynicism, infatuation and negativity.

Freedom means being free from the attachment to one's addictions--including food, alcohol, money, and drug addiction. Freedom is being free from suffering, whether it is from psychological wounds or painful memories. Freedom is being free from perversion, an immature fascination with sex and from other obsessive behaviors. Detachment and non-attachment to our ego is the freedom the sages refer to.

To be free from the confines of the mind, ego and *maya*, of what we think "is", is the ultimate freedom. On a shallow level, we think that freedom means we have license to do whatever we want to do, but there is a deeper meaning than that. Bliss happens only when we get out of our ego, and out of our head, when we open our heart and learn to surrender, honor and trust our own divinity and the divinity in our partner.

Tantric sex starts at this stage, not sooner.

What has happened is that people believe that "ego tantra" is authentic tantra. This has given tantra its undeserved notoriety and has cheapened what is a very divine and sublime path.

To add to this confusion, many well-meaning people believe that spirituality and spiritualism are the same. Tantra is about spirituality; it is not new-age metaphysics, sex therapy or spiritualism. Spirituality is about becoming one with God, with the goal that every action undertaken will merge us with the Supreme. Spiritualism, on the other hand, is about connecting with nature, contacting spirits and ghosts, or gaining insights in our lives through tools (such as cards and dowsing). While these tools may be very helpful, spiritualism and spirituality are distinctly different.

Tantra is an initiatory path demanding intense preparation before undertaken. It is a spiritual path requiring strict external moral disciplines, and internal moral strength. It is not for the timid, weak, or easily intimidated. There are no easy short cuts on the tantric path.

Tantra is the science of a spiritual journey. The discipline rigorously explores all energies and applications associated with human existence and is not limited to the intellect but for enriching our lives in every dimension.

All teachings of the Tantra tradition are in preparation toward our unfoldment of self-realization. The Tantra tradition uses two main approaches to the realization of Brahman: the first one is simply a gradual effort to release oneself from habitual or addictive behaviors. The second spiritual consummation is the direct experience of the bliss body leading to the dissolution of individuality.

Living souls are prisoners of the joys and woes of existence.
To liberate them from nature's magic
The knowledge of the Brahman is necessary.
It is hard to acquire this knowledge,
but it is the only boat to carry one over the river of Samsara.
A thousand are the paths that lead there,
Yet, it is one, in truth
Knowledge, the supreme refuge.
…Yoga Upanishad

The Paths Of Tantra

My dearest ones! Do not give up your worldly life,
your near and dear ones.
Do not waste yourselves away, rushing around in search of God
in the four directions, nor lose your own souls
while seeking inner peace and comfort.
Live in your own homes with your spouses and children,
making full use of your artistic talents,
or running your businesses or factories.
In whatever position your destiny has placed you,
whether you are millionaires or laborers, kings or beggars,
God belongs to you all. If you call Him with love,
thinking about Him with devotion,
He will reveal Himself to you.
He will grant a vision of the divine light of His love.
Then you will know that you are an embodiment of bliss.
You will realize, I am Shiva! Yes I am! Yes I am.
…Baba Muktananda

The Kingdom (of Heaven) is inside you and it is outside you.
…Jesus of Nazareth, Gospel of Thomas

The tantriks developed three paths of self-realization and each of these placed an emphasis on worship--either internal or external. Meditation and textual studies are internal, while sexual union, Goddess worship, and elaborate rituals, are some of the external methods of worship.

All tantric techniques fall into one of three categories--self-realization, transcendence, and the mystical path. Within these basic three categories are numerous branches and schools of practice.

The most austere path is the *Samaya* path, which strictly focuses on internal meditation in the *Sahasrar* (the crown chakra), after the *Kundalini Shakti* (the divine feminine energy) has been awakened. *Samaya* practitioners are absorbed in the ideal of *Moksha* (liberation), and dismiss the necessity of worldly needs.

The *Samaya,* or self-realization path, is a path of completeness in this lifetime, an effort to avoid another birth. The goal of this path is to be removed from this world, denying the senses, and practicing austerity. To become one with the Divine within is the ultimate goal of human life. *Samayans* believe their path is the highest of the three paths.

The transcendence, or *Mishra* path, is dedicated to *seva* (selfless service to humanity). Believing that this is the only way to free their karma from debt, this middle path participates in both internal and external worship of the *Kundalini*, situating the goddess upon the heart. *Mishra* practitioners believe their path is the highest because they exercise both internal meditation and external worship.

The mystical path of tantra, called *kaula* or *kula*, finds wonder and delight in mundane day-to-day activities, such as working, making a living, marriage and raising a family. Life is organized so that every action is sacred and nothing is condemned. This is the path for the householder to discover the divinity and role we play in the Universe.

Kaulas practice external worship and elaborate rituals. The path is further divided into two parts, *vama marg* (the left-hand path, which includes sexual practices and elaborate rituals), and *dakshina marg* (the right-hand path that does not glorify sex but does not condemn it either).

Vama marg followers look upon sex as a divine method for achieving realization in this lifetime. They believe that worldly pursuits and *Moksha* do not contradict each other. The Divine Mother is worshipped at the *Muladhar chakra*, the energy center at the base of the spine. Purified liquor, meat, fish and sexual union are often used during worship.

Kaula tantra is the path of enlightenment through the senses, involving the magical, mystical union of the opposite poles of *Shiva,* the masculine consciousness, and *Shakti,* the feminine energy. This tradition teaches that to know the body is to know the Universe. As a microcosm of the Universe, the body is worshipped and utilized as a tool for reaching enlightenment.

The profound science and practices pertaining to meditation and hundreds of esoteric practices for generating worldly and spiritual prosperity blend perfectly in the tantrik disciplines.

Kaulas identify with:

1. The Self (the Universal *Brahman*).

2. The Guru (coming through a lineage) is believed to be an incarnate of Shiva, bestows *shaktipat* (transmission of divine energy) upon the devotee through will, word, look or touch.

3. The Goddess, is worshipped through elaborate rituals involving:

- *Mantras,* (as the goddess in verbal form), which are imparted during initiation, by the Guru
- *Yantras,* which are a geometric representation of the body of the Goddess
- *Mudras,* the hand and body positions
- The system of the *chakras* (which includes the *tattvas)* and the *Sanskrit* alphabet establishing the goddess in various parts of the body

Jyotish, a highly effective and predictive system of astrology, *Ayurveda,* a holistic healing system, and *Hatha Yoga* are also important Tantric practices.

Within the *Kaula* path, there are numerous schools. *Shaivites* worship Shiva, Shakti, and their union. *Shakta* practitioners worship the Goddess. On the far-left, we have the *Ghoras,* who have a reputation for bizarre practices. The right-hand schools include *Kundalini yoga, Bhakti yoga,* and others. Left-hand practitioners say that only those who have first been initiated in the right-hand practices can progress on to the more advanced discipline of the left.

The *kula* path is considerably difficult because the aspirant is challenged on a daily basis, by not having the safety of living as a recluse, or in an *ashram* with other like-minded devotees. The *kaulika* lives at home with family, has friends and neighbors (who may or may not be seekers). Living and working in a mostly non-spiritual environment, the householder must maintain equipoise, without allowing any distraction to take away from their path.

Although there are many schools and branches in tantra, they share some basic commonality as well. There is a path suitable for each individual, and what works for one person may not work for another. We only need to listen to our intuition and follow our heart. Deepak

Chopra says that prayer is the way we talk to God, and intuition is the way God talks to us. Therefore, following our heart and trusting our intuition will guide us to the path that is perfect for us.

If a man is a yogin, he does not enjoy sensual pleasures;
while one who enjoys them cannot know yoga.
That is why the kaula way,
containing the essence of sexual enjoyment and yoga,
is superior to all paths. In the kaula approach,
sexual enjoyment turns into yoga directly.
What in conventional religion is considered sin becomes
meritorious.
…Kularnarva Tantra

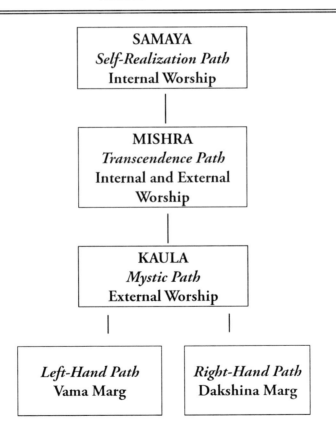

The Three Tantric Paths

Finding a master in the left-hand path is very difficult because they usually practice in secret. The left-hand path can lead to over-indulgence by those who want to justify sexual addictions and sense gratification; therefore, masters do not divulge their association with tantra. Their teachings are reserved for devotees who prove to be physically fit, emotionally stable, and mentally competent--those who have outgrown an adolescent obsession with sex.

Because of the power and potential for abuse, tantric masters will initiate only those who have already undergone intense preliminary practices and have sufficient self-discipline and control over their body and senses. If tantra were only about sex, all the complicated, elaborate and exceedingly difficult process would not be necessary at all. If tantra was used just to gratify an individual's sexual desire or sexual addictions, or if sex was the main objective for the tantrik, all this preparation and trouble would hardly be necessary, as there are so many easier ways to get sex.

Excess generally causes reaction,
and produces a change in the opposite direction,
whether it be in the seasons, or in individuals, or in governments.
…Plato

The Guru Principle

Gururbrahma gururvisnurgururdevo maheshvara
Gurureva parabrahma tasmai shrigurave namah.
The Guru is Brahma, the Guru is Vishnu, the Guru is Lord
Maheshvara.
The Guru is the Supreme Divinity, and therefore we bow down to the
respected Guru.
…Guru Gita[2]

---

[2] Permission Swami Satyananda Saraswati

The term *Guru* means "one who gives light by eradicating the darkness of ignorance". *Gu* means dispeller, and *Ru* means darkness. According to the *Malinijayotttara Tantra*, the *Guru,* or teacher, is defined as one who knows all the principles of *sadhana* in their true perspective. He or she is reincarnated from Shiva and is, as such, the revealer of the potency of mantras. At his mere touch, the people get purged of all sins.

The guru principle is essentially an ancient Indian concept, having no parallel in the spiritual tradition of other societies. The only other close equivalent to the guru-ship concept arose in early shamanic cultures. For example, in indigenous Native American, Aztec and Mayan civilizations, "holy" men or women became the spiritual reservoir of their society, petitioning their gods through prayer, dance, and song. As the intermediary between the two worlds of spirit and matter, these shamans conducted rituals for healing, winning battles, food, and favorable weather conditions. The mystical customs of these tribes were passed on in an oral tradition for generations from master to disciple.

If "mastery" is obtainable only through a teacher or guru, why do we bother to learn from books? We learn from books in order to "prepare" ourselves and expand our basic and fundamental knowledge. Prior to finding a guru, books can assist us in determining whether or not a path or discipline is our calling. It should be noted that it is not always necessary to meet the Master in physical form. You may have his *darshan* (a vision) long after his bodily death. If it is your karma, a guru will eventually appear, either in person, in a dream, a photograph, through his writings or discourses, through the sound of his voice, or his will. However, your principles of faith and devotion must remain present.

Faith in the Master and devotion to him are the vessels that can carry us across the ocean of this illusory world. This Sea of *Samsara* (the illusory world) flows ceaselessly in and around us, always threatening to engulf us.

The tradition of devotion to the guru goes back a long way in *Maharashtra,* in the central-western area of India, where many of the greatest masters lived. In this tradition, God, Guru and Self are always taken to be the same.

Tukaram Maharaj, a great saint from *Maharashtra* said, "When you meet a saint, he makes you a saint". When we meet a guru that we consider a saint, and we feel is the right teacher for us, then, automatically, we try to be as much like him as possible. At the same time, the master is telling us that there is no difference between him and us. Disciples differ in their ability to accept and understand what the guru is saying. Those who are ready to accept the lessons of the guru become masters themselves.

Show me the man you honor, and I will know what kind of man you are.
...Thomas Caryle

The teachings of *Tukaram*, and his *Guru, Sri Siddharameshwar Maharaj*, follow tradition and place great emphasis on the guru-disciple relationship, regarding it as a sacred bond through which the ancient wisdom can be transmitted.

By his mere glance,
Bondage becomes liberation,
and the knower becomes the known.
He distributes the gold of liberation to all,
both the great and the small;
it is He who gives the vision of the Self.
As for his powers,
He surpasses even the greatness of Shiva.
He is a mirror in which the Self
sees the reflection of its own bliss.
...Jnaneshwar Maharaj, in praise of his Guru, Nivritti

Although the ultimate goal is to eventually become our own gurus, when we begin on a path, we need a teacher because he will reveal to us our own "inner" guru. The external and internal Guru is the same because the Guru is a *principle*.

Bodhidharma, a famous Indian Buddhist monk, founder of the Zen school of Buddhism, declared, "If you don't find a teacher soon, you'll live this life in vain. It is true, you have the Buddha-nature, but without the help of a teacher, you will never know it. Only one person in a million becomes enlightened without a teacher's help."

Lao Tsu, the Chinese philosopher who is traditionally regarded as the founder of *Taoism* writes in the *Hua Hu Ching,* "Find a teacher who is an integral being, a beacon who extends his light and virtue with equal ease to those who appreciate him and those who don't. Shape yourself in his mold, bathe in his nourishing radiance, and reflect it out to the rest of the Universe."

In the "Tibetan Book of Living and Dying", it is stated that there is only one way of attaining liberation and of obtaining the omniscience of enlightenment; and that is to follow an authentic spiritual master.

In the West, the term "guru" is used frivolously. It is a term used to describe anyone who has some expertise in any area, for instance, there are investment "gurus", exercise "gurus", self-help "gurus", fashion "gurus", child-raising "gurus", homemaking "gurus", cooking "gurus" and everything else under the sun. There are also many "false" gurus.

A guru is *not* just a teacher or expert. A guru comes from a lineage of enlightened masters and has the gift to transmit his spiritual light to the seeker. The guru has the ability to purify, transform, and spiritualize the life of the devotee. The guru may act like a mirror; drawing the reflection of our own mind out in the open for us to see, and he helps us attain victory over our thoughts and ego, so that we can experience the bliss of detachment from the ego, through the art of surrender.

Even if all the trees in the Universe are made into pens
and the whole of the seawater converted into ink
still it will be insufficient to illustrate fully the glory of the Guru.
…Kabir

In the west, we have an aversion to the concept of "surrender". Surrender does not mean being at the mercy of another, or being subservient to anyone. It does not mean we will be brainwashed, or be in some sort of weird cult, or in a passive/dominant relationship or in a superior/inferior situation. We can have teachers and still have complete control, power and will over our own lives.

Our ego resists surrender to someone who has more knowledge than we do. The ego, ingenious and cunning as it is, imagines that it is superior and does not need the guidance of a more experienced person. Somehow, the ego deludes and manipulates us into thinking that surrender indicates weakness of will, while it simply means we relinquish our ego.

The *Tantra Sastra,* Shiva's treatise on tantra, states that the true guru is one who is tranquil, able to control her mind, is humble and modest, earns a living in a proper way, and is a family person. Versed in metaphysical philosophy, the guru teaches the theory and practice of meditation, and loves and guides her disciples.

If you cannot find an already enlightened master, that should not stop you. You should look for a teacher who displays a firm devotion to Shiva and Devi, who has the ability to yield success with the recitation of mantra, has impeccable integrity and knowledge to assist you on your journey.

Shiva maintains that it is even harder for a guru to find a worthy student. He describes the three types of students.

If you take a glass and place it in a bowl of water downward, the glass will appear to be full, but when you take it out, it is, of course, empty. This is like the student who only practices when the teacher is around. As soon as the teacher is gone this student discontinues the practices altogether and does not apply any of the teachings to everyday life.

The second type of student is like a glass placed in the bowl of water at an angle. The glass appears to be full, but when you remove it from the bowl, it loses most of the water. This student will practice when the teacher is around, but when the teacher leaves, this student gradually loses interest and stops doing any of the practices.

The best kind of student is like the glass placed in the bowl of water in an upright position. When it is in the water it is full, when it is removed, it is still full. This student practices in the presence of the teacher and continues to practice even when the teacher is not around.

The *Bhagavad-Gita* in Chapter 12, *sloka* (verses) 13-20, describes *bhakti* (spiritual love and devotion), the qualities a devotee should have to gain the grace of God. Rishi Gyan Rajhans, a scientist and broadcaster, translates these traits as follows:

1. A devotee has no hate for any living being
2. Cultivates friendship and compassion
3. Give up the feeling of "I and Mine"
4. Is unmoved by happiness or misery
5. Is forgiving
6. Strives for self-control
7. Is always content with what he has
8. Has a strong determination
9. Surrenders her mind and intellect to God
10. Is not afraid of anyone; and none in the world should fear him
11. Desires nothing
12. Is pure and efficient
13. Is free from elation, anger, fear and turbulence of mind (accepts "what is")
14. Is indifferent to what befalls her
15. Is free from weakness of mind
16. Is free from the feeling that he is an independent agent
17. Has no feeling of elation and enmity or desire. (That is, is unaffected by pain or pleasure.)
18. Develops an attitude of mind that rejects good as well as bad things. (Unattached to pain and pleasure)
19. Has no attachments and should accept pain and pleasure, honor and disgrace, heat and cold equally as his portion (Does not mean he owns nothing, or has no relationships. Simply means he is not attached to results of actions, behaviors and habits).
20. Looks upon friends and foes alike. (Is not judgmental, but uses discretion)

21. Does not indulge in idle talk (a busy mouth indicates one whose mind is not still)

22. Is not attached to any fixed abode. (They can be happy anywhere.)

23. Is steadfast in mind

Adapting these guidelines from the *Bhagavad-Gita* can benefit not only our spiritual self; it can enhance the way we approach our relationships and life, in general.

The guru guides and inspires the student along the path, setting an example to follow. The road can be precarious without the guidance of a teacher, and any distraction could easily steer us in the wrong direction. We can minimize and even avoid a certain amount of risk when we are cognizant of what is involved.

There is a confusion that you have to have sex with a Tantra guru before you can learn it. In truth, you need the guru to show you your *divinity*. You need the guru to help relieve you from wrongful thinking.

All animals know how to procreate. What makes us different from animals is that we have the ability to make sex divine by doing it with consciousness. The guru shows us the light of consciousness, then it is up to us to practice every day, if possible, with a partner who is our equal. (Please see section on partner selection in Chapter Five)

The bliss of the sex act is the *result* of the preliminary practices. It is the result of *sadhana.* The bliss of tantra is not just ejaculatory relief or release.

The most important thing is to have an understanding and application of a new way of thinking, feeling and acting. This is what a guru does. He awakens you to truth and consciousness.

Once you have this understanding, you can apply this to everything you do in life. Your intuitive sexuality is awakened and your bliss life unfolds automatically.

Ramakrishna said, "Some realize the Self within them through the practice of meditation, some by the path of wisdom, and others by selfless service. Others may not know these paths; but hearing and following the instructions of an illumined teacher, they too go beyond death. The roof is clearly visible, but extremely hard to reach. But if someone who has already reached it drops down a rope, he can pull another person up."

All the Masters had a guru guide them on their sadhana. Christ's guru was John the Baptist; *Krishna* had a guru, the sage *Sandipani.*

Babaji taught *Yogiraj Lahiri,* who became the guru of *Shri Yukteshwar,* who became the guru of *Bhupendranath Sanyal,* who in turn became the guru of *Paramahansa Yogananda,* author or "Autobiography of a Yogi". *Yogananda* mesmerized the West with recounts of miracles by saints, and the physical manifestations of *Babaji,* the *mahaavatar* who re-introduced to the world all the branches of yoga that Shiva originated thousands of years prior, for the upliftment of humanity.

Vivekananda was the first Hindu to bring Indian teachings to the West in the late nineteenth century. Although he was not college educated, he astonished Western scholars with his profound understanding and knowledge of theology. A disciple of *Vivekananda,* *Ramakrishna* became *the guru* of many great beings, including *Shree Maa,* who is the guru of *Swami Satyananda Saraswati,* the author of the *"Chandi Path".*

Abhinavagupta, called the most prominent scholar and philosopher in history, studied under several *Gurus,* including *Narasimha Gupta, Bhuti Rajatanaya, Sumatinatha,* and *Shambhunatha.* From the lineage of *Vasugupta* and *Somananda,* he devoted his entire life to the worship of Shiva and Chandi, and wrote many authoritative texts of Tantra, including the *"Tantraloka".* He was the most prominent proponent of *Kashmir Shaivism,* the philosophy of tantric non-dualism--the principles of Supreme Consciousness manifesting itself as the universe. It is said that he never died, but he and a few of his disciples entered a cave, never again to reappear.

Magga Baba, Pagal Baba and *Masta Baba (Masto)* were the gurus of *Osho, Bhagawan Shree Rajneesh. Osho* was the controversial guru who openly criticized organized religion and governments, and was much misunderstood by both his critics and followers alike. This prolific master was dismayed that the press hailed him as the "sex" guru (because he talked openly about sex), and called him the "Gucci" guru not only because many of his devotees were wealthy, but because he also loved to dress well. Later in his life, when he saw how his teachings had been so misinterpreted and misunderstood, he encouraged his followers to follow the path they had mostly ignored, meditation. (After *Osho's* death, many meditation masters have deliberately avoided discussing the role that sex plays, even in a spiritual context, because of the hysteria and misunderstandings it might generate.)

Shankaracharya, the great Indian philosopher said, "There are three things that are rare indeed and are due to the grace of God: the human birth, the intense desire for liberation, and the protecting care of a perfected sage--a guru."

All great beings, even after reaching their own enlightenment, surrendered their egos to their gurus.

Om Guru Om.

Shiva, Lord Of The Universe

Mahadeva, Rudra, Ishwar, Mahayogi.
The formless God of regeneration,
as represented by the three tilaks.
They represent the union between Shiva and Parvati
resulting in creation.
All other Hindu Gods are believed to have descended from Him,
the Supreme Being.
… Anonymous

Tantra is based on the contention that Supreme Consciousness is divided into three principles of nature:

- Creation--Brahma
- Preservation--Vishnu
- Transformation--Shiva

Of this trinity it is Shiva who is worshipped in tantra.

The Puranas claim that Brahma created Shiva, but archeological discoveries indicate that Shiva preceded Brahma and Vishnu since both Brahma and Vishnu have their roots in the *Vedas,* and not before.

Shiva's images are both iconic (anthropomorphic) and aniconic. As an icon, he is a human being, but in his aniconic form, his abstract image is the cosmic pillar, which also evokes his phallus, or *lingam*.

Shiva is of pre-Vedic origin. Some scholars and teachers contend that around the year 7000 BC, Shiva, meaning "he who is always absorbed in consciousness", manifested himself in human form.

By uniting sounds and rhythms, he instituted music and dance to humankind, a contention supported by archeological explorations in the area. Combining certain sounds together, he created scales, called *ragas,* together with *tala,* the rhythm. These melodies were sung at the same time everyday, evoking certain emotions, such as deep spiritual longing, ecstatic celebration, auspiciousness, and divineness of the guru or deity.

Shiva is considered the originator of all the Tantra and Yoga systems.

He introduced and developed tools, such as the concept of marriage and the mutual responsibility of the couple, the equality of men and women regardless of caste, and the system of Guru-ship. Shiva also founded *Vaedyak Sastra,* or *Ayurveda,* the system of Indian medicine, but perhaps his greatest contribution was to introduce the concept of *dharma,* signifying the "innate characteristic" of human beings.

Shiva asserted that humans deserved more than just sensory gratification, and that through his teachings we could all attain the goal of Supreme Consciousness. This Supreme Being bridged the phenomenal and spiritual worlds and systemized it into the path that exists till this day.

Shiva's teachings were first taught in oral form to his wife, *Parvati.* Eventually, his disciples finally transcribed his teachings, and the *Tantra Sastras* became the basis for many of the formal yoga practices still in existence today.

The infinite Supreme Being manifested in two polar, but interrelated ways: Shiva, the Eternal Consciousness, and Shakti, his Creative Power--but both of these principles are not separate entities--they are actually two poles of the One Being experiencing itself. Humans feel incomplete when they identify with just the material and mental objects created by Shakti, the Divine Energy. Whether they realize it or not, they search all their lives for a connection with Shiva, Eternal Consciousness.

The *sadhana* of meditation reveals that all manifested objects are a play of Shiva and Shakti, and that both are simply two faces of one Supreme Being. This realization restores living beings to their original state of the *Brahman*. In fact, it is said in *Sanskrit*, "Eternal Bliss is called *Brahman*". We are able to experience this bliss through direct perception deep within our own mind. Well-performed spiritual practices help explore and master the mind that will eventually lead to the realization of our inherent eternally blissful existence.

Shiva gave us five spiritual teachings, called the *Five Makars*. He taught different versions of the *Five M's* according to the development of the student. The five *makars* have been subject to criticism, but since tantriks were always anxious to keep their highly powerful mode of worship a close secret, the criticism has not been a source of anxiety for them.

The first *M* is called *Madhya*. For the students dominated by physical instincts, Shiva told them to drink a specially prepared "wine", which had to be consecrated by the Guru. This wine was symbolic of being intoxicated with the Divine. (Like drinking the blood of Christ, the drinking of wine is a symbol of salvation.) For the more developed yogi; *madhya* refers to the *amrita*, the divine "nectar" that is secreted from the pineal gland every month. It also can mean honey from flowers that attracts bees. The Devi is also known as "She Who has a Bee-Like Nature" so this nectar attracts her presence in our lives.

The second *M* is *Mamsa,* the eating of meat, fruits, or vegetables. This is the reverent act of accepting the nutrition of the bounty of the earth. The Goddess promised to nourish the world with vegetables from her own body, thus she was famed as *Annapurna*, or "She Who Nourishes with Vegetables". The food we eat is her gift to us and so we honor her with rituals. Another meaning of *mamsa* is "tongue", meaning we should control our speech. This included using *mantra*, the recitation of power charged sounds.

The third *M* is *Matsya,* the eating of fish, which is partaking of the body of the Universal Life Force, as we swim through life on the ocean of *samsara*. The waves of the illusion are five in number:

1. *Klesa*--misery or suffering

2. *Avidya*--ignorance

3. *Asmita*--confusing the non-*Atman* with *Atman*

4. *Raga*--attachment

5. *Abhinivesa*--fear of death

In subtle tantra, "fish" refers to the two subtle nerves along the spine--the *ida* and *pingala*--which cross and end at the nostrils. Through *pranayam,* or breath control, we control the nerves and calm the mind for meditation.

The fourth *M* is *Mudra*, referring to a symbol or positioning of the hand or whole body, to exact states of bliss within. *Mudra* also means this inner state of bliss as we meditate on the *bindu*. "*Mud*" is joy or pleasure and *"ra"* means to give.

The last *M*, probably the most misunderstood is *Maithun*, the marriage of Divinity that resides within and without. Shiva taught that sex should bring forth an elevated state of purpose, that is, for spiritual growth, and that gradually the sexual instinct should be controlled. The union that Shiva taught to his more advanced yogis was the union of the *jiva* (the individual) with the Supreme, by raising the *Kundalini Shakti* at the base of the spine, until it reaches the *Sahasrar chakra,* near the pineal gland.

Two of the foremost texts on tantra offer an explanation on *maithun*. The *Kularnarva Tantra* says, "As for the last *M*, it symbolizes the cosmic process of creation". The *Mahanirvana Tantra* makes the emphatic assertion that in *maithun*, the participant should only be a *Swakiya*, the lawfully wedded wife, and no one else:

---

0 Consort of Shiva! In this strong Kaliyuga which has an enervating effect,
for the remaining fifth tattva viz 'maithun',
only the lawfully wedded wife should be made the participant
as she alone is free from all blemishes.
...Mahanirvana Tantra Chap. VI- 14

A commentary by Justice *Shiva Nath Katju,* a proponent of *Kashmir Shaivism,* regarding the *maithun* follows. He states, "The *Veerachar Sadhana* and the subsequent stages leading to *Kaulachar* can only be safely performed by a householder. In such worship, it is necessary for the practitioner to have a female partner as his Shakti and the wife is the safest Shakti. Solo efforts in Shakti worship are always fraught with risks and dangers. Wife, as his Shakti acts as a shock absorber and safety valve and provides a shield against adverse currents that often come in his way, besides helping him in his sadhana. But Shakti worship with another woman who is not the wife - a *parkiya* –is fraught with great dangers that may unhinge the practitioner's mind or may even prove fatal. It may be frankly stated that the worship involving sex union with wife is always in privacy of the two and any suggestion that such acts are indulged in groups is patently absurd and needs no comment."

There is still a third "secret" meaning of the five *Makars,* which was reserved for the advanced tantrik. Shiva stressed the necessity of a guru/disciple relationship because the tantric path was as thin as a razor's edge. He warned that without the guru/disciple relationship seekers could easily deviate from the path.

Om Namah Shivaya.

Devi, The Goddess Chandi

Tu hi sata chita sukhamaya
Shuddha brahmarupa mam
Satya sanatana sundara
Para shiva sura bhupa
Om jaya Chandi jaya jaya.

You are the essence of Truth, Consciousness, Happiness,
The form of Pure Conscious Being.
You are the beauty of Eternal Truth.
Beyond Infinite Goodness, you rule over all the Gods.
Be Victorious!
…Chandi Maa Ki Arati[3]

---

[3] Reprinted with permission from "Chandi Path" by Swami Satyananda Saraswati

She is Many, yet she is One.

In the tantric philosophy of the principles of the universe, there are two identities-- masculine and feminine--for the manifestion of that formless, nameless, unspeakable, unknowable force--God. We worship and identify with this formless force in two aspects. One is through Shiva, the male aspect of this Divine Consciousness; the other is through his feminine counterpart, Goddess Chandi, *She Who Tears Apart Thought.*

Chandi is the Vital Energy, the Creative Force identified with God. She is the Grantor of the highest attainment of perfection, who is described as the Supreme Lord of the Universe, represented by "ninety million divine mages" in her manifest forms.

Chandi represents the Mother Goddess of all creation. Through Her, all life emanates, and all forms manifest. She is also known to the west as Mother Nature, but Her realm is more than just nature. She is the life principle of the cosmos. Shiva, the consciousness and Divine intelligence of all beings, is portrayed as the sleeping godhead, inert until awakened by the magnetic energy of the Goddess. Through their Divine Union, life as we know it, is manifested. (Tantric union strives to replicate their heavenly union on an earthly, microcosmic level).

Chandi and *Mahalakshmi* are the same. Chandi, however, is "hidden" and is not widely known. Overt texual reference to her is rare, so she may appear to be nowhere, but since everything is derived from her, she is everywhere. Because of Her immense power, it became necessary to keep Her hidden, because power, in the wrong hands, could be disastrous. So, a "curse" was placed on the "*Chandi Path*"; requiring an "armor", "bolt" and "pin" to release its secrets. Till today, many Brahmins will not do any of Her pujas publicly, and there are very few temples devoted to Chandi, although, by comparison, there are hundreds of temples throughout the world devoted to Her worship as *Kali.*

In the popular books on Tantra, Her name is never mentioned. Instead, She is referred to by Her other names and forms, most notably, *Devi, Shakti, Kali, Durga, Parvati* and numerous others.

The Goddess is the wellspring of all energy of all life. Just as the sun warms and nurtures us, all energy emanates from Her. Shiva's energy is reflected from the light of Devi, like the sun and the moon. Together, they radiate the duality of the cosmos on a grand scale. They are the dance of life, the harmony of the masculine and the feminine, moving in perfect rhythm to the beat of time.

The Devi is the ultimate representation of infinite power, purity and strength of purpose. Although she is One, She manifests as many, and each manifestation has a specific purpose. The consort of Shiva, the unmanifest Goddess destroys the *asuras* (our inner enemies), such as, desire, anger, delusion, pride, greed, and envy and replaces it with peace, love and bliss.

Devi pervades her three incarnations. *Mahakali* destroys the darkness of our ignorance and *Mahasaraswati* conveys knowledge and creativeness upon Her devotees. Her function as *Mahalakshmi* bestows prosperity and beneficence. (We all assume many roles in the play of life. For instance, we may identify a woman as wife, seductress, mother, daughter, doctor, lawyer, etc.; still she is the same person--dressing, speaking and playing her many roles at the right place and time.)

Of this trinity, *Mahalakshmi* reigns Supreme, for the other two Goddesses emerged out of her body. We call Her The Divine Mother, *Tripura*, (the Three Cities), *Lalita* (She Who Plays), *Gayatri* (the Mother of the Universe), *Mahadevi* (Supreme Goddess), and we worship her in her sub-forms as the sixty-four *yoginis*, the eight *matrikas*, 16 *yoginis*, eight very secret *yoginis*, fourteen *yoginis*, ten *Kula Kaula* shaktis, ten shaktis of the vital fires, eight *vasinis*, the fifteen *nityas*, the *mahavidyas* and multitudes of other goddesses.

Tripura is the ultimate, primordial Shakti,
the light of manifestation.
She, the pile of letters of the alphabet,
gave birth to the three worlds.
At dissolution, She is the abode of all tattvas,
still remaining Herself.
… Vamakeshvaratantra

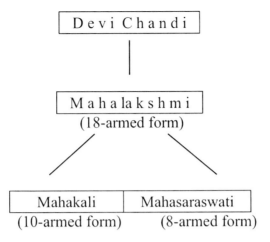

The chart above, according to *Bhaskararaya*, the foremost authority on Shakta Tantrism, shows Chandi as the *samasti*, unmanifest form of the Goddess. *Mahalakshmi* is *vyasti*, manifest; still she is pre-eminent over the other two *vyasti* forms of *Mahakali* and *Mahasaraswati*, who were created from her body. *Mahalakshmi* is foremost because she possesses the three *gunas* (attributes, qualities, styles and types of life):

- *Sattva guna*--truth, sweetness, intelligence-stuff, thought
- *Tamas guna*--inertia, darkness, obstruction, mass-stuff
- *Rajas guna*--power, energy-stuff, activity

Mahakali represents *tamas guna,* and *Mahasaraswati* has the quality of *rajas guna.*

The entire Universe is Her Divine *Lila*, Her play, and display. While Shiva is *Purusha,* Supreme Consciousness, Devi is *Prakriti*, the Principle of Nature. She is inseparable from He. Neither can exist without the other.

Tantra is a matriarchal practice, in which the Devi is the fruit of our karma. Shiva is our free will.

Om Aim Hreem Kleem Chamundayei Vicce.

The Chandi Path and our Inner Enemies

Our inner enemies are all manifestations of our ego. Through spiritual practices, we learn to combat the entities depriving us of recognizing the true nature of our Self. As manifestations of our mind, these enemies stalk us, tease us, taunt us, and threaten to strike at every opportunity.

The mind is a remarkable organ capable of creating a world of heaven or hell. It can be our best friend, and our worst enemy. It is our agony and our ecstasy.

Goddess Chandi, *She Who Tears Apart Thought,* slays the negativities of our thoughts and shows us that we, too, can defeat our self-created foes and establish a palace of shimmering light in the temple of our hearts. She lovingly tells us to give all our problems to her.

The *"Chandi Path" or "Pathah"* also known as the *"Durga Saptasathi"* or the *"Devi Mahatmya"*, is the majestic, poetic Epic in Sanskrit, based on the thirteen chapters of the *Markandeya Purana,* dating between 900 and 500 B.C.

Shri Chandi is the basic authority and essence of the Tantras; it is to Tantra what the *Bhagavad Gita* is to Vedas. The *Chandi Path* is a story of the conflict between man's animal instincts and morality, which results in internal chaos and disharmony. The three stages of life: creation, preservation and transformation are described in the three sections of the Chandi; each section dedicated to the corresponding manifestation of one of the three Goddesses. To solve and transcend this unending strife, we are directed towards a goal of spiritual and psychological evolvement through awareness, reason, mindfulness and creative imagination. The Chandi identifies Devi's defeat over the enemies, reminding us that we, too, can emerge victorious over the negativities that prevent us from owning our own bliss.

Each *sloka* or verse in the Chandi is a *Mantra Sastra* in itself, having an outer, more apparent meaning, hidden within a deeper, inner significance, completely undecipherable without spiritual illumination. This grandiose Epic is an esoteric, spiritual text in the form of occult teachings.

We shall describe the outer significance of the characters in the *Chandi Path*, reminding the reader that these characters, the inner enemies and internal demons, are within us all.

- Too Much--As we acquire things, greed sets in. Instead of being satisfied with our gains, we desire more and more and still we have no peace. Thinking we need more security, we hoard; still, we are never satisfied, because the grass is always greener on the other side. We live in competition, instead of peace. We fill our minds with unnecessary thoughts that bring us anxiety and stress. Spiritual wealth should be our aspiration.

- Too Little--If we don't have enough of anything, we become "stingy", and deny others and ourselves the right to receive respect, love, joy. If we have no mindfulness, we walk on the path of life with no gain. We are devoid of love, prosperity or abundance, and we become spiritually bankrupt.

- The Great Ego--Our greatest foe has only one purpose--to defend and protect the personality. It deprives us from realizing our true divine nature; for when we do, it becomes suddenly unemployed.

- Devoid of True Understanding--*Maya* veils consciousness, and we have not the ability to discriminate between reality and illusion. We lack *viveka*, discrimination, and we suffer needlessly.

- Haughtiness-This is a cousin of pride and self-importance. We get stuck on ourself; this is self-indulgence, so we can't find who we are.

- Fickleness, the Great Deceiver--With fickleness, we have a lack of *viveka*, and a lack of ability to choose. The will is compromised. If we have no commitment or purpose, our mind becomes unstable, our actions unsteady, and so we have no peace. We are constantly searching for something outside of us that we think will bring us happiness, not realizing all along that happiness is within.

- Memories--To dwell on the past is a futile exercise preventing us from living in the moment. We cannot embrace the future by regurgitating our past, blaming others, or ourselves or comparing our present experiences to our past. To do so tempers our judgment. We can be self-reflective, but not to the point of centering our life on the past. This steals our life when we can't enjoy the present.

- Wandering To and Fro--When we have no moral compass, or intellectual compass, we are easily influenced by the winds of time, easily swayed in every direction. We just run around in circles, but never get anywhere.

- Hypocrisy--If we preach what we don't practice, who are we fooling but ourselves? We may think we can hide from others, but we cannot hide from ourselves. We are so full of self-deceit or arrogance that our judgment is impaired or compromised. We are blinded by *maya* and hold on to our own dogma. We hold on to rigid beliefs even in error, and become blind to our own actions.

- Disbelief--This is refusing to accept a new reality, because we are stuck in routine and habits, or we keep our mind and heart closed due to fear of change. We typically don't accept our own grace because we do not think we are worthy.

- Arrogance--When we think ourselves superior to others because we believe we know more than they, or we think we are better-looking, more educated etc. we are living a life of competition rather than a life of creation. Self-righteousness and a superiority complex stem from our insecurities. By over compensating for our own inferiority, we create a superiority complex to protect ourselves from a sense of worthlessness.

- Anxiety--This usually occurs when we have irrational fears, when we are not present. We worry about something that has already passed or something that is in the future. This is a symptom of an overactive, runaway mind.

- Blindness--Being so trapped in *maya* we are unable to see the truth. We may look but not find, listen but not hear, witness but not see. We are blinded by illusion and self-denial.

- Temper--Rage is the result of unresolved anger, repressed fears and the frustration of not being able to find a meaningful expression or outlet for our pain. It is a way to compensate for our lack of self-worth. Usually it stems from an unjustifiable punishment, hurt or abuse, when we were most vulnerable, thus, we cannot embrace more positive emotions.

- Irresistible Temptation--We are so easily led astray by momentary gratification that we lose all sight, hindsight and insight without thought of the consequences. We do things without concern for the consequences, without considering the ramifications, whether the action is illegal or immoral. We are persuaded by the thought of getting something good with hardly any effort, like stealing, cheating, doing drugs, or other adharmic activities. We easily succumb to the siren of temptation, led by her sweet song and promise.

- Foul Mouth--Not only is a foul mouth disrespectful to yourself and others, but it is debasing to blurt out words without any control or consciousness. "Diarrhea of the mouth" is a disease that contaminates the outer and inner environment. Making false statements, lying, and gossiping are all components of the same dis-ease. Control your thoughts and your mouth will follow suit.

- The Great Frustration--When we exert our will and it is not fulfilled, frustration sets in. It comes from being overwhelmed and buying into the illusion that we need to be in control. This is the grandfather of anger.

- Want of Resolution--We want resolution and an outcome of a situation that is aligned with what we want, not necessarily for what is best. We want to force a sense of completion, rather than allowing something to gracefully resolve itself. This is how we try to control a situation, as long as it is to our liking. A *lack* of resolution is also undesirable because it leads us on a trail of unfinished or unresolved situations.

- Self-Conceit--This is not self-love, but false love, vanity and narcissism. Actually, it reflects a person who is very insecure, thus, has a need to exhibit a false sense of superiority. Because we feel unworthy, we compensate by thinking ourselves superior to others.

- Self-Deprecation--This is the opposite of self-conceit. When we deny our own worth, we create feelings of inadequacy and inferiority. We put ourselves down and have no self-respect or healthy appreciation for our gifts and talents. We see others as greater, smarter, better looking than we are. When we do this we dishonor the God dwelling within. There may be a "false" modesty, or a feeling of guilt and unworthiness for having special gifts or talents.

- Sinful Eyes--We deliberately use people, with a shrewd eye to deceive. When we have an ulterior motive, another agenda, with an intention to screw someone over, we have sinful eyes. Or, we look at situations, people and things only from our own viewpoint, without consideration of where someone else is coming from. This is sheer selfishness. We are unable to see the truth of anything.

- Passion--Here they are talking about an unhealthy kind of passion that creates egotism and duality. It is actually an *obsession,* accompanied by greed, excessiveness, and a selfish desire for gain without consideration. Positive passion, on the other hand, is *joie de vivre.* It is having enthusiasm and will to pursue your goals.

- Anger--Anger boils under the surface--silent and more insidious. It is a reactive emotion owned by ego, which hangs around undetected. People with a lot of anger have a short fuse, they are reactive and everything upsets them and sets them off. Unresolved issues cause anger, which cheats us out of happiness. "Holding onto anger is like grasping a hot coal with the intent of throwing it at someone else; you are the one who gets burned", said Buddha.

- Seed of Desire--Every desire we have sprouts more desires. The more we have, the more we want. We live in this world and by necessity, have material needs. It is okay to have desires, if they are from the authentic self and necessary for your survival. All desires are not bad. The authentic self thirsts for God. True desire is the thirst of our soul, a quest for love, knowledge and peace. Inauthentic desire comes from ego's needs that artificially drive us. Accumulating material objects: a big house, new car and other status symbols, drives us to want more and more. We are never satisfied. Hoarding and competition replace humility and gratitude.

- Confusion—Having no clarity or understanding of any idea or situation that arises creates a muddled mind. When we entertain contradictory thoughts we cannot make sound decisions. We have an absence of understanding because we are in overwhelm mode.

- Thoughts--These are the *asuras*, the demons or forces that obscure our divinity. Thoughts create our reality and must be brought under our control. If we do not control them, they will control us. Our thoughts dominate our consciousness and mindfulness, because we trust our intellect and reason. We are obsessed with our own thinking, which blinds us from seeing the truth. Ego drives our thoughts, and runs amuck if we allow it. We can use our intellect as a tool to solve problems, but we are not a summation of our thoughts. On a regular basis, we need a procedure to stop thoughts and the mind machine, in order to "feel". Through meditation, we give permission for the intuitive wisdom from our soul to emerge into full consciousness.

Om Hrim Chandikayei Namaha.

Mahaavatar Babaji, Guru of Saints

Love and serve all mankind, Assist everyone
Be cheerful, be courteous
Be a dynamo of irrepressible happiness
See God and good in every face
There is no saint without a past
There is no sinner without a future
Praise every soul
If you cannot praise someone, let them pass out of your life
Be original, be inventive
Dare, dare, and then dare more
Do not imitate. Stand on your own ground
Do not lean on the borrowed staff of others
Think your own thoughts. Be yourself
All perfection and all virtues of God are hidden inside you,
reveal them
God is already within you, reveal Him
Let God emancipate you. Let your life be that of a rose
Through silence it speaks in the language of fragrance
…Babaji

7000 years prior to the birth of Babaji, Lord Shiva incarnated in human form in order to give humanity his Supreme teachings through *agamas*, oral discourses, to his Goddess wife, the beautiful Parvati. Shiva laid the foundation for all yogic practices, indelibly imprinting the principles of the Divine for the benefit of all humankind.

Much later, an avatar named Babaji, of Nagaraj, together with his consort, Mataji, re-introduced many systems of yoga to the world, through the initiation of advanced yogis.

Babaji of Nagaraj
(203 AD)

In this system of guruship, Mahaavatar Babaji prescribed divine transmissions:

- Hatha Yoga--bodily postures through *Maha Buddha Baba*

- Mantra Yoga--chanting through *Neem Karoli Baba*

- Bhakti Yoga--the path of devotion through *Paramhansa Brahmananda*

- Jnana Yoga--the path of knowledge through *Dakshina Nurti*

- Raja Yoga--the path of the mind through the lineage of *Sankara* and *Kabir*

- Kriya Yoga--through *Lahiri Mahasay* in the late 19th century, who subsequently transmitted it to *Shri Yukteshwar*, the saint who was the guru of *Yogananda Paramahansa*, who, in last century, immortalized Babaji in his book, "Autobiography of a Yogi". The Kriya Yoga path utilized kundalini sexual energy for achieving Oneness with the Supreme.

- Tantra Yoga--Babaji initiated a woman into the path of Tantra. *Brahmani*, also known as *Bhairavi,* was a saint from Bengal who, in turn, transmitted tantric knowledge to *Paramahansa Ramakrishna* and a few other masters. Many of her teachings have become the basis for the Tantra that is practiced today.

Babaji's greatest contributions to yogis are probably the highly secret Cobra Breaths, which open the chakras through transmutation and transformation of sexual energy. At the first level Cobra Breath, each breath is considered equal to one year of spiritual evolution. So a regular practice of the breath will accelerate spiritual progress by years. Varying versions of the first three levels of Cobra Breath are taught at some tantric workshops or available for a fee. However, Cobra Breath practice without *sadhana* is not recommended, for reasons mentioned in other sections of this book. There are seven different levels of Cobra Breath, with each level corresponding to one of the seven chakras. These advanced practices are directly received through intuitive or divine initiation from a Satguru or Babaji himself.

Till this day, Mahaavatar Babaji lives in a cave in the Himalayas, choosing to appear on occasion, in order to give his timeless teachings and initiations to devotees worldwide.

Om Kriya Babaji Namah Aum.

Tantric Scriptures

*In turiya state, the aspirant is identified with Shiva consciousness.
The common man simply calls it the turiya or fourth state,
because it is beyond the three known states of waking, dream, and deep
sleep.
He has no experience of the turiya state.
...Introduction to Shiva Sutras, Jaideva Singh*

Tantra had its basis on oral transmissions from guru to disciple, even after sages had already transcribed numerous texts and scriptures. These transcriptions were written in a "twilight language", that is, language veiled in secrecy (utilizing metaphors, allegory, symbolism, and contradictions) so they could not be understood by the uninitiated or unworthy. The sages deliberately cloaked the teachings to preserve their sanctity, or, as we have seen in the *Chandi Pathah,* placed a "curse" on them, removed only through secret methods.

The *Tantra Sastra* is a presentation of Vedantic truth, which through modes of life and ritual meets the characteristics and infirmities of the *Kaliyuga* (the age of darkness). The *Tantra Sastra* prescribes a *sadhana* of its own for the attainment of the common end of all *sastras*--that is, a happy life on earth, Heaven thereafter, and at length, Liberation. Religion is in fact the true pursuit of happiness, called *sadhana sastras,* that is, practical Scriptures prescribing the means by which happiness, the quest of all mankind, may be attained. And as lasting happiness is the attainment of God-ness, they teach how man, through worship and by practice of the disciplines, may attain a divine experience.

The speaker of the Tantras and the revealer of the *Shakta Tantra* is Shiva Himself or the Devi Herself. When Shiva teaches the practices and the Devi listens, it is called *Agama,* and when they reverse roles and Devi assumes the role of Guru and teaches the principles to Shiva, it is called *Nigama.* For the Two are One. Sometimes there are other interlocutors. Thus, one of the Tantras is called *Ishvarakartikeya-samvada,* where the Lord addresses his son, *Kartikeya.* The *Tantra Sastra* therefore claims to be a Revelation, and of the same essential truths as those contained in the Eternal Veda, that is an authority to itself *(Svatah-siddha).* Those who have had experience of the truths recorded in *sastra,* have also proclaimed the practical means whereby their experience was gained.

"Adopt those means", they say, "and you will also have for yourself our experience." This is the importance of *sadhana* and all *sadhana sastras.*

The Guru says, "Do as I tell you. Follow the method prescribed by scripture. Curb your desires. Attain a pure disposition, and thus only will you obtain that certainty, that experience which will render any questionings unnecessary."

The practical importance of the *agama* lies in its assumption of these principles and in the methods that it enjoins for the attainment of that state in which the truth is realized.

=====

*As long as you are contaminated with notions of me or mine,
the self will not be found for it lies beyond cognition
and cannot be realized as "my" self.
… Tripurarahasya IX, 13*

=====

Gandharva Tantra is another important work having a left slant. It is from the school of *Shri Vidya.* The last chapter deals with the description of the physiological and spiritual phenomena known in Tantrik lore. It is given in the form of question and answers. Devi asks the following questions and Shiva replies.

1. "Where does speech originate and how does it disappear?" Shiva replies, "Speech comes from and merges in the mind through the instrumentality of *Avyakkta* and the vital breath."

2. "Who feels appetite and thirst and who sleeps and wakes up?" "Vital breath (wind) feels desire for food and drink and bodily fire enjoys them. Wind causes sleep and waking."

3. "Who sins and is bound and who is emancipated?" "Mind is responsible for sins and bondage."

4. "How is the etheric side of the soul to be accounted for in the body?" "When the soul being under control ceases to function, it becomes free. The soul has three sides, aerial, astral and etheric as breathing, digesting and speaking."

5. "How does the soul assume the physical body?" "The soul appears in the physical form under the influence of matter as *sattva, rajas,* and *tamas* and it is centered in the tip of the nose and heart. It lives as embodied so long as the heart and the head continue to function."

6. "Who is the soul?" "The supreme reality is the soul."

7. "How does the soul see?" "It sees through the body."

8. "How does it become *Sakala* (bound) and how *Nishkala* (released)?" "It becomes *Sakala* when it comes under the influence of *Prakriti* and *Nishkala* when it realizes its unity with the Transcendental Self."

9. "How does it get sustenance and what accounts for its physical appearance and disappearance?" "It gets sustenance through its actions, and appears and disappears through the presence or otherwise of limitations caused by action. It rises and falls like a ball in the scale of life."

Mahanirvana Tantra--It is not necessary to go to the Himalayan *Kailas* to find Shiva. He dwells wherever his worshippers, versed in *Kulatattva,* abide. We can seek him in His mystic mount, the *sahasrar-padma,* the thousand-petalled lotus through meditation.

Shiva promulgates His teachings in the works known as *Yamala, Damara, Shiva Sutra,* and in the Tantras that exist in the form of dialogues between the *Devata* and his *Shakti,* the Devi in Her form as Parvati. According to the *Gayatri Tantra*, the *Deva Ganesha* first preached the Tantra to the *Devayoni* on Mount Kailas, after he had himself received them from the mouth of Shiva.

After a description of the mountain, the dialogue opens with a question from Parvati in answer to which Shiva unfolds His doctrine on the subjects with which this particular Tantra deals.

Abhinavagupta's *Tantraloka* (the body of *Kashmir Shaivism),* is the basis for the *Malinivijayottara Tantra,* said to be of "divine" authorship (as revealed to the sages), and an indispensable tool for understanding the *tattvas* (principles), the *Sanskrit* letters, and mantras. Thus, it occupies a pre-eminent position among tantriks.

The *Atharva Veda* (from the *Rig Veda*) is a compilation of 5,977 verses to benefit the householder in his daily life, giving guidance in agriculture and herbs, trade, health and medicine, love and relationships. But since the path was besieged with thorns (over-indulgence, temptations and justification), the seeker was warned not to contaminate his body, mind or soul by associating with *adharmic* persons who could cause his fall.

The *Kaulajnananirnaya Tantra* is a text by *Siddha Matsyendranath* that unites the *Natha* path with the *Siddha* tradition. It discusses the worship methods, flowers, *linga* and chakras.

The *Kaulavalinirnaya Tantra* is a text on the *Kaula* system of worship.

Kundalini Shakti, The Life Energy

By what men fall by that they rise.
...Kularnava Tantra

It has been universally recognized by many spiritual and religious traditions throughout the ages, that the awakening and ascendance of *Kundalini,* the Supreme Energy, leads us to unity with God. The Chinese alchemists call this energy *"chi";* the Japanese know it as *"ki".* Christian mystics, describing their enlightenment, refer to it as the "Holy Spirit".

During the medieval period, Jacob Boehm related, "For the 'Holy Ghost' will not be held in the sinful flesh, but rises up like a lightning flash, as fire sparkles and flashes out of a stone when a man strikes it. The 'Holy Spirit' rises up, in the seven unfolding fountain spirits, into the brain, like the dawning of the day, the morning redness, though an angel from heaven should tell this to me, for all that I could not believe it. But the Sun itself arises in my Spirit, and therefore I am most sure of it." John in Revelations makes reference to "seven churches" and "seven seas", and the "mystery of the seven stars" are said to represent the seven chakras. The "Tree of Life" in Judaism also corroborates the *Kundalini* and chakra system.

Tantriks accept Kundalini as the microcosmic version of Shakti, who is known as *"Chiti"*, the Universal Consciousness. Kundalini is represented as a sleeping serpent coiled three and a half times at the base of the spine in the body of the *jiva* (individual). Chiti Shakti in her external aspect is all-pervasive, thus she is already awake. She is the creator of the Universe and she is the creator of our human body. It is this aspect of Kundalini within that the *jiva* needs to awaken.

Tantriks understand the union of Shiva, the male principle of universal consciousness, with Shakti, the female principle of nature and energy, gives birth to creation. This union awakens our potent but latent power and opens the portals to psychic states, which results in manifestation of our deepest desires.

Kundalini can be aroused in several ways, such as through meditation, mantras and tantra *asanas*. The flow of Kundalini with a partner sends the Shakti in an upward flow to unite with Shiva at the *Sahasrar* (the crown chakra). The individual then undergoes a progressive transformation. This blissful unity can also be experienced without a partner through an internal union.

Asanas are meant to control the body and mind, and a new unit comes into existence in which the old two are lost. This is the essence of sexuality and spirituality. *Osho*, the enlightened meditation master, states that tantric sexual union is falling in love with the Whole Cosmos. It is a total surrender to the Whole Cosmos. He says, "The inner life-force is aroused to its full potential through the mystic process of awakening the Kundalini Shakti".

The awakened Kundalini can alter our lives in many beneficial ways. It can motivate us and give us the ability to achieve excellence in whatever we do. By releasing this sleeping creative pool of Shakti, we can become the best we can be at whatever we do. She can improve our health and maintain our youthful vitality. When she fully envelops our being she awakens all our senses and energizes the chakras--the energy centers of our being--making us more effective. She can keep our bodies and minds ever youthful. She will improve our personal relationships, re-acquaint and re-affirm our relationship to the Supreme Consciousness.

We benefit from awakening our sexual energy because she is the creative energy reservoir that is within us all. As she fuels our creative processes and opens the doors of awareness to our higher consciousness, we become aware of who we are and all we can be. She gives us the method and the means to be That--I am That, That I am, *So'ham, Ham'sa.*

After having learned a few techniques it is possible to experience temporary, premature Kundalini and partial third eye openings, but without discipline, early Kundalini openings will dissipate and not have the potential for achieving higher states of consciousness. Instead, it can create anguish, mental disorders and anxiety.

It came as a flash and disappeared as such.
That which has a beginning must also end.
Only when the ever-present consciousness
is realized will it be permanent.
Consciousness is indeed always with us.
…Bhagavan Ramana Maharshi

Tantra is about sharing sexual energy, but more importantly, tantra is about achieving enlightenment with our partner. When we engage in any kind of relationship with another, we absorb each other's energies. This is one of the reasons we sometimes feel uncomfortable when in the presence of certain people; we are feeling discomfort energetically and psychically. When that relationship is sexual, the energies exchanged are much more intense.

Union should be practiced as often as possible with one partner, because each encounter will build a reservoir of energy, a storehouse of Shakti. When we invest all our energy in our relationship, the dividends will grow.

The Tantric System Of The Chakras

The knowledge of chakras and the Kundalini is essential to manipulate the energies of the subtle body through yoga, sexual union, and meditation.

The Kundalini in medical science is the caduceus, the serpent traveling upwards along the spine, piercing each chakra, exemplifying good health and well-being.

Tantra chakras, or wheels of life, are energy centers located along the spine in the etheric body at the intersecting points of the *ida, sushumna* and *pingala,* the subtle energy channels.

The *ida* runs along the left side of the vertebrae, moving upwards, on the left or the negative pole. The *pingala* or positive pole runs downwards alongside the right side of the spine. The *sushumna* is the central pole that is contained within the vertebral column.

When this energy moves thru this system she awakens our senses, our sexuality, the power of our will and the compassion of our heart. She gives us wisdom and intuitive knowledge and ultimately awakens in us the consciousness of Shiva.

A healthy chakra, or plexus, should be spinning rapidly with each chakra moving the next one along. A weak chakra spins very little, if at all, and can therefore slow down or halt the spinning of the subsequent chakras. When any chakra is halted or slowed down, illness sets in because the flow of energy is impeded. Active, healthy chakras not only stimulate our physical being, but they also keep us healthy and balanced emotionally and mentally.

Each plexus corresponds to a particular endocrine gland, sub-gland and nerve ganglia. These chakras affect our health and our physical, mental, and emotional states. In an underdeveloped or unhealthy person the spinning of the chakras is slow and unsteady. In a healthy person, the chakras are full of vitality and energy.

As we activate our energy centers, we will experience a rush of energy, and an overall sense of well-being. This is often described as sexual energy; a dynamic force that when used properly can awaken the creative potential within all of us, and lead us to states of bliss and ecstasy.

The human mind is never at rest and we hear constant inner dialogue. Using Kundalini to open the chakras improves our health and minimizes the self-defeating propensities of our minds. The propensities and expressions that control our thoughts are dependent upon the vitality of the chakras. The faster the vibrations, the more hormonal secretions are released.

In the Sanskrit language, there are 51 letters. Each of these letters represents a *vritti,* or propensity, of the human condition. Each chakra is represented by a *yantra,* a mystical diagram, with a specified number of petals. Within each petal is a letter, each with an acoustic root that represents each propensity.

Whenever there is any movement, or vibration, there is a sound, and that is the acoustic root. The vibrations emanating from the movement of the chakras cause secretions from the glands and sub-glands. The expression of the propensities depends on the normal or abnormal secretion of the hormones.

The movement and opening of the chakras begins at the *Muladhar,* the first chakra, at the base of the spine. The Kundalini ascends to the next chakra, the *Svadhistan,* only when the first chakra propensities are under control. In this manner, she will gradually work her way up to the seventh chakra, only to repeat yet another cycle. Each chakra may take months, and each cycle may require years to refine. With each cycle, there will be greater depth of understanding, and eventually, the propensities of all the chakras will become purified. Although the following charts depict a highly involved study in a simple manner, please be aware that there are more subtle meanings involved and their importance should not be underestimated, particularly in tantric study.

Other traditions, including other yoga or new age traditions, may assign different attributes to the chakras. We have, in some instances, included the corresponding astrology, tarot or other equivalent, since the reader may already be familiar with these tools, and would thus be able to make an instant connection. However, we would urge caution about "mixing" different theories about the chakras from various traditions, as it would be like mixing oil with water. All the contradictions from the new-age genres can be confusing. Our chakra descriptions are based on traditional teachings and personal observation. We have found there is less discrepancy among traditional teachings than the new age thought.

Kundalini release can occur through any of the yogic practices, including hatha yoga, meditation, mantras, tantra, even drugs and by accident. The possibility of a premature Kundalini awakening exists when the seeker has not had advanced spiritual preparation. It is generally agreed that a tantrik must be morally aware and responsible, and do his or her practices in a sensible manner. Tantra is not to be practiced in a frivolous manner.

Yoga is a deadly serious business, requiring more courage,
more intelligence, more will power,
and even more solid common sense
than most of us possess.
There is more to it than vague speculation
or iridescent dreams.
Not less but more, hard, daily grind;
not less but at times, more discouragement and flatness;
not less but more, study, more patience, more self-control.
Modesty, purity, complete and unostentatious sincerity,
that inward loveliness which perfumes the whole being that is something
of yoga.
Nothing is more quickly felt, more remarkable,
than the intense sweetness,
the touching simplicity of the true yogi.
It is already becoming clear that a chapter which had a Western
beginning
will have to have an Indian ending if it is not to end in self-destruction of
the human race
At this supremely dangerous moment in human history,
the only way of salvation is the ancient Hindu way.
Here we have the attitude and spirit
that can make it possible
for the human race to grow together in to a single family.
…Toynbee

Muladhar Chakra

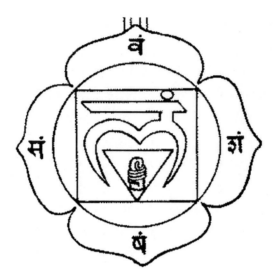

Muladhar Chakra

The discovery of the original man is the discovery of the eternal element in you.
And once you have discovered it and allowed it spontaneously to go anywhere it wants to go -- without bothering about your parents, your well-wishers, your teachers, your preachers – you may find that your original being in its ultimate fulfillment, flowering, is the buddha.
The buddha is nobody else.
…Osho

Sanskrit	*Muladhar,* root support
Mandala	Terrainian Plexus, Pelvic Plexus
Location	Base of the spine, sacro-coccygeal
Gland	Prostate
Organ	Male reproduction organ, the spine, blood, testes, vagina,
Function	Survival, possessions, early life, the "tribe", including family, church, teachers and others who influenced us as children and molded us, making us conform to the rules and traditions of so-called acceptable behavior, the status quo. These impressions are called *samskaras.*
Inner state	Stability, security
Number	One
Element	Earth
Kingdom	Mineral
Sense	Smell--perfumes, incense, genital odors produce excitement. The sense of smell is the first station, the lower soul
Musical note	C
Color	Red
Petals	4
Letters	*vam, sam, sham, ssam*
Vrittis (Propensities)	*dharma* (ethics and morality), *artha* (wealth), *kama* (physical desires), *moksha* (spiritual liberation).
Essential oils	Frankincense, amber, rose

Organ	Nose
Shape	Square
Lesson	Stability, materiality
Gemstone	Ruby, garnet
Astrology	Taurus
Angel	Auriel (rules earth)
Sephira	Malkuth
Tarot	Pentacles
Characteristics	Money, material comforts, possessions, support, home, job, vigor, heredity, security, passion, and trust
Healthy	Grounded, centered, belonging, pride, fully alive, able to trust, independent, determined, trusts in self and others, secure, patient, constant, ambitious, passionate, committed, survival. Sexually--plenty of energy, ability to orgasm naturally
Imbalanced	Weight problems, problems with feet, legs, instability, and eating disorders, obsession with money and material things, lack of financial security. Severe perversions, fascination with death, such as serial killers who rape.
Excessive	Greedy, egotistic, domineering, bossy, addicted to possessions, greedy, high strung, hyperactive, violent, dishonest, cunning, promiscuity, fascination with pornography, unable to focus on partner

Deficient	Can not reach goals, lack of confidence, feel unloved, not grounded, no confidence, suicidal, sexually inadequate, fearful, frustrated, alienated, separate, sexually lethargic, low energy, can't reach orgasm
Bij	*lam* (pronounced lung)
Motto	I have
Deity	Dakini

First Chakra Manifestations:

Cinderella Man, boxer Jim Braddock, exemplifies someone with a strong and healthy Muladhar. In combination with a strong third chakra, he possessed an indominable spirit to survive the depression. Anne Frank's will to survive the holocaust also is an example of someone who has strong survival skills, accompanied by the determination and will of the third chakra.

Five Minute Exercises to stimulate the first chakra:

1. Stand with feet about shoulder width apart, hands at the side. Rise up on balls of the feet, massaging the bubbling spring (the cavity below and in the center of the ball of the feet) and raise both arms above the head. Hold this position for a few minutes, and come back slowly so that your feel are flat on the floor. Repeat.

2. Stand with feet shoulder width apart, exhaling as you lean forward and touch both hands to the floor. If you cannot reach that far, just "hang" for awhile and let the gravity of your weight pull you down further. Take a breath in and bend the knees. Exhale and straighten the knees but do not lock them. Feel the energy moving in the legs after a short while.

3. Other grounding exercises are stomping, jumping, jogging, running, kicking or any activity that uses the legs.

4. A good sexual exercise for the *Muladhar* is to thrust the pelvis forward while contracting the anal sphincter muscles. Try to move just

the pelvis area. Thrust forward and exhale. Inhale and bring the pelvis back to the normal position. Do this exercise while standing, or sitting on the floor cross-legged, on the knees or even on a chair. Do this to music with a throbbing beat, close the eyes, and concentrate on the breath. Feel a surge of sexual energy.

5. A simple way to meditate on this chakra is to apply some frankincense oil on your forehead, close your eyes and see the color red in the mind's eye. Repeat the *bij mantra*, and direct your focus to the base of the spine.

Svadhistan Chakra

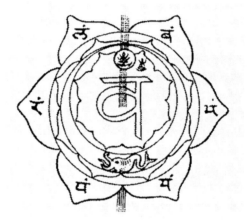

Svadhistan Chakra

Furthermore, the people who say that sex has no relation to religion are entirely incorrect, because it is the energy of sex, in a transformed and sublimated form that enters the realm of religion. The sublimation of this vital energy lifts man to realms about which we know very little. The transformation of his sex energy raises man to a world where there is no death, no sorrow, to a world where there is nothing but joy, pure joy. And anyone who possesses that energy, that life force, can uplift himself to that realm of joyous, truthful consciousness, to sat-chit-anand.
...Osho

Sanskrit	*Svadhistan,* sweetness
Mandala	Fluidal Plexus, Hypogastric Plexus
Location	The testes or ovaries at the abdomen
Gland	Suprarenal glands
Organ	Spleen, kidneys, skin, ovaries, testicles
Function	Sexuality, creativity, emotions, feelings, creative energy, women's power, creative ability, physical health, sex and reproductive center, conscious or unconscious memories from this lifetime or past lives.
Inner state	Feelings, clairsentience
Number	Two
Element	Water
Kingdom	Plant
Sense	Savoring skin and genitals with tongue and mouth creates excitement
Musical note	D
Color	Orange
Petals	6
Letters	*bam, bham, mam, yam, ram, lam.*
Vrittis (Propensities)	*avagina* (indifference), *murccha* (fainting, swooning breath), *prashraya* (over-indulgence), *avishvasa* (distrust, disbelief), *sarvanasha* (fear of annihilation), and *krurata* (crude manners).

Essential oils	Amber, rose, and musk
Organ	Tongue
Shape	Crescent
Lesson	Peace and wisdom
Gemstone	Carnelian, Tiger-eye, coral
Astrology	Cancer
Angel	Gabriel (rules water)
Sephira	Yesod
Tarot	Cups
Characteristics	Sexuality, creativity, emotions, sensuality
Healthy	Shows concern for others, friendly, creative, intuitive, good humored, balanced, desire for pleasure, vitality, sexual satisfaction, natural urges and pleasures, moderate and controlled, naturally orgasmic
Imbalanced	Mistrustful, introverted, unable to show emotions, worrying about what others think, anti-social, addictive behavior, fear of sex and intimacy
Excessive	Self-serving, manipulative, selfish, arrogant, lustful, conceited, addicted to food, sex, can't get enough, uses others just to get sex
Deficient	Frigid, distrustful, shy, overly sensitive, timid, weak sex drive, can't reach orgasm, obsessed with food or sex
Bij	*vam* (pronounced vung)

Motto	I feel
Deity	Rakini

Some second chakra manifestations:

Cleopatra used her sexuality and captured the hearts of the two most powerful men, Caesar and Marc Antony. Marilyn Monroe had an imbalanced second chakra, as do many in the porn business, people with addictions, especially food and sex addictions.

Five Minute Exercise to stimulate the second chakra:

1. Stand with both feet slightly apart, placing hands on the hips, bend the knees and rotate the hips from the right, going around to the left, then to the back and to the right. Try not to move the torso and do not bounce. Do in front of a mirror to music.
2. When meditating on this chakra gaze at the lotus with its six petals as long as possible without blinking, then gently closing the eyes, see the color orange emanating from the abdominal area, and repeat the *bij* quietly or aloud.

Manipur Chakra

Manipur Chakra

> *Remember: if you can cease all restless activity,*
> *your integral nature will appear.*
> *…Hua Hu Ching*

Sanskrit	*Manipur,* lustrous gem
Mandala	Igneous Plexus, this is the area of intense "heat"
Location	Navel area
Gland	Pancreas, adrenals
Organ	Digestive, liver and pancreas
Function	Will power, determination
Inner state	Laughter, joy
Number	Three
Element	Fire, heat
Kingdom	Animal
Sense	Sight--behold partner's body in awe and adoration
Musical note	E
Color	Yellow
Petals	10
Letters	*d'a, d'ha, n'a, ta, tha, da, dha, na, pa, pha*
Vrittis (Propensities)	*lajja* (shyness), *pishunata* (sadistic tendency), *iirsya* (envy), *susupti* (inertia), *visada* (melancholy), *kasaya* (ill tempered, peevishness), *trsna* (yeaning for acquisition), *moha* (attachment), *ghrna* (hatred), *bhaya* (fear)

Essential oils	Amber, rose, and sandalwood
Organs	Eyes
Shape	Triangle
Lesson	Human and divine love
Gemstone	Amber, citrine, yellow topaz
Astrology	Aries
Angel	Michael (rules fire)
Sephira	Hod, Netzach
Tarot	Wands
Characteristics	Outgoing, respects self and others, skillful, spontaneous
Healthy	Cheerful, open and expressive, intelligent, strong nerves, self confident, flexibility, decisive, happy, orgasmic
Imbalanced	Timid, fearful, much anger and rage, hate, isolation, judgmental, dogmatic, thrives on attention, cold, uptight, sexual predator
Excessive	Very demanding, workaholic, perfectionist, critical, overly ambitious, uptight, rigid, critical, power seeker, bullying, unyielding, wants to fight, controlling, reactive, explosive, aggressive
Deficient	Depressed, blames others, no confidence, confused, poor digestion, fear of failure, apathy, feeling deprived of recognition, aloof, feeling isolated, psychosomatic problems, no will
Bij	*ram* (pronounced rung)

Motto	I will
Deity	Lakini

Third Chakra Manifestations:

Donald Trump, Henry Ford, Alexander the Great are examples of people who possess strong will and determination, persistence and one-pointedness to reach their goals. Tyrants like Hitler and Mussolini, seized with power and aggression in combination with spiritual unconsciousness, created a madness and chaos that can never be described or fully understood.

Five Minute Exercises to stimulate the third chakra:

1. Stomach crunches or sit-ups are excellent exercises to strengthen this chakra, as well as your lower back.
2. The "bow" pose in yoga is also beneficial. Lie on the stomach, inhale, lift the head, press the sacrum down, grab the ankles and lift the chest up. Balance on the belly.
3. If this is the chakra that needs to be strengthened, close the eyes, feel heat in the navel area, see the color yellow radiating from this area, repeat the mantra "rung", apply some cassia or lemongrass on both wrists.

Anahat Chakra

Anahat Chakra

Gamble everything for love.
If you are a true human being.
If not, leave this gathering.
Half-heartedness doesn't reach into majesty.
You set out to find God, but then you keep
stopping for long periods at mean-spirited roadhouses.
Don't wait any longer. Dive in the ocean, leave and let the
sea be you. Silent, absent, walking an empty road, all praise.
…Rumi

Sanskrit	*Anahat*, unstruck
Mandala	*Saora Mandala, cardial plexus*
Location	Upper chest
Gland	Thymus
Organ	Heart, respiratory, hands
Function	Love and devotion
Inner state	Compassion, love
Number	Four
Element	Air
Kingdom	Human
Sense	Touch- sensations felt through skin, hands, clitoris, lingam and tongue
Musical note	F
Color	Green
Petals	12
Letters	*ka, kha, ga, gha, una, ca, cha, ja,jha,ina, ta, tha*

Vrittis (Propensities)	*asha* (hope), *cinta* (anxiety), *cesta* (effort to arouse dormant potential), *mamta* (love), *dhamba* (arrogance), *viveka* (discrimination), *vikalata* (psychic depression), *ahamkara* (conceit), *lolata* (avarice), *kapatata* (deception), *vitarka* (argumentativeness), *anutapa* (repentance)
Essential oils	Lavender, jasmine, henna, sandalwood
Organ	Skin
Shape	Hexagon
Lesson	Compassion, love, devotion
Gemstone	Emerald, jade
Astrology	Gemini
Angel	Raphael (rules air)
Sephira	Tipharet
Tarot	Lovers
Characteristics	Compassion, sees God within all, feels gratitude and unconditional love. First step to enlightenment

Healthy	Open heart, grateful, appreciative, compassionate, philanthropic, humanitarian, sees the good in others, balanced; desire to nurture others with no expectations of their own. in touch with own feelings, empathy, adaptable, generous, pure, gentle and innocent, sexual energy transforms to love, volunteer work.
Imbalanced	Frigid, devoid of compassion and morality, financial and emotional insecurities, jealousy and possessiveness, mistrustfulness, self doubt, blaming others, guilt, shame, contracted
Excessive	Overly critical, possessive, manic depressive, angry, jealous, accusatory, miserly, stingy, overconfident, grandiose attitude, on a personal religious crusade to have sex with many partners under guise of "helping" them, by "teaching" them "Tantra" and taking on the role of a "pseudo" guru

Deficient	Self-pity, afraid of letting go and getting hurt, paranoia, indecisive, needs reassurance and constant confirmation of self worth, uncertain, possessive, self doubting, feels unloved, can't feel love for partner, can't commit or have intimacy because of fear, sensitive, no *bhakti*, devoid of devotion
Bij	*yam* (pronounced *yung*)
Motto	I love
Deity	Kakini

Fourth Chakra Manifestations:

Mother Theresa, Joan of Arc, President Jimmy Carter (Habitat for Humanity), Joy Adamson, conservationist, and Dian Fossey, who saved mountain gorillas from extinction. The latter two brought to our attention the necessity for animal welfare, conserving endangered species and protecting wildlife habitat. Religious zealots are the result of a very imbalanced Anahat chakra.

Five Minute Exercises to stimulate the fourth chakra:

1. The Cobra. Lie flat on the belly. With arms bent at each side, lift the chest, head and shoulder and looking at the ceiling, stretch back as far back as possible. Repeat.
2. To open the hand chakras, stand with both feet slightly apart; stretch both arms out to the sides at shoulder height. Keeping the elbows straight, rotate the arms from the shoulder forward. Then reverse the rotations.
3. Spread fingers apart and slowly move each finger one at a time, baby finger, ring finger, middle finger, index finger and thumb. Then

reverse. Do this anytime, when working on the computer for a while or using the hands a lot.

4. Meditate on this chakra by breathing the color green into both lungs, inhale some lavender essential oil, and repeat the mantra "yung". Any of these chakra meditations can be made more elaborate by using the appropriate colors, sounds, and scents for each chakra

Visshuda Chakra

Visshuda Chakra

Oh Devi! Oh Saraswati!
Reside Thou ever in my speech.
Reside thou ever on my tongue tip.
O Divine Mother, giver of faultless poetry.
...Swami Sivananda Radha

Sanskrit	*Visshuda,* purification
Mandala	Sidereal Plexus, Pharyngeal Plexus
Location	Throat
Gland	Thyroid and parathyroid
Organ	Throat, neck, shoulders
Function	Communication
Inner state	Transforms ideas into symbols, clairaudience
Number	Five
Element	Ether
Kingdom	Human
Sense	Sound, vibration
Musical note	G
Color	Indigo
Petals	16
Letters	*a,a', l, li, u, u', r, rr, lr, lrr, e,a e, o, ao, am', ah*
Vrittis (Propensities)	*sadaja* (peacock), *rsabha* (bull), *gandharva* (goat), *madhyama* (horse), *paincama* (cuckoo), *dhaevata* (ass), *nisada* (elephant), *om* (acoustic root of creation), *hum* (sound of kundalini), *phat* (fruition), *vaosatha* (development of mundane knowledge), *vasata* (welfare), *svaha* (surrender to Supreme), *namah* (surrender to the Supreme),*visa* (repulsion), *amrita* (attraction)

Essential oils	Rose and amber
Organ	Ears, mouth
Shape	Hexagon
Lesson	Communication
Gemstone	Quartz, turquoise, blue topaz
Astrology	Mars
Angel	Geburah, Chesed
Characteristics	Good communicator, truthful
Healthy	Contented, centered, good speaker, inspired, grasp of spiritual teachings, speaks and knows the Truth, can speak and converse about sex, expresses easily to partner, honest and natural expression about sex
Imbalanced	Arrogant, self-righteous, talks too much, dogmatic, gossips, lies
Excessive	Seduces others through speech, sell themselves through lies and dishonesty, domineering, fanatical, over-reacting, speaks harshly
Deficient	Scared, timid, quiet, weak, unreliable, devious, can't verbalize feelings, inconsistent, dependent, lack of creative expressions, suppressed feelings, resistant, melancholy, slow to respond
Bij	*ham* (pronounced hung)
Motto	I express

Deity	Shakini

Fifth Chakra Manifestations:

Martin Luther King and Gandhi inspired masses through their speech, due to the awesome power of their fifth chakra. Beethoven, who was deaf, listened and heard his music within and was able to communicate and express himself effectively, creating the greatest masterpieces ever. Helen Keller was deaf and blind, still she became a great speaker and writer. Ray Charles communicated through a language of music that was understood and felt worldwide.

Five Minute Exercises to stimulate the fifth chakra:

1. Neck rolls. Bend head gently to the right side of the shoulder; slowly bring it around to the front all the way to the opposite side. Roll the head back and then to the right side. Make the circles smooth and gentle. Do a few times and repeat in the opposite direction.

2. Shoulder rolls. Keeping the back straight, lift up both shoulders and then roll them to the back and drop. Now, reverse the shoulder rolls by lifting them up and rolling them to the front.

3. Meditation suggestion on this chakra: The mantra of the Goddess is "hung" at the throat area. Sit quietly and listen to the sound of the natural breath. Picture a smoky hexagon vibrating at your throat.

Ajna Chakra

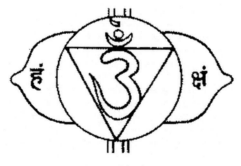

Ajna Chakra

*The intuitive mind is a sacred gift
and the rational mind is a faithful servant.
We have created a society that honors the servant
and has forgotten the gift.
…Albert Einstein*

Sanskrit	*Ajna,* to perceive
Mandala	Lunar Plexus (*Chandra Mandala*)
Location	Between the eyebrows
Gland	Pituitary
Organ	Eyes, intuition
Function	Seeing, intuition, visualization
Inner state	Clairvoyance
Number	Six
Element	Light, ether
Kingdom	Angelic
Sense	Sight-images, lights, colors
Musical note	A
Color	Violet
Petals	2
Letters	*ha, k'sa*
Vrittis (Propensities)	*para* (spiritual knowledge), *apara* (mundane knowledge)
Essential oils	Patchouli
Organ	Sense organs
Lesson	Insight, non-duality
Gemstone	Clear crystal, moonstone

Astrology	Jupiter
Characteristics	No fear of death, can receive guidance, astral travel
Healthy	Charismatic, knows "truth", high consciousness, intuitive, has wisdom, perception, spirituality, idealism, ability to heal
Imbalanced	Worrisome, fearful, oversensitive, spaced out, belittling, absent-minded, no focus
Excessive	Egomaniac, religiously dogmatic, feels it is their "duty" and karma to "help" others with sexual hang-ups through sex, the messiah syndrome.
Deficient	Undisciplined, afraid of success, doubtful, envious of other's talents, forgetful, superstitious, no intuition or insight of sexual needs of partner, can't connect with partner's soul
Bij	*Om* (pronounced ong)
Motto	I know
Deity	Hakini

Sixth Chakra Manifestations:

Religious and spiritual fanatics, false gurus, cult leaders David Korresh, Jim Jones, and Charles Manson, all seem to have some sort of "sexual dysfunction", indicative of a sixth chakra gone awry. Catholic Priests use their positions to molest the young and weak, which is abhorrent to their "religion", not to mention a complete and inexcusable abuse of power.

On the plus side, we are blessed to have had Ralph Waldo Emerson, Joseph Campbell, and many saints and sages grace us with their insight, wisdom, intuition and presence.

Five Minute Exercise for opening the sixth chakra:

A simple meditation at this chakra is as follows: with your eyelids closed, roll your eyes back as far as you can. Visualize the moon surrounded by a violet light shooting out from the center of your forehead between your brows. Repeat the mantra *"Om"*. Hold this image for five minutes or more.

Sahasrar Chakra

Sahasrar Chakra

Only a knower understands
what our supreme home is like
Lightning flashes without any clouds
There is no sun, yet there is brilliant light
The pearl in that realm appears without a shell
There is no sound and yet the Word reverberates.
All other forms of light are humbled by
the Lord's effulgence
The Indestructible, Unfathomable lies beyond.
Kabir says, That is my home.
Which only disciples of the Guru can perceive.
...Kabir

Just as a river flowing for a long time, merges,
n the ocean and becomes the ocean,
when Kundalini has finished Her work and stabilized in
The Sahasrar,
you become completely immersed in God
All your impurities... are destroyed, and you take complete
Rest in the Self. The veil which makes you see duality
drops away
And you experience the world as blissful play of Kundalini,
A sport of God's energy. You see the universe as supremely blissful
Light, undifferentiated from yourself,
and you remain unshakeable in This awareness.
This is the state of liberation, the state of perfection.
...Baba Muktananda

Sanskrit	*Sahasrar*, the thousand-petalled lotus
Mandala	Shunya Mandala
Location	Cranium
Gland	Pineal
Organ	Cerebral cortex, central nervous system, brain
Function	Higher self
Inner state	Wisdom, cosmic consciousness
Number	Seven
Element	All
Kingdom	Cosmos
Sense	All
Musical note	B
Color	white, clear, gold
Petals	1000
Letters	All
Vrittis (Propensities)	Contains the vrittis of all the chakras
Essential oils	Lavender, rosewood, frankincense
Organ	All, the Self
Shape	Space
Lesson	Divine Union, surrender
Gemstone	Diamond, sapphire
Astrology	Saturn
Sephira	Kether
Characteristics	Divine Awareness, Higher Self, and Miracle Worker

Healthy	Feel divinity in soul and in partner's soul, total access to the unconscious, transcends the laws of nature, perform miracles, spiritual, faithful, peaceful, refined, joyful, grateful, love of beauty, sexually mature
Imbalanced	Kundalini psychosis, frustration, unrealized power, depression, frequent migraines, full of despair, destructive, egotistical
Excessive	Destructive, unrealized power, delusions of grandeur, spiritual conceit, seeks sexual union with anyone without connection to God
Deficient	Indecisive, dull
Bij	AUM
Motto	I Am That
Deity	Shiva and Devi

Seventh Chakra Manifestations:

Yogananda, Jesus, Buddha, Muktananda, Vivekananda, Ramakrishna are perfect examples of seventh chakra manifestations. On the other side of the coin, many psychotics have dysfunctional seventh chakras, with no balancing at the lower chakras to ground them.

Five Minute Exercise for opening the seventh chakra:

Meditate every day for five minutes, gradually increasing to an hour or longer. One day, an effulgent, shimmering blue pearl, the size of a sesame seed, will appear and dance before your eyes. This pearl contains the entire universe. Swami Muktantanda describes it as the light of the Self within you. He says, "Everything you seek is within you." When you have experienced this state, you will be transformed, living in God and moving in God every moment of every day. This is the state of perfection, the state of enlightenment and self-realization, the purpose of life.

Yin And Yang, The Attraction Of Opposites

*The ideograms indicate the sunny and shady sides of a hill, fou,
and they are associated with the masculine
and the feminine,
the firm and the yielding, the strong and the weak,
the light and the dark, the rising and the falling,
heaven and earth, and they are even recognized
in such everyday matters as cooking as the spicy
and the bland.
...Alan Watts*

Duality is everywhere in the world. Everything has an opposite, a polar complement. Duality is also called yin/yang. There are many examples of duality, for example, feminine/masculine, mother/father, passivity/ activity, dark/light, body/mind, intuition/logic, night/day, soft/hard, internal/external, wet/dry, follower/leader, receptive/creative, and nature/technology.

We can view the complementary relationship in their mutual dependence; *yin* and *yang* cannot exist without the other. For people who desire wholeness, this means that we cannot have good without evil, or life without death, nor growth without decay. Thus, we should stop trying to annihilate a polarity's unpleasant half.

Yin/Yang

Everything that exists in this world contains energy that can be recognized as yin or yang, feminine or masculine energy. The Chinese concept says that everything in this world exists in a continuum, like black to white, up and down, right and left, good or bad. These are the polarities that exist in this physical world and within each man and each woman.

Yin is the feminine quality, the softness, the sweetness, and subtleness. Yang is the masculine energy that is the opposite of yin. If we have a very feminine energy, we need to find someone who has a dominant masculine energy to balance out the yin and yang in both partners. The key is to find balance between these two forces—between each other and within ourselves. We can balance both of these energies within our own body through meditation and breathing exercises such as *Nadi Shodana*, which is explained elsewhere in this book.

The art of Chinese *Taoism* is the philosophy of harmony and balance, where everything in nature is balanced.

Balance creates harmony when extremes brought together create a dynamic exchange of opposite forces that attract each other like a magnet, or like electricity, which has a positive and a negative force.

In electricity, two positive forces become neutral. There is no attraction or desire to come together. If we have two negative polarities, the same is also true. Like the concept of voltage in electricity, there should be equal and opposite charges. One positively charged 10,000 volts and the other only negatively charged 1,000 volts does not create a balance. There is an attraction, but no balance. In relationships, we need to find one who possesses opposing features and qualities, but not so much that they dominate us. A balance of yin and yang energy swirls around to create a wonderful dance of harmony and nature.

One exercise is to become aware of energy within our partner and us. Analyze whether the activities we participate in are yin or yang. Moreover, consider why that may be so? Do our partners reflect the energies we lack? What is it like to have a yang/yang partnership or yin/yin?

Almost everything can be categorized as embracing yin or yang energy. Some things are both. It has nothing to do with soft, weak, or harsh. Energy can often be hard to discern. Males can be *yin* dominant, and females can be *yang* dominant. Notice if the activities you participate in are more feminine in principle or masculine.

Here are some examples:

Countries and Cities:

India	yin
France	yin
USA	yang
Russia	yang
San Francisco	yin
New York	yang
Honolulu	yin

Musical Instruments:

Piano	yin/yang
Harp	yin
Drums	yang
Violin	yin
Brass	yang
Bass	yang

Religions:

Muslim	yang

Buddhist	yin
Christianity	yang
Paganism	yin
Hinduism	yin
Wicca	yin

Animals:

Eagle	yang
Butterfly	yin
Brown Bear	yang
Bee	yin
Snake	yin
Dog	yang
Cat	yin
Koala Bear	yin
Horse	yang
Cow	yin
Tiger	yin

Transportation:

Truck	yang
Airplane	yang
Sailboat	yin
Powerboat	yang
Motorcycle	yang
Train	yin

Landmarks:

S.F. Bay Bridge	yin
Pyramid	yin
Empire State Bldg.	yang

Activities:

Football	yang
Ice Skating	yin
Weight Lifting	yang
Jogging	yang

Dancing	yin
Yoga	yin
Volleyball	yang
Basketball	yang
Gardening	yin
Cooking	yin
Hunting	yang
Meditation	yin
Shower	yang
Bath	yin
Boxing	yang
Karate	yang
Tai Chi	yin
Gym workout	yang
Horseback riding	yang

Languages:

English	yang
Sanskrit	yin
German	yang
French	yin
Latin	yin
Japanese	yin/yang

Elements:

Fire	yang
Earth	yin
Air	yang
Water	yin

Signs and Planets:

Taurus	yin
Scorpio	yang
Virgo	yin
Sagittarius	yang
Libra	yin
Moon	yin

Sun	yang
Venus	yin
Mars	yang

Food:

Tea	yin
Steak	yang
Salad	yin
Rice	yin
Potato	yang
Beer	yang
Tofu	yin

Misc:

Tattoo	yang
Mehendi	yin
Jewelry	yin
Computer	yang
Color Pink	yin
Mountain	yang
Sea	yin
Valley	yin
Clouds	yin
Thunder	yang
Lightning	yang
Guns	yang
Tidal Wave	yin
Hurricane	yin
Earthquake	yang
Television	yang
Radio	yin
Mathematics	yang
Literature	yin
Writing	yin
Buying	yin
Selling	yang
Cigarettes/smoking	yang

Sex	yin/yang
Republican	yang
Democrat	yin

There is a basic premise about the energy emitted and stimulated through sexual activity of different combination of couplings. The power of the Shakti lies in its subtlety, not in the gross demonstration of that energy.

There are three principal *nadis* that run along the spine. The central pole is called the *sushumna,* which is within the vertebral column. The left pole, or the negative pole is the *ida,* which runs along the left side of the vertebrae, moving upwards. To the right lies the *pingala,* the positive pole, running downwards alongside the spine.

In the sexual position with the man on top, his *pingala* (on his right) pushes Shakti's *ida* (on her left) upwards, and when her *pingala* descends (on her right), it pushes his *ida* (on his left). With the man entering the *yoni* from behind...his *pingala* descends from his head, (Shiva consciousness), causing her *pingala* to rise from the *Muladhar* up her spine. This is the circuit of energy that is activated during sex and it is something we can observe.

Some people have imbalanced *chi,* which manifests as energy that is slow, low or dark. These are people who exhibit poor decisions, get involved in bad situations, and are unlucky, unhappy, mean-spirited, or angry. They often will suck the energy from someone who has some light. This draining effect is the vampire phenomena and should be avoided at all costs. This is, no doubt, the reason the scriptures admonish us over and over again to keep in the company of dharmic persons only.

Mingling with people who have no path is risky--physically, psychically, mentally, emotionally, and spiritually.

Karma, The Fruit Of Our Action

We may accept the idea of karma only if we understand it as 'psychic heredity' in the very widest sense of the word.
...Carl Jung

Carl Jung saw karma as the motivation for knowledge that leads from past life into this life and onto future lives.

There are four kinds of karma, but the simple explanation is that it is the law of cause-and-effect, or action and reaction. The cause can be any type of action, including a person's thoughts and behaviors. The effect is the action's consequence, including the material and psychological conditions of our life. Every action creates an effect; thus, we are constantly creating karma.

Gahana Karmano Gatih
The effects of Karma are unfathomable.
…Bhagavad-Gita 4:17

In studying the dynamics of the universe, science continually deals with the cause and effects of events. This principle is stated most directly in the Second Law of Thermodynamics: "For every action, there is an opposite and equal reaction."

In metaphysics and the occult, these fields examine the principles of spirit and the human psyche. In particular, we learn how our thoughts and actions manifest our world; from this perspective, we are studying karma as a creative process--performing a specific act to cause a specific effect.

In everyday life, we frequently refer to karma in every aspect of life. For example: "You made your bed; now you have to sleep in it" or "taking responsibility for our life is a sign of psychological maturity." "You didn't pay your electric bill, so we're turning off your power" or "she dumped you because you cheated on her." "You are grounded because you lied to me", "you violated a law, so you are going to prison"; and "what goes around comes around."

Our family, teachers, and church influenced us in our most formulative years. These early impressions, called *samskaras,* form some of our karma. The elements will affect our behavior during future encounters with the *samskaras.* The amount of karmic effect will depend upon our compliance with intuition during the current encounter.

Shallow men believe in luck.
Strong men believe in cause and effect.
...Ralph Waldo Emerson

Karma is simply feedback that shows us the effect of particular actions; i.e., we discover that when we do a particular act, we experience a particular result. Life is thus viewed as a classroom. Karma is a means by which our tests are graded.

Through our encounter with karma, we study responsibility. We realize that we are responsible for the conditions that are in our life. We have no one to blame; we have no justification for complaint; we are not victims. There are no mistakes; there are no accidents.

Karma is usually viewed as a destructive force that interferes with our creativity. However, the underlying principle is merely cause-and-effect, the same principle that is involved in all forms of creativity. When we accept the idea that our actions create our personal world (and thus we willfully direct our thoughts and images and energy and actions toward a constructive goal), we can use this principle to create the type of personal world that is best for us. Our karmic education can be one of happiness and fun.

When we do not accept the idea that our actions create our personal world, our actions are still creative--but, because of our lack of focus and discipline, our thoughts tend to be a mishmash of conflicting directions that contradict and weaken one another.

Love, for example, is not something that we do, or something that we have to learn; instead it is one of the innate qualities of the life-energy (spirit). It occurs naturally when the contents of our archetypal fields allow this flow, such as when our thoughts, images, energy, and actions are not blocking the flow.

If we indulge thoughts that someone does not deserve love, we intentionally generate thoughts, images, energies and actions that prevent us from behaving in a loving manner. The love is still there, because spirit always connects us to everyone and everything, but we have created unnatural blockages to the flow in this material situation.

This love is not a sentimental type of human love; instead, it is simply the natural dynamic of the impersonal life--energy that flows between souls

Karma is not based on law in the human sense of the word. If we use the word law, we might tend incorrectly to correlate spiritual law with human law, and thus imagine that we can avoid consequences with the cosmic equivalent of a shrewd attorney, or plea-bargaining, or a bribe, or an emotional appeal to a judge and jury. None of those things exist in the concept of karma.

Beyond the superficial appearances of our material world, karma teaches us about the traits of spirit. It is holistic. Its wholeness contains, balances and unites the dualities of action/reaction, attacker/prey, yin/yang. It is authoritative. It does not yield to our whims, our desires, our terrors, our human powers, or our social institutions. When our life is tragic, it is tragic only to the extent that we have presumed to act in a manner that is contrary to the irrepressible dynamics of spirit.

Karma is known as punishment and reward. We might think of bad karma as a punishment, and good karma as a reward. However, there are problems in this reasoning. The concepts of punishment and reward are merely value judgments that are based on our emotional, egoic, and feeling reaction to a phenomenon; they are based on whether we like the phenomenon. However, from an impersonal viewpoint, there is neither punishment nor reward; there is simply a result.

Some people intentionally create good karma (through generous acts) so that they will gain the corresponding rewards. However, other people (such as the practitioners of karma yoga) strive to create no karma, because they believe that all karma is restrictive; that "bad karma is an iron shackle, and good karma is a golden shackle".

Karma is a healing process. A karmic payback can be destructive and painful (and even fatal). Yet it is a healing--a balancing, a re-uniting, a restoration, and a regaining of wholeness. The pain in karmic paybacks is part of the healing process. The part drives us to seek relief in spiritual understanding by which we learn about the principles that must be obeyed in order for the pain to cease.

Ultimately, the goal is not to ease the pain of karma but to understand the larger dynamic of life in which karma is only one part, and in which the pain is only a motivator for us to get on with our lessons in life.

Karma follows man like his shadow.
It sits with him while he sits,
moves with him while he moves.
It works on even while he is working.
Just as fruits and flowers come to the trees in their appointed time
unimpelled by any one, one's past Karma never transgresses its appointed
time.
…Mahabharatha

Karma causes many problems. Despite the assertion that karma is part of an ultimately benevolent system by which we gain our spiritual education, we tend to view karma as an unwanted guest in our lives. However, it is simply the result of our actions. Some of our actions create pleasant conditions, and some create unpleasant conditions. For example, when we perform well at our job, our karma is expressed in our big paycheck. Our actions (i.e., our creation of karma) have made our life the way it is (for better or for worse), in terms of our relationships, our financial state, our physical health, our skills, our personality, our psychological and emotional traits, and our other conditions.

The correct response is to intuitively deal with each situation in its uniqueness, considering the blend of the situation's requirements and our psychological and material needs (including, but not dominated by, the need of our a-field elements to discharge their residual charge from previous encounters with this archetype). We are still creating a-field elements (because the mind continues to record our behaviors for future reference in case this type of situation happens again), but the elements have such a slight charge that they will be mere non-compelling reference points when the circumstance recurs.

Perhaps spiritual freedom occurs when all of our unwanted debts have been paid. The only conditions in our life are the ones that we want at this moment. We have not eliminated all of our karma. If it is simply an effect from action, we still need to create effects in order to create our human life--our home and our relationships.

We understand the dynamics of awareness such that our actions do not create unwanted karma, which would bind us to any corresponding unwanted circumstances in the future.

Karma is one of the reasons why we are reincarnated. If we believe in reincarnation, we can see it as a progression of lifetimes, each of which furthers our spiritual education and which also provides an opportunity to pay back karmic debts from previous lifetimes.

Not In the sky, not in the midst of the sea,
not if we enter into the clefts of the mountain,
is there known a spot in the whole world,
where a man be freed from his deeds.
... The Lord Buddha

Many people dislike their human existence, and so they dislike the karma, which retains them in this world for a continual series of karmic paybacks. However, after the death of the physical body, their archetypal fields remain intact and so the unresolved charge from the field's elements requires a rebirth in which they will recreate the same unsettled circumstances so that the charge might be dismissed. Other people appreciate their human existence as an arena in which to learn about life and they accept and are even grateful for karma and reincarnation as a part of the process.

Karma can cause us to be afraid of life. Some people are so afraid of karma (and the possibility of reincarnation) that they hesitate to commit any action at all. (At its extreme form, some practitioners of the Jain religion, generally just sit in a chair all day, because any action at all would create karma.)

However, we can choose other perspectives. We are here to learn about life through action and interaction. To be inactive is to betray our very reason for being in this world. Life itself is constantly changing, constantly active, constantly giving intuitive messages, which guide us in each moment. If we ignore this guidance and choose instead to be inactive, we create karma through the inaction itself, because karma is created whenever we fail to obey intuition.

Karma can be painful but our love of life can be so great that we are willing to tolerate the bruises. As we learn more about life, through our experiences, we are likely to experience less of the pain.

We can act without creating extraneous karma. Every action creates karma i.e., it creates an effect. Our goal is to act in such a way that we create the appropriate karma--a productive conversation--without extraneous karma.

We can develop our ability to recognize karma. We can look for the results of any action. As we study the cycle of cause-and-effect in regular life, we are more likely to see it in more subtle manifestations. For example, regular-life karma is exhibited if we fail to pay our telephone bill and then the telephone company cancels our service. We can notice the effects of everything that we do--physically, emotionally, mentally, socially, and financially.

We can consider the possibility that reincarnation occurs. People who do not believe in reincarnation will not recognize a cause, which was created during a previous lifetime.

Our past-life karma determines the conditions into which we are born--the particular family, any birth defects, some of our childhood illnesses, and some of the conditions with arise later in our life. One common belief is that we continue to reincarnate with the same people in order to resolve the karma from our previous, and on-going conflicts; for example, our spouse in this lifetime might have been one of our parents in a previous lifetime. We choose when we will be born, and who our parents will be, where we will live, and when we will die.

We can consider the idea that we do not need to know the specific cause of all phenomena in our life. Although a problem might be resolved more easily if we know the cause, we can manage it without having that information.

Sometimes the cause is obvious, but sometimes it is not. Our karma is intertwined with the karma of everyone and everything. We are part of a complex fabric of cause-and-effect, which ripples throughout the universe, such that--to some extent, individually--we are the cause of everything, and we are the effect of everything. Cause and effect tend to perpetuate themselves. If we look at a cause, we see that it is the effect of a previous cause, and so on, extending backward in time. We cannot isolate any event as pure cause or pure effect.

The cause might have occurred during a past life. If we look for the cause within our current lifetime, we will not find it.

Not only do we have our individual karma, but we also partake in the collective karma of every group to which we belong--our family, our community, our nation, our corporation, the human race, etc. Thus, an effect in our individual life might be due primarily to the actions of our group, although our individual karma determines the impact of this group karma upon ourselves. Group karma can be manifested in economic depression, prosperity, war, and other group-wide events.

In order to see our karma clearly, we need to have humility. Our delusions of holiness are shattered if we acknowledge that our suffering might be due to the suffering that we have inflicted. An awareness of our wholeness allows us to view the idea that we have the potential for any possible action, including, for example, a brutal action which might be responsible for our current problems.

If we recognize our capacity for maliciousness, the only way in which we can go on with our lives is to accept our past and our present. This acceptance does not mean that we like what we did, but merely that we still love ourselves as we learn about the nature of life. If we deny ourselves that love--if we shame ourselves and we hate ourselves--our own protective mechanisms will prevent us from seeing the parts of us which trigger that shame and hatred.

We can diminish or eliminate the effect of unwanted karma, the extraneous effects that we created in addition to our intended effects. In each of these methods, intuition--the communication mechanism that translates spirit's perspective into human understanding--can assist us in resolving our existing karma.

To resolve our karma we can approach it from various perspectives. Straight payback is the standard means by which we repay karma usually unwillingly, and usually without knowing the reason why we are experiencing the particular hardship or bounty. For example, if we have been dishonest in our finances, we will encounter financial hardship, probably because we have implanted that idea that it is okay to steal and then people have adopted our thought in their dealings with us. In payback situations, we can use our intuition.

It can tell us the cause of our present circumstance; for example, "My relationships have been unsatisfying because I have been cruel to people". With this knowledge, we might be able to change our behavior so that we are no longer perpetuating the situation. Our intuition can direct this change by suggesting thoughts, images, energy, and actions. As those elements change, we change, and our karma changes.

It can tell us whether a present circumstance is a resolution of old karma or the creation of new karma. For example, if someone is hurting us, intuition indicates whether this is our old karma that we are resolving (and thus we should simply accept the injury, without retaliating against the person) or new karma that the person is creating with us (and thus we should act to create a resolution, perhaps through a lawsuit).

It can tell us whether we need to enforce a payback. We might usually think of karma as something that happens to us--but sometimes we need to be an agent in someone else's karma (either "good" or "bad"). For example, perhaps we are usually a gentle person, but intuition might tell us to speak harshly to someone, because that person needs to resolve some unpleasant karma.

Some people believe that we can resolve karma through *seva*, the giving of love, service, money, and other commodities. Through our sacrificial giving, we repay the energy and substance that we unfairly received. To resolve good karma, we would open ourselves to receive the pleasant goods that are due to us. When we decide that we want to resolve our existing karma, we usually engage a scatter-shot method-- doing random deeds of kindness and generosity.

In some types of healings, we are apparently relieved of the ailment; i.e., the karma is apparently resolved. However, in many instances, our ailment recurs, because the underlying karma is still there. The "healer" experiences the ailment, perhaps years later. Despite the good intentions, the healer has interfered with the karmic process, and so he or she pays this penalty.

We can balance reciprocal karma (i.e. good and bad karma). Our good thoughts do not destroy our previous bad thoughts. However, these new elements (i.e., our good karma) discharge the residual energy from the existing contrary elements (i.e., our bad karma)--as in a contact between matter and anti-matter--such that the existing elements no longer have a dynamic charge by which they can influence our life; they remain as mere memories.

We can summarize by classifying all karma in four categories:

1. *Sanchita Karma*--is the accumulated *karma* of this lifetime and previous lifetimes that are affecting us in this lifetime.

2. *Prarabdha Karma*--is the portion of *sanchita karma* that is affecting us in the present moment. We cannot do much about it, but we can meditate, repeat *mantras* and undergo actions, such as wearing gemstones, or participating in *pujas* (ceremonies) or *homas* (fire rituals), that can directly affect changes in this life, by making offerings with a clear intent, to the deities.

3. *Kriyamana Karma*--is the result of our present actions that will take effect in this lifetime. This is sometimes called "Instant *Karma*".

4. *Agami Karma*--is the action that we perform in this lifetime that will affect our future incarnations.

No creature remains even for a moment without being engaged in Karma
... Shrimad Bhagavad-Gita

The Four Aims of Life

The scriptures of all yogas, including Tantra, maintain that there are four aims of life:

1. *Artha*--physical resources, daily comforts, money. Material wealth and prosperity are necessary because without the means to pursue our goals the other three aims cannot be achieved. Without financial means, it would be practically impossible for the seeker to pursue any *sadhana*. *Artha* is also interpreted as spiritual wealth. However, we must always keep a balance and not let the quest for comforts overrule love, virtues and pursuit of liberation.

2. *Kama*--our desires, love. In tantra, everything we do in life has one purpose--to lead us to liberation. As long as we are earthbound, we will have our desires, including our sexual desires, and that sexual energy can be evoked as a means to higher consciousness.

3. *Dharma*--self-regulated morality, ethics, ideal. Our actions and morals influence our karma. Having a clear understanding and unselfish

intention, being aware of the four kinds of karma, we realize that all of our actions, past and present, determine our experiences in life. Living dharmically is at the core of life itself and the tool for attaining *moksha* (liberation). There are ten characteristics of dharma and they are:

- *Dhrti*--patience
- *Ksama*--forgiveness
- *Damah*--control over the inner enemies
- *Asteya*--not to steal anything physically or mentally
- *Shaoca*--cleanliness (external and internal cleanliness of the body, environment and thoughts)
- *Indriyanigraha*--control over the five sensory organs (hearing, feeling by touch, seeing, tasting, smelling) and controlling the five motor organs (speech, grasping, locomotion, excretion, procreation- mentally and spiritually)
- *Dhii*--benevolent intellect
- *Vidya*--spiritual knowledge
- *Satyam*--love or truth
- *Akrodha*--non-anger

4. *Moksha*--self-realization, higher consciousness, the attainment of powers brought about by meditation. Moksha liberates us from the three debts of karma:

- Debt to the gods--discharged by doing something good for the world
- Debt to our ancestors--repaid through respect to our elders
- Debt to our gurus--which is discharged by imbibing and living in accordance with their teachings.

The Eight Limbed System of Yoga

The practice of yoga consists of eight systems.

1. *Yama*--external moral/ethical discipline.
2. *Niyama*--internal moral/ethical strength.
3. *Asana*--yogic postures, sitting in God's presence, bodily positions.
4. *Pranayam*--proper breathing, retention and control of the breath, altering breathing patterns.
5. *Pratyahar*--withdrawal of senses from the external world to internalize your consciousness for meditation, vision, hearing, mantras, having the image/picture internally and externally, knowledge and understanding the meaning of the mantras, chanting, inscribing *yantras* (geometrical designs) on copper sheets, performing *pujas* (rituals).
6. *Dharana*--concentrating or extended mental focusing on physical sensations in body. Performing the *bandhas,* locks, while establishing the deities in the chakras within the subtle body, called *nyasa.*
7. *Dhyana*--process of meditation, the principal practice of bringing your mind to ideate on Oneness, understanding of what you are doing and why, application of what your understanding is.
8. *Samadhi*--experience of becoming One with Consciousness, the feeling of Infinite Peace.

The Eightfold Path of Buddha

There are eight requisite factors in life. These are the principles by which we should live our lives, according to Buddha. You will notice that there is no difference in principle from the various spiritual paths.

1. *Samyak Darshan*--be selective about the things you look at (books, pictures, movies), and how you look at them. See through the eyes of God. When you change the way you look at things, the things you look at change, having spiritual insight.
2. *Samyak Sankalpa*--all of our actions should reflect a proper intention. Have a firm determination to do only worthwhile activities that are for the good of all.

3. *Samyak Vak*--means that expression of the motor organs--hands, feet, tongue and our speech, what we choose to hear, should be clean and clear. Being truthful and honest.

4. *Samyak Ajiiva*--proper and harmless "occupation" (for instance, not exploiting others for profit or pleasure). Occupation includes the psychic and mental realms. Our thoughts can harm or help others and we should control our actions and intentions. Our goals should be for the betterment of all.

5. *Samyak Vyayama*--taking care of our physical, psychic and spiritual body through exercise, proper foods and nutrition.

6. *Samyak Karmanta*--finishing anything we have started, so that we have no unfinished business. This includes having proper conduct, actions, seeing things through completion.

7. *Samyak Smrti*--having control of our minds and thoughts, retaining good things in our memory and releasing whatever is not congenial to our spirit. Watching and being ever mindful of our thoughts.

8. *Samyak Samadhi*--suspending our mind in spiritual absorption. Meditation.

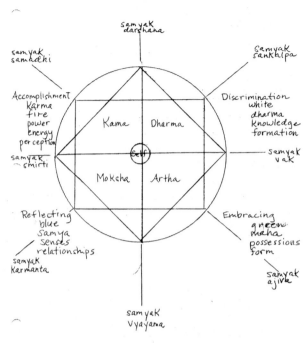

Samyak

The Tao

> *The Tao that can be spoken of is not the eternal Tao.*
> *The name that can be named is not the eternal name.*

As in other mystical literature, the *Tao Te Ching* (the principal text of Taoism) claims that its ideal is not definable or describable. Nevertheless, for the sake of discussion, we might say that the Tao is spirit or the underlying principle of life or the way of the universe. Although we cannot define the Tao intellectually, we can experience it intuitively.

This is not a self-conscious type of practice with techniques and goals; instead, we learn to relax into the course of events, and we become more aware of our place in those events (while paradoxically becoming *less* aware of ourselves as being separate from the events themselves). As we discover ourselves within the Tao, we find a type of inner guidance that presents us with an ever-changing role within the larger drama of life. Until we have an intuitive awareness of the Tao, we can explore clues from the intellectual and metaphorical explanations.

We follow the promptings of our natural self. Taoism honors simplicity, ordinariness, self-acceptance, humility, and unsophistication; it rejects the traditionally western values of logic, effort, ambition, goals, and self-improvement--all of which are viewed as futile, self-conscious counterfeits of our innate qualities and activities.

> *Virtue comes after loss of the Way,*
> *humanity comes after loss of virtue,*
> *duty comes after loss of humanity,*
> *courtesy comes after loss of duty.*

In other words, when we lose contact with spirit, we try to prop up ourselves with *concepts* of spirituality, and then we manipulate our behavior to try to conform to those concepts; then, as we identify ourselves with this fabricated self, we become even farther removed from our true spiritual nature.

Taoism offers relief from the pressures of society; we can be ourselves, instead of striving to be more than that. Further, Taoism offers a vision of a different kind of society in which people are at peace with themselves, and therefore they exhibit an organic morality because they do not fight to accumulate the goods and qualities, which might otherwise be judged especially important.

> *Not exalting cleverness causes the people not to contend.*

Rather than being a *passive* viewpoint, this is a vibrant responsiveness to the impulses of life; if we look for passivity, we find it instead in the sluggish, encrusted intellectualizing which we employ in our mimicking of life through possessions, social positioning, and vain creations. *Wu-wei*, the Taoist doctrine of "non-doing" does not mean that we do not act, but rather that our actions are intuitive, holistic outgrowths of the needs of the moment such that we have a sense that *we* are indeed not doing but instead that life is doing itself *through* us, without our self-monitoring, personal exertion or pressure, or pre-planned scheme or intent.

The *Tao Te Ching* uses many metaphors from nature; nature exemplifies a way of being which is not forced or externally regulated. Primarily, the book examines *water*, whose dynamic is analogous to that of the Tao:

1. Water moves in a non-linear fashion (in contrast to the course of the mind's logic, which can be viewed as a straight line on a predictable course).

2. Water assures its forward motion by non-confrontationally seeking paths of least resistance; it is willing to go around or over or under its barriers (e.g., rocks and low-hanging tree-branches).

3. Water has no objectives that could be crystallized into words; instead, it simply participates in a process in the moment (i.e., flowing).

4. Water exemplifies humility as it allows gravity to draw it toward the lowest level, but doing so does not degrade it.

5. Water displays surrender as it generally concurs with the shape of the river and the stones. Having no rigid form of its own, water adapts itself to the contour of its container without betraying its nature.

Despite all of these non-forceful qualities, water gradually wears down all blockages in its path, and it achieves its end.

When we accept the natural impulses of life from inside of us and from outside of us, we find that these impulses rise and fall in harmony, synchronicity, equilibrium, order, and pattern. This is not the type of harmony in which we would sacrifice our soulful qualities in order to fit our perverse, complex-ridden self into an intellectually designed conglomerate of other perverse, complex-ridden selves, but instead it is the type of harmony which is orchestrated by life itself, such that each living thing can express itself fully, because none of us are making the outrageous demands which would be generated by loose-cannon goal-making from dysfunctional elements in our archetypal fields.

When we explore the Tao, we discover that the process is that of *life*--a benevolent macrocosm that mirrors our own exuberant self, so we yield to the inevitable surge of what is; we stop fearing what had seemed to be chaos, and we begin to trust the process.

The Tao is not reducible to a formula. From those descriptions, we might believe that we can know the Tao through:

1. Psychological self-acceptance
2. Behavioral imitation of nature
3. Amiable cooperation with the life around us.

We might conclude that the Tao is naturalness, and that we ought to discard that which is *un*natural. However, a text titled the *Chung Yung* shatters these easy answers by saying, "The Tao is that from which one cannot deviate; that from which one can deviate is not the Tao."

Alan Watts said, "This sentence suggests that there is no analogy between Tao and the Western ideas of God and of divine or natural law, which can be obeyed or disobeyed. The saying is a hard one, because both Lao-tzu and Chuang-tzu speak of forced actions, which are at variance with the Tao. You may imagine that you are outside, or separate from, the Tao and thus able to follow it or not follow; but this very imagination is itself within the stream, for there is no way other than the way. Willy-nilly, we are it and go with it. From a strictly logical point of view, this means nothing and gives us no information. Tao is just a name for whatever happens, or, as Lao-tzu put it, 'The Tao in principle is what happens of itself [*tzu-jan*].'"[6] In other words, sometimes it is natural for us to be unnatural; sometimes it is harmonious for us to be inharmonious; sometimes it is balanced for us to be unbalanced; it is all a part of life.

Ego

Most of the shadows of this life are caused by standing in one's own sunshine.
…Ralph Waldo Emerson

---

[6] From ***Tao: The Watercourse Way***. Copyright 1975 by Mary Jane Yates Watts.

The ego has been defined in many ways. In the following definitions, we are examining the ego as our identity in the human realm.

In Western psychology, the word ego refers to a part of the psyche. Although the word is just a label, there is something underlying the label, which is real, definable, continual, and dynamic. In Eastern religions, however, ego refers to something entirely different. It is only the label that we put onto ourselves.

The ego is our self-image. It is our armor, protecting us from our pains, hurts, and vulnerability. The ego as our center of consciousness is an eye from which we look at the world. This ego creates boundaries; providing our sense of being separate from other people and from the world in general.

In that separateness, our ego distinguishes itself as being unique. As our identity, it sets us apart from other people's identities. Without ego's protective shield, we are devastated by criticism, or ridicule, but we revel in praise, pride, vanity, and accomplishment. It is the façade of our soul, that which prevents us from realizing our true nature. It can either minimize or maximize our faults or assets. It puts us in denial, makes us defensive, deludes us, and flatters us.

Ego exists in the form of the mind; hence it is imperative and important that we purify our minds and our thoughts, through *sadhana*, or spiritual practices. Only when we recognize when ego is reacting can we learn to control it. This is not an overnight process.

The ego makes our decisions and implements our will. It makes a distinction between the inner world and the outer world, and it notes our perceptions from both. Then, by conceptualizing, labeling, and organizing those perceptions, it tries to make sense of them, and it files them in various contexts, where we can make considerations regarding their value, potential threat or benefit.

The ego is our continuity. The ego says, "I am this type of person." This continuity gives the ego a sense of security and stability, but it is an ungrounded sense, because there is actually constant change. The continuity is sustained through various means.

Our habits, which suggest, through their repetitiveness, that we are indeed a particular kind of person, are also our ego. However, reality actually exists in our constantly changing world of our current actions.

As a sentry, the ego analyzes situations as threatening or beneficial, largely on the basis of the possible impact to its images of us, but also to the resources that allow it to operate in the human world. Thus, it reacts to insults and challenges to its circumstances and habits (physical or mental). Contrarily, threats to the body are managed largely by instinct, such as the fight-or-flight impulse.

The ego is a constellation that is composed of particular elements from within every archetype. For example, we might identify ourselves as a husband and a computer programmer.

Eastern thought is that the ego causes all our pain and that the only way to true happiness is to eliminate it.

In the West, we believe we should develop a healthy ego for a well-developed ego can help us to develop a sense of individuality, independence, self-esteem, and self-respect, create personal boundaries, and assertiveness. It can help create our presence, values, conviction, opinions and perspectives, tastes and preferences, and freedom from the contrary inner psychological forces that would dominate the ego.

When we have these qualities, we have an ego that can be termed well developed, well defined, or strong--indicating poise and confidence.

From the western perspective, a strong ego enables us to approach people from a position of strength, abundance, and vigor, rather than from neediness and emptiness. We can build relationships between two whole people, rather than trying to manipulate the other person into filling our voids. A well-defined ego is fulfilling and comfortable.

We develop humility, the knowledge of what we are and what we are not. Humility is based on an accurate perception of ourselves--neither inflated nor degraded. A weak ego uses conceit, arrogance, and pomposity to try to compensate for its lack of fulfillment and comfort.

As long as we manage the ego's archetypal field properly, we do not develop constellations of conflicting elements that will need to be expressed. We are likewise protected from external influences; we know ourselves, so people cannot easily sway or persuade us with their opinions. When our ego is in charge, we can be relatively consistent, stable, and trustworthy in our behavior.

A well-developed ego does not succumb to intellectual slavery or dogma. While we are not overcome by the internal and external influences, we can accept the valid input from them. A weak ego necessarily closes itself off, to protect itself. However, a fully formed ego stays intact when it considers the antithetical perspectives of the shadow and the soul.

Because an undeveloped ego has empty spaces--e.g., a poorly defined relationship with our parents--the other parts of the psyche rush in to fill the spaces; for example, the shadow or the inner child might fill that void with some repressed anger from our childhood. If we have a weak ego, we need people to say that we are worthwhile or interesting or possessing whatever other trait we cherish. We betray our own identity, trying to be the type of person who would receive approval, to gain that assurance, and we manipulate other people because we are fishing for a compliment instead of engaging in honest conversation.

Strong ego boundaries protect us against the everyday insults and injustices from other people and from the self-condemnation, which we would inflict upon ourselves if we had dysfunctional elements in the ego's archetypal field.

Because we have a clear sense of who we are, our persona, which presents who we are to the world, can be crisp, definitive, and genuine. A vague ego can create only a vague persona, which lacks energy, attractiveness, and distinct attributes with which people can interact.

When we have a healthy ego, even our appearance is improved, with a relaxed grace of movement, eyes that are bright and alert--and, very likely, a smiling face.

The goal of many people who seek psychological or spiritual fulfillment is transcendence of the ego. As Jack Engler, Harvard psychologist and Buddhist teacher said, "You have to be somebody before you can be nobody". We need a strong ego before we can properly transcend the ego. With transcendence come peace of mind, broader perspectives on life, a type of spiritual consummation, and a calming of the ego's storms, which resulted from our misunderstanding and misapplication of the function and range of the ego.

To create a healthy ego, we can enhance independence. We can establish our own income and housing and other foundations of adult life. In addition, we are emotionally independent, feeling free to love and to seek sources of love in our own way, and intellectually independent in developing our own viewpoints. However, we realize that we do need people in order to be a complete person, so we find a balance between independence and interdependence.

A healthy ego means we have good self-esteem. We believe that we have innate value and that we have a right to be alive.

When we are where we are supposed to be, we have a sense of presence, belonging here, and of having a right to be here, instead of indulging excessive shyness and uncertainty. Even when we are not talking or doing anything, people notice us, because our sheer willingness to be a part of it all grants a degree of charisma.

The ego has a limited function. When we believe that the ego is our only identity, we naturally assign all administrative functions to it, including our small choices (e.g., deciding how to react to an indignity) and our big choices (such as our direction in life, including career, relationships, etc.). Throughout our life, much of our frustration and failure occur because the ego has accepted duties for which it is unqualified (and for which it has no authority, hence the conflicts when the ego tries to impose its will); the ego lacks the information, perspective, and power that are available to the higher Self.

The ego is insatiable and we are justified in regarding the ego as a truly unmanageable distraction, to be assaulted with austerities that would simply exterminate the ego along with its unquenchable desires.

A man is like a fraction whose numerator is what he is
and whose denominator is what he thinks of himself.
The larger the denominator the smaller the fraction.
...Leo Tolstoy

The Master of Disguise is brilliant and relentless; it will do everything and anything to prevent its demise and prevent our growth. Not only does it play tricks on us, it manipulates us into believing it has our best interests at heart, preventing us from surrendering to our higher consciousness or a higher source, such as a teacher. Our ego makes us feel we do not need anyone or anything else; that we are perfectly able to take care of our own needs. Conversely, our egos tell us we are weak, helpless, needy, and hopeless, dwelling in conceit or self-pity effortlessly. Ego knows how to operate effectively, adjusting itself to suit each individual's circumstance.

It sneaks up to us in the form of helpfulness--feeling, needing and wanting to help others for our personal gratification. Ego says, "I can make a difference. I can help this person". It is deceptive, cunning and full of trickery. Whether we feel distress or satisfaction, both are the work of a skillful ego. The ego tells us we are inadequate, it tells us we are superior.

So how does one know whether it is ego reacting or the Self? When we perform actions without any expectations whatsoever from the fruit of our work, that is the Self. When we have no expectation that our deeds that will somehow benefit us in the process, or someone will like us or do things for us in return, that is the Self. The Self is not the doer, but the witness of the doer. The Self has no attachment to the end result.

When the Self appears, the ego becomes frightened, agitated, insecure, and vulnerable. Negative emotions may emerge and bring to the surface all the darkness we have been avoiding since childhood. When we are exposed, the sense of whom we thought we were deteriorates. This can be a most difficult phase to go through. Even when we think we know what is happening, it does not make it any easier. It is terrifying, confusing, disconcerting, not just for us but for those closest to us.

At this time, we need an anchor of stability, someone who knows the process, and preferably someone who has also traveled that road. Having the examples of our *Gurus* and teachers, knowing they too have been through this, is reassuring. We need a guide to light the way.

When we are able to let neither pain nor joy affect our state, when we can always maintain a state of equipoise, amidst turmoil or peace, we know we have control over ego. We will feel a profound sense of peace, and more notably, others will feel and sense that somehow we are "different". We will have no attachment to our previous habits, and neither praise nor criticism will affect us in any way because we will have found our center. We know we are not the ego.

The only way to win the battle against the ego is to become fearless, to recognize when it is creeping up on us, whether in the form of words, actions or feelings. Ego can be subdued, through self-effort, humility and surrender. Ego cannot survive in an environment of unconditional love and compassion. When the ego dissolves, the old *samskaras* are replaced with a new awareness and we discover that love that was there all long. Through unwavering devotion, our heart opens and we will attract into our lives, not our soul mate, but the one who is our equal-- our "twin soul", our *spiritual* counterpart. The one with whom we will experience a mutually profound rapture.

Only when the individual ego has been obliterated, will we experience the pure, unaffected, undifferentiated Self, the state of *Satchitananda* (existence, consciousness, bliss absolute).

There is one more distinction between the East and West. To repeat what we said earlier, in Western psychology, ego refers to a part of the psyche. Although the word is just a label, there is something underlying the label, which is real, definable, continual, and dynamic.

In Eastern religions, ego refers to something entirely different--it is only the label that we put onto ourselves.

Kriya

Kriya means to do, to act, or take action. It also refers to physical or emotional involuntary *reactions* that become activated when the *Kundalini* starts to awaken. Even one who has been practicing awhile will find that as the body begins to purify itself in the inner fire, or *yajna*, they will experience enormous heat. The *Shakti* literally stirs the energy, which can actually be felt moving inside the body. On an emotional level, unpleasant stuff may surface, which can cause distress and discomfort. This stuff comes up for our purification. We must first empty our vessel before we can fill it.

A tantric relationship brings out our best and worst, and everything out there in the world is played out internally within us. We experience the light and the dark simultaneously.

It helps to talk to someone when stuff comes up, someone who has undergone and experienced some of the same things. And this is one of reasons why a person pursuing tantra, or any yoga, should have a *sangham* (a community or support system), or someone who understands the process, who can help by holding space for us during difficult times. Holding space can be defined as *allowing* and *witnessing* from a non-judgmental perspective.

Kundalini psychosis, or spiritual emergence, the term used in psychiatry, is the result of awakening this emotional energy before we have prepared ourselves for it. We have to work through this energy of new perceptions to reintegrate our personalities, bringing the pieces back together. Any major trauma, near death experience, or use of drugs can have a similar effect of disintegrating our personality. Like scattering our marbles, it loosens us all around, which may be good if we are stuck in rigid patterns of belief systems that are faulty. Along with professional guidance, this can give us an opportunity to reintegrate and rebuild a more coherent and truthful reality.

Maya

If the doors of perception were cleansed
Everything would appear as it is...
Infinite.
...William Blake

The term *maya* means illusion resulting from the ignorance of the *jiva*. The illusion of the gross body (our physical self) is the *maya* most of us relate to. *Tamas guna*, the principle of staticity or dullness is a feature of this *maya*. This is the *maya* of ignorance and forgetfulness, the illusion that obscures the reality.

This *maya* separates us from our divinity. The veil of obscurity prevents us from being conscious of our thoughts, actions, and deeds. Through this veil of illusion our minds create false images of ourselves, those around us, the events, our character and our behavior, hiding us from the truth of who we are, what we do and what we think. Through practices, the veil is lifted, allowing us to experience the Divine. The scriptures tell us that our ignorance affects seven generations before us and seven generations after us; thus, through the fruit of our karma, we can purify fourteen generations.

We see the world, not the way it is, but the way we are.
...Talmud

The gross body (our physicalness) is composed of all the elements, which has no real existence because they are ever changing. This *maya* is an attribute of the mind, which is the cause of our attachment, or bondage to our pain and suffering. When we go beyond *maya,* what remains is the soul.

In the subtle body, *maya* is perceived as the spiritual energy of *Prakriti* (embodiment of nature) and *Purusha* (the individual). This is the *maya* of union where Divine Mother is the measurement of existence, not an illusion. All knowledge at this level leads to unity; therefore, this is the *maya* of tantra. *Rajas guna* is the principle of energy attributed in the subtle body.

The energy of the infinite Self is the *maya* of the causal body, the soul of true existence, and the intuitive supreme. This is the maya of Vedanta, where there is only one reality, the One Infinite Consciousness in harmony with its Self. *Sattva guna* is the principle of sentience.

Although we relate to all three forms of *maya* as long as we are embodied, humans are primarily attached to the *maya* of the gross body.

Our soul can be held hostage by illusion and inner demons, however, we can learn to free ourselves from our bondages, and find joy in life.

....

PRACTICE

....

Challenge For Her:

We have a tendency to over think and get trapped in negative thoughts and emotions about ourselves, our partners, our friends, our work, our life and our appearance. As a daily practice, get a journal and write the positive things about yourself, your partners, your friends, your work, your life and your appearance. Even if feels untrue at first; align yourself with the best of everyone and every situation and think in a more positive manner.

1. Examine all the positive things in your life, and list everything you are grateful for. Every day add five more things, and meditate on this for five minutes daily.

2. Meditate on this teaching from Christ, "Finally, brothers, whatever is true, whatever is noble, whatever is right, whatever is pure, whatever is lovely, whatever is admirable--if anything is excellent or praiseworthy--think about such things."

Challenge For Him:

Become the Buddha and be aware of living the way of *The Noble Eightfold Path:* Right Views, Right Thoughts, Right Speech, Right Conduct, Right Livelihood, Right Effort, Right Mindfulness, Right Concentration. Make a conscious effort to do this daily basis.

Practice For Couples:

1. Sit facing each other either on a chair or cross-legged on the floor. Sit with your spine straight, knees touching, and holding hands. Locking eyes, name three things that you appreciate in each other. Coordinate your breaths so that when she inhales, he exhales, and then reverse the process. Continue for as long as desired, then embrace and take a deep breath. You will be left feeling very connected to each other.

2. After you have read the entire book, make it a practice to read one segment every day. You can choose it at random if you wish. You will be amazed how your subconscious mind will alert you to passages that may be answers to questions you may have. Develop the habit of devoting just five minutes a day to meditating, doing an exercise, reading a section of this book, or focusing your attention to whatever is needing your attention.

//om//

Chapter Two:

The Practices

Tantra is the study and practice involving Shakti and all the senses to activate and transform energy into higher states of consciousness. Hence, this tantric sex is often referred to as "sacred sex" and "spiritual sex". In Tantra, we use lovemaking as a means to experience the subtler aspects of energy within.

This chapter explores and prepares the body, mind and spirit for receiving and containing this sexual energy. Through the continuous practices of tantra with one partner, the reader will develop a more experiential understanding of energy movement throughout the body through sound, sight, taste, touch and smell.

Contemporary psychologists like Piaget, in concurrence with the ancient sages, established that we learn best through our senses and our personal experiences.

The following practices are essential in developing skills for a more complete and intimate bonding with your beloved.

Here's a Quick Tantra Tip:

How to energize and activate energy in your hands:

With palms facing each other, held shoulder width apart in front of the abdominal area, gaze at the space between the palms. Now "pull" the invisible energy apart, stretching it about two or three feet apart, and contract the energy as you slowly bring your palms together until they are about six inches apart. Continue doing this for five minutes and notice any sensations. You may feel tingling, needles and pins, heat, cold, numbness, and any number of sensations. It could be very subtle at first, and you may be tempted to just disregard it as "imagination". As your become more proficient in your practice, any initial skepticism will turn to trust.

Play with this energy everyday and get to know it. Learn to trust this energy.

Meditation

Meditation is the ultimate music.
It is the music that is not created by any instrument;
it is the music that arises in your silence.
It is the sound of silence.
It is the harmony that is heard when all noise has disappeared.
When the mind with its thousands of voices is gone
and your inner space is utterly empty, silent, still,
that stillness itself has a tremendous music to it.
And out of that music is all creativity, true creativity.
…Osho, from "Nirvana, Now or Never"

Why meditate? We meditate to develop objectivity of our *asuras*, the inner enemies that lurk within. We learn to see them objectively and separate from whom we are.

Just to know these inner enemies intellectually is not sufficient. To be fascinated with the metaphors and texts serve no purpose until we become mindful of the threats they pose to our inner peace and joy.

It all begins with meditation and mindfulness. Having awareness all the time and recognizing our inner foes when they try to seize control over our consciousness, is the only way to overcome their influence.

To effect changes we need to develop a mindful objectivity of our thoughts and behavior, and either recognize them or be under the spell of a vicious enemy. We must become a spiritual warrior who literally protects and defends a state of bliss and happiness. We must take a position of strength and actually fight the *asuras* with our will and purpose; otherwise they will continue to attack our consciousness. The inner enemies are insidious, sneaking into our psyche at every opportunity. Eventually through our will and inner strength, they can be subdued. By taking the stance of the *Bodhisattva,* the spiritual warrior, we can defend our state, and be victorious.

We do this in two ways; we meditate, and we practice mindfulness.

Meditation is the quiet space that is within us all. It is the place of silence, the state of non-doing, the music of the inner space. Meditation is the absence of the chatter of the mind. Every masterpiece, whether it is a painting, music or writing, comes not from the mind, but from meditation.

Meditation is the path, the inner journey from our mind to our soul. It is a path to find our true nature, beginning by first stilling the mind and becoming comfortable with the emptiness and the silence of the universe. Once we achieve this silence, we can journey inward to the very core of our existence.

If they ask you,
"What is the sign of your Father in you?"
say to them, "it is movement and repose"
…Jesus Christ

Before we meditate, we need to find a safe and comfortable place where we will not be distracted or disturbed. Many saints sought serenity in the heart of a mountain or a cave, where there was ultimate security and silence. Today, it would be difficult and impractical to find a cave or mountain, so we have to create our own refuge, usually somewhere in our home where we will not be interrupted. We sit in a yoga posture, an *asana,* allowing the mind to enter the space easily, forcing the body to sit quietly. It may take awhile but the regular practice of these yogic postures will still the body and mind. (See section on yoga asanas.)

Some meditations are more passive and some more active. The most powerful and active meditation is the tantric union with our beloved, where body, mind, and soul are actively engaged in a divine connection with our partner.

The journey is within. Too often when we try to meditate with a partner we become absorbed either in our senses, our ego, or our partner, and we cannot find this true inner sanctum. It is necessary to master meditation on our own before attempting the dynamic meditation of union with a partner.

Meditation is so important that it has entered the mainstream of health care as a method of stress and pain reduction. For example, in an early study in 1972, transcendental meditation was shown to effect the human metabolism by lowering the biochemical byproducts of stress, such as lactate (lactic acid), and by decreasing heart rate and blood pressure and inducing favorable brain waves.[8]

Dr. James Austin, a neurophysiologist at the University of Colorado, reported in his landmark book *Zen and the Brain*, that *Zazen or Zen* meditation rewires the circuitry of the brain. This has been confirmed using sophisticated imaging techniques that examine the electrical activity of the brain.

Dr. Herbert Benson of the Mind-Body Medical Institute, which is affiliated with Harvard and several Boston hospitals, reports that meditation induces a host of biochemical and physical changes in the body collectively referred to as the "relaxation response". The relaxation response includes changes in metabolism, heart rate, respiration, blood pressure, and brain chemistry.[9]

Regardless of our reason for meditating, we can apply many of the same principles to our daily life. When we do this, we multiply the rewards simply because we are increasing the amount of time during which we are attending to our inner states, and we are sustaining the momentum that we cultivated during meditation. We also have the opportunity to test and apply any revelations that we acquired during meditation. We receive feedback and confirmation that adds new dimensions to our understanding of abstractions such as "divine

---

[8] Scientific American 226: 84-90, 1972
[9] Wikipedia.orgGNU Free documentation License

love", and we can see how this "divine love" takes form in our everyday activities, our home, our friendships, our finances, our physical health, and other situations.

The activities of our everyday life are not a distraction; rather they are that which attracts our attention. Our interest, our desire, our emotional response is not a diversion from some ideal spiritual state. On the contrary, we might find that the reason we are enticed to meditate specifically is because there is something for us to learn--a spiritual principle, a *karmic* or fateful situation, which we have created, or an attachment that needs to be released with love.

When we bring meditation into our daily existence, we learn more about dualities and the common ground that lies beyond them. We become mindful of every activity that we undertake, such as walking or dancing,

The outflowing of loving energy that results from mediation, helps us to live fully in the world and yet simultaneously to experience the loving divinity beyond this world.

Basic activities and responsibilities of life, like eating and sleeping, will not change after enlightenment. However, these positive energies will alter our outlook on life, by maintaining qualities, such as love, devotion, mindfulness, bliss and clarity, compassion, and maintaining equipoise in the midst of challenges. Our spiritual evolution might be based on acceptance, transcendence, and witnessing our personal world, but with an expanded awareness.

As we experience the enjoyable states that occur during meditation, we naturally want to recreate those states throughout the day. We look for ways to change our outer life and release lethargy and heaviness that diminish the sweet lightness that we found during meditation. In addition, meditation increases our sensitivity to subtleties. For example, we might choose to stop eating meat, because we discover that the digestion of meat causes friends to become abrasive and energy draining in ways that we hadn't noticed previously.

We may change our life, career, and associations, to resonate with our new experience of vitality. We might become more outgoing, active, and adventurous, or, contrarily, we might quit some of our involvements in order to have a quieter, simpler lifestyle.

Nothing in this world is inherently more spiritual than anything else. If we are true to ourselves, we find and use whichever elements will enhance our growth, regardless of any stereotyped ideas regarding the proper lifestyle of a meditator. Our needs will change constantly, so we must monitor ourselves, and find enjoyment in the freshness of each new development of ourselves. Some changes, perhaps all of them, will happen automatically. Meditators often say that their destructive habits, like drugs or smoking simply dropped away, for now they have an inner strength and alternative to establish new ways of being.

Meditation gives us a larger perspective of life, increasing the clarity of our thinking and enhancing such qualities as detachment and love.

To materialize spiritual realization and experience the bliss body, a *sadhak* (seeker), should do the practices of meditation, surrender and worship before advancing to the study of tantra.

Great beings like the Buddha, Jesus, Moses, and Mohammed, all made *sadhana* (spiritual practices) a necessary part of their lives.

Mindfulness

To enjoy good health, to bring true happiness to one's family,
to bring peace to all, one must first discipline
and control one's own mind. If a man can control his mind
he can find the way to Enlightenment,
and all wisdom and virtue will naturally come to him.
...Buddha

Mindfulness is the attentive and conscious effort of regulating our own thoughts, moods, words, and deeds. It is having an awareness that does not wane, but is always consistent, self-regulating, and self-adjusting.

It takes this mental awareness and conscientious effort on our part to break free from our emotional scars and self-induced torments. Being ever mindful can shortstop the ego by enabling us to become less reactive, to see the truth, to adjust our thinking, and find effective solutions to every problem. When we are able to control our thoughts, we can become more authentic, and more successful in whatever we do.

By becoming more loving, giving and honest, we receive, by default, more love, devotion and respect.

To apply mindfulness we can utilize tools such as silence, meditation, contemplation, journaling, self-analysis, or other activities that require concentration and diligence, such as yoga, golf etc. Making love is the ultimate form of mindfulness, where we must be not only aware of our partner's feelings, thoughts and actions, but we must be conscious of our own state as well. While making love requires mindfulness, it does not require that we live "in our head"; rather, our center should be in our *heart*.

Mindfulness is a moment-to-moment alertness to the events of our world. We cultivate bare attention; our mind merely observes, without elaborating. Mindfulness meditation is a practical form of meditation for busy people, because it does not require us to set aside any time for it; instead, we are simply mindful of whatever activity we are doing. Although that might not seem like meditation, mindfulness, *satipatthana*, is practiced in many Buddhist sects.

In mindfulness, we are aware of whatever is happening. Rather than concentrating on a particular object (e.g., a candle flame), we allow our attention to shift continually from one object to another, in the natural course of our daily actions; we do not direct our attention toward anything in particular. We can be mindful of our thoughts, feelings, emotions, sensory input, bodily sensations and external phenomena such as people, objects, and movements. As our attention moves from one object to another, we can mindfully notice both the object and the reason why our attention was drawn there.

In mindfulness, we merely observe our thoughts as they pass through us. However, sometimes we benefit from lingering with our thoughts, to delve into them more deeply. This is analytical thought.

Sometimes we might need to daydream in reverie and fantasies; we shut off the input from the external world and become functionally mindless.

Instead of merely observing, we might need to affirm our human identity and boundaries by indulging our personal reactions, opinions, liking or disliking, and our intent to change certain elements in our life.

We gain benefits from mindfulness, by acting consciously rather than automatically. This enhances our spontaneity, flexibility, creativity, and freedom of choice. From this position of centeredness, we are ready for anything. We notice our behavioral habits and the thoughts or emotions that propel them. With this awareness, we might modify the habit to one that is more productive, or we could lift the behavior from the realm of the habitual altogether and perform it with full attentiveness.

Eventually mindfulness itself becomes a habit; it is the natural state of the mind.

We become more aware of our emotions and thoughts. We notice them as soon as they arise, so we are less likely to become lost in them and thus to perpetuate nonproductive habitual emotional responses or trains of thought or fantasies or compulsions. This awareness of our inner world might be developed more easily in thought meditation, when we are turned inward specifically to observe our thoughts and feelings, but we can also observe them during mindfulness of our daily activities.

Our senses become more acute and we notice both the beauties and the dangers around us. For example, we have a greater enjoyment of a delicious apple, and we are more conscious of the circumstances when we are driving.

Mindfulness increases our understanding of our physical body. As we become more mindful of our body we can enhance its energy, pleasure, comfort, breathing, relaxation, efficiency of movement and posture--and thereby increase our healthfulness. We notice more of the tensions and pains that alert us to situations that need to be corrected, and we discern our reactions to specific foods, or to bad habits, such as overeating, or smoking, or taking drugs.

The present is where we find joy and life itself. We attend to the current process rather than fantasize about the eventual goal. In mindfulness, the past and the future do not exist (except perhaps in a sense of flow from one moment to the next). Contrarily, our thoughts are never in the present; even when we are thinking about a present occurrence, the amount of time in which we process the data about the occurrence has already made it a thing of the past.

Some people think too much. They allow a continual flood of thoughts--labeling and judging and over-analyzing everything around them, processing regrets about the past, and worries about the future. The mind creates thoughts constantly; sometimes we need to attend to those thoughts. But at other times, we can direct our attention to other valuable interests. We can decide instead to be attentive to the refreshing and stimulating objects of the senses--the cool breeze, or the background music, or the warm sensations of our body, or our feelings regarding our surroundings, or our imagination.

Only that day dawns to which we are awake.
... Thoreau

In mindfulness, we are accepting and *self*-accepting, regardless of whatever is presented to us. With this acknowledgment of things as they are, we do not become immersed in thoughts of interpretation, judgment, reaction, opinion, expectation, liking or disliking, or wanting to change anything. In mindfulness meditation, everything is equal; it is simply an occurrence to be observed in what the Buddhists call "choiceless awareness". For example, if we feel unhappy, we behold the unhappiness; if we are excited, we behold the excitement. We surrender to the experience of our life, rather than denying or avoiding, but if we find ourselves denying or avoiding, we can be mindful of those activities, too.

When we can maintain mindfulness continually, it matures into insight meditation, *vipassana*. Because our mindfulness is constant, in regard to all that we encounter, we begin to perceive these elements' interplays and patterns. We have no distractions that would cause us to miss a moment of the action (and which would leave us with the absence of important pieces from our puzzle). Thus, we gain insight into the general nature of our world and ourselves.

We can maintain mindfulness during sleep. We develop this ability in lucid dreaming and in Tibetan dream yoga, to be conscious during the entire sleep-period. During some lucid dreams, we are as mindless as we are during wakefulness; however, we have the option of practicing mindfulness as we pursue activities within the dreamscape. Some people are able to maintain consciousness 24 hours per day. They are lucid during their dreams, and aware also during the non-dreaming periods. When they awaken, they are fully refreshed, because their body has had a natural sleep and their mind, too, has recharged itself.

Mantra, The Mystical Power of Sound

*In the beginning was the Word
and the Word was with God and the Word was God.
…John 1:1*

Tantra is designated as the *Mantra Sastra* (study of the mantra), a tradition involving incantations, philosophy, principles, ceremony, initiation, worship, mental and bodily discipline, and observances. Mantra is a word, phrase, or sound that is repeated for harmonizing the body through the rhythm of the breath, focusing the mind towards the higher Self. The mantra is the audible form of the deity.

The major focus with which the Tantras are concerned is in the power of mantras. Mantras are certain scientifically arranged formulas, which, if practiced according to the Tantrik precepts, bring about certain results conducive to the fulfillment of the chanter's wishes. Every *Matrika* (a, A, etc.) is a living energy in itself; and should not be mistaken, for a mere *Varna,* or letter. Every *Matrika* is a mantra. The subtle combinations of the Sanskrit syllables are associated with spiritual propensities of the mind. The *Sadhak* creates a living force by placing the letters in a certain systematic order.

Although many words and sounds of the universe are meaningful, they cannot be called mantras unless they possess the capacity to liberate a person from bondage. Only sounds and sound waves that can stimulate the subtlest portion of the human mind and unite it with the supreme can be a mantra. Other words are mere words, ordinary syllables, and nothing else.

The mantras are nothing but the harmoniously living forces strong enough, no doubt, to accomplish even the most difficult undertakings of those dedicated to the Tantras. The arrangement of letters in a scientific procedure assists the worshipper, during Tantric ceremonies. To understand the hidden secrets of the mantra, Tantra and yantra

may work wonders, and gradually liberate us from the confines of the world.

The liberation of the kundalini can be interrupted by a single stroke of a siddha mantra, a 'proven' or effective mantra.
A mantra is a collection of sound waves that can produce a powerful resonance, or sympathetic vibration. The scriptures say "Only that mantra which is received through the Grace of the Guru can give all fulfillment".
...Kularnarva Tantra

In virtually every type of meditation, we use an object, e.g., our thoughts, our environment (as in mindfulness), or a visually perceived object (as in concentration meditation). In mantra meditation, the object is sound. Mantras have the power to harmonize our mental, emotional, and physical forces, elevating our consciousness that transforms us from ordinary to the divine.

The repetition of Sanskrit mantras provides us with the power to attain our goals, giving us the power to heal, ward off evil, acquire supernatural powers, and wealth. In other words, mantra can effectively alter our karma. In tantra, the mantra is in the form of a Sanskrit letter, or combination of words. According to the *Shaiva Upanishads*, the Sanskrit language was developed such that each letter is associated with a particular state; thus, every letter can be used as a mantra.

Mananaat traayate iti mantrah
... That which uplifts by constant repetition is a Mantra.

Don Campbell, author of the "Mozart Effect", lists the benefits of using our voice (singing, chanting etc.) He says "toning" for just five minutes a day can help people relax, center and balance their emotions. Toning balances brain waves, deepens the breath, and reduces heart rate, Campbell says.

The mantra "Ahhhh" evokes a relaxation process. "Ah", the first letter in the Sanskrit alphabet represents Shiva. "Ah" is the sound present in all the names of the Lord--God, Shiva, Krishna, Jehovah,

Buddha, Allah, Ishvara, Rama, Brahma, Chandi, Kali, Lakshmi, and Durga to name a few.

Chanting focuses and opens our mind. The special rhythm brings about a sense of tranquility, altering our mood.

Mantra is a word or phrase to experience a particular state of consciousness. For example, we might want to experience bliss, *samadhi,* or mental alertness. Each mantra has a unique effect; one mantra might be stimulating, while another mantra is relaxing. With this discernment, we can select a mantra that is appropriate for our current needs; however, many people feel comfortable using the same mantra whenever they chant.

Mantras assist in our breathing cycles. While the average person takes in fifteen breaths per minute, researchers have found that recitation of the mantra brings the breath down to six breaths per minute. Doctors from Italy and Peter Sleight, of the John Radcliff hospital in Oxford, noted these results in the British Medical Journal. They monitored the blood pressure, heart rate, and breathing of 23 healthy men and women.[10]

Traditionally, seekers receive their own mantra from their guru in the context of a formal initiation. In the absence of a guru, however, intention and faith can make the sound vibrations of these powerful mantras effective, and they can easily become a part of our life.

During meditation, you might hear a sound or a word that seems appropriate to be used as a mantra. If you repeat the mantra, later, you are likely to return to the state in which you originally heard it.

The body is both stimulated and calmed by the physical vibration of this audial massage. A high pitch resonates in the head. This pitch might help to stimulate and clear the mind. A variable pitch changes its resonance. For example, you can start low and then gradually raise the pitch; or spontaneously raise or lower the pitch, to create a pleasing melody.

If you want to commit to a particular number of repetitions, you can count them with a rosary, or prayer beads, a *mala* (which is a rosary of 54 or 108 beads). With each repetition, move one bead through the

---

[10] Mike White, executive director of "Optimal Breathing School and author of "Secrets of Optimal Breath Development"

fingers. You can use the thumb and the ring finger to move the bead forward. Avoid using the index finger because it is the finger of the ego.

Our potentialities lie dormant in the *Muladhar* chakra. When we raise the kundalini, we start to awaken our creative potentialities. Through the mantra, we open the first stage of vocality. Next, we visualize what we are going to vocalize. This stage is at the *Svadhistan* chakra. The third chakra, the *Manipur* is the center of the luminous energy where we maintain our body's balance. At the *Anahat* chakra, we try to give vocal expression to our mental idea, and at the *Visshuda* chakra, the abstract idea turns into vocal expression.

If the mental repetition of a mantra continues all the time, day and night, the kundalini remains perpetually awakened.

One of the most prominent mantras is called the *Gayatri*, "The Mother of the Vedas". The practice of this mantra enabled the sages to receive revelation of all other mantras, for this mantra calms mental noise, washes off karmic impurities, purifies the ego, sharpens the intellect, and illuminates the inner being with the light that flows directly from the Source. This mantra connects us to the guru within and helps us receive inner guidance and inner inspiration. One may not notice an instantaneous transformation, but the effect of this mantra is immense and everlasting. The process of purification through this practice begins in the deep unconscious and gradually pervades all aspects of our personality. We become new and fully transformed, from inside out.

The *Gayatri* is traditionally recited at sunrise and sunset facing the direction of the sun.

Om bhuh bhuva swaha
Tat savitur varenyam
Bhargo devasya dhimahi
Dhiyo yo nah pracodayat
…I meditate on the radiant and most venerable light of the Divine,
from which issues forth the triple world (heaven, atmosphere, earth).
May the Divine Light illuminate and guide my intelligence.

A mantra recited while focusing on a corresponding yantra is a powerful practice, promising great rewards, whether the purpose is for spiritual enlightenment or mundane needs. Mantras are used to find a marriage partner, win lawsuits, attract wealth, gain protection, remove diseases and problems, and fulfill all desires.

Aum

AUM is a bow,
The arrow is the self,
And Brahman (Absolute reality) is said to be the Mark.
… Mandukya Upanishad

Aum

The goal which all the Vedas declare, which all austerities aim at,
and which men desire when they lead the life of continence is OM.
This syllable OM is indeed Brahman.
Whosoever knows this syllable obtains all that he desires.
This is the best support; this is the highest support.
Whosoever knows this support is adored in the world of Brahma.
… Katha Upanishad I

"Aum" or *"Om"* is the primordial sound, the sound that has its origins at the very creation of the Universe, when the "Big Bang" occurred. The sound stands for creation, preservation, and transformation.

In Sanskrit the vowel 'o' is a diphthong compound of a + u; hence *Om* is represented as *Aum*.

"*A*" is the sound, the acoustic root of creation.

"*U*" is the sound of preservation.

"*M*" is the acoustic root of transformation, annihilation.

In Sanskrit, *Aum* is symbolized by four strokes, and a dot, each representing manifestations of consciousness.

The large lower curve represents *jagrat,* the waking state of consciousness that the majority of people belong to.

The upper curve symbolizes the state of *sushupti.* This is the deep sleep, or the unconscious state, where desires and dreams no longer exist for the individual.

The middle loop on the right is *swapna.* In this dream state, the individual is turned within, between deep sleep and the waking state

The fourth state of consciousness, known as *turiya* is represented by the *bindu,* the dot, where the states of peace and bliss are the ultimate goal. The *bindu* is the unmanifest universe.

The semi circle, *nada,* which separates the dot from the other three curves, symbolizes *maya,* the illusion that prevents us from realizing our divineness. The semi circle does not touch the dot, indicating that this highest state that is not affected by maya.

Chanting *Om (Aum)* creates a vibration that merges the *jiva* with the Infinite. The momentary silence between each repetition becomes apparent until the sound ceases and all thought comes to a standstill. The mind is transcended as we merge with the Supreme Conscious Being.

The essence of all beings is the earth.
The essence of the earth is water.
The essence of water is the plant.
The essence of the plant is man.
The essence of man is speech.
The essence of speech is the Rigveda.
The essence of Rigveda is the Samveda.
The essence of Samveda is Om.
…Chandogya Upanishad

So'Ham, The Natural Mantra

So'Ham is a mantra in meditation. It is the natural sound of the Self. It is the sound of the natural breath meaning, "That am I" or "I am the breath". " *So*" signifies God or Guru, and "*ham*" denotes "I" or "me".

When we inhale we can hear the "So" and when we exhale the sound we hear is "hum". The mental repetition of this mantra will balance our emotions, resolve past traumas, and bring awareness to the Supreme Consciousness. After awhile So'Ham becomes "Hamsa."

Do this a few minutes every morning. It does not sound like much, but done regularly you will notice changes and will look forward to meditation.

Kirtan-Singing the Names of God

Music is the science of vibration. It is called *Nada Brahma*, the sound of God.

Vibration is root of all creation. The positions of the stars, planets, individuals, and everything on this planet were created from vibratory conditions. Every pitch noted in Indian music relates to the vibration of a planet, color, plant or animal, affecting corresponding chakras.

Kirtan is the glorious spiritual practice of singing and dancing to God's names with other seekers. It can be an ecstatic and enlightening experience.

Raga is an assembly of melodic patterns, colors or tones that elicits certain emotional states, strictly using only the notes that correspond to that state. There are about 231 *ragas* in Indian music. Here are a few:

1. *Bhimpalasi Raga*--melody invokes tranquility and yearning for God

2. *Shiva Bhairav Raga*--this melody brings forth the tenderness of new day and devotion and longing for God. This raga can be listened to or chanted at any time to bring forth this feeling.

3. *Darbari Raga*--traditionally sung in evening to evoke *bhakti*

4. *Bhupali Raga*--having supreme joy and honoring of the Lord

5. *Malkauns Raga*--feeling valor, courage, joy

6. *Yaman Raga*--melody that is stately, auspicious, pleasurable

7. *Jivanpuri Raga*--summoning the Lord

8. *Bilaaval Raga*--tender repose, blissful prayer

9. *Desh Raga*--tender feelings, light, and delightful

Singing has been known to strengthen the immune system. Researchers found that concentrations of immunoglobin A (proteins in the immune system which function as antibodies) and hydrocortisone, an anti-stress hormone, increased significantly during singing.

Studies have shown that choral singing improved physical and emotional health. These studies have taken place at the University of Frankfurt among choir members, and in England at the *Journal of the Royal Society for the Promotion of Health* where choir members reported that they developed better lung capacity, more energy and confidence. In a questionnaire, 89% reported intense happiness while singing, while 79% said they felt less stressful, and 75% experienced heightened adrenaline.[11]

Singing uplifting songs is of great benefit. As a spiritual practice, kirtan increases inner radiance, keeps the mind one-pointed, fights against mundane difficulties, and brings one closer to the Supreme.

During kirtan, when devotees assemble, their collective energies--both physical and psychical--function in unity. They focus on the Supreme collectively, and this concentration of energies removes all afflictions and worldly obstacles. There are instances where it has even prevented disasters and other calamities of nature. Chanting benefits

---

[11] "The Lantern: The Student Voice of Ohio State University", published Tues. Jan. 20, 2004

even those who are not singing. Simply listening to the chanting can also dispel miseries and restore our balance.

> *Divine sound is the cause of all manifestation.*
> *The knower of the mystery of sound knows the mystery*
> *of the whole Universe.*
> *…Hazrat Inayat Khan*

When we are troubled, listening to the chanting of a great being can bring relief, confidence, and peace of mind. In fact, it is a good practice to have spiritual music playing softly in the background all the time. In muscle testing, it has been shown that people are strengthened just listening to this music. On the other hand, when rap or heavy metal music was played, they were weakened.

It is important to surround ourselves with good energy people, books, music, food, and drink. Everything we see, hear, eat, and drink affects our body and our experiences. As we progress in our spiritual practices we become increasingly sensitive to energy, and we must be very prudent and cautious about the type of energy we surround ourselves with and put in our bodies.

Swadhyaya, Recitation of Texts

Swadhyaya is the sacred practice of chanting and reciting ancient texts, such as the *Guru Gita* and the *Chandi Path,* which are comprised of hundreds of verses, or mantras. The practitioner usually does the practice every day at a given time in a clean room.

Sit in *padmasana*, holding the book in the right hand, with eyes fixed on the material. Free the mind from distractions and focus on the mantras with reverence and devotion.

As you recite, your mind becomes purified, your heart becomes a vessel of nectar; you feel radiance, vigor, love, and great peace of mind. You feel the inner bliss, the state of completeness, and a state that will be recognized and again experienced when you are in meditation or in divine union with your partner.

Shri Yantra, Visual Perfection

A yantra is a pattern of symmetrical geometric designs of power zones that create a balanced picture with a dominant theme in the center. Generally, yantra refers to any such design that is used in meditation and rituals.

Yantras are symbolic. Each part of the yantra represents one of the forces in our lives; the linear pattern depicts the interplay of these forces. These elements are arranged symmetrically, to express the ideally organized, balanced, and unified functioning of our mind, our affairs, and the universe.

Shri Yantra is a geometric design that binds an inner connection with the Supreme Principle. *Shri* is an honorific term of respect, *Yantra* means, "to bind". *Shri Yantra* (also referred to as *Shri Chakra*) is the embodiment of the Goddess *Lalita* in visual form--a powerful mystical diagram to channel psychic forces.

The two bindus, white and red, are Shiva and Shakti,
who in their secret mutual enjoyment are now expanding and now contracting...
the Sun is Kama, which is so called because of its desirableness;
and Kala is the two bindus that are Moon and Fire.
...Kamakalavilasa

Shri Yantra

The different parts or petals and lines of the yantra are arranged in concentric circles, *mandalas,* and contain rays or sub-limbs of the Goddess. *Shri Yantra* has nine of these *mandalas,* each filled with various aspects of the Devi. *Shri Yantra* is said to be a geometric form of the human body, which implies that goddess, as Macrocosm is one with the human being as Microcosm.

The consort of Lord Shiva, Goddess *Lalita* is identified in the *bindu* as three manifest forms of the goddesses *Saraswati, Lakshmi* and *Kali,* the three forces of the three cities--creation, maintenance, and dissolution. In the *bindu,* Shiva and the Devi are in divine union. The five triangles of Shakti facing downwards is the *kamakala,* the aspect of desire, and the four triangles facing upward represent Shiva's *lingam.*

Shri Yantra consists of triangles, *trikonas,* the outer gates of three lines, *bhupura,* and circles.

The five Shakti triangles also symbolize the five elements of earth, water, fire, air and ether, identified with creation and the human body, while the Shiva triangles have to do with dissolution and marrow, semen, breath and life.

The circles represent the macro state, the universal state, to the microstate, the most microscopic form of life. *Shri Yantra's* meaning is therefore, both microcosmic and macrocosmic. Each triangle, sub-triangle, lotus, circle and line is identified with specific attributes, powers, goddesses, Sanskrit letters, propensities, speech, and attractions.

The point or dot in center is the *Bindu* of Pure Bliss. Here sits the Goddess *Lalita,* the *Mahatripurasundari Devi,* in sexual union with *Shri Mahadeva,* Shiva.

The technique for using a yantra in meditation is this--gaze at the center of the yantra. With your peripheral vision, see the outer images of the design. Starting at the center let your eyes wander throughout the yantra to its edges; then gradually return your attention to the center. Look at it just long enough to become familiar with it, then close your eyes and re-create the image in your imagination. Sit for as long as you desire. Then, bring your awareness back to where you are and gently open your eyes when you are ready.

There are yantras for every possible purpose. Mantras increase their effectiveness, and help fulfill our purpose and desires.

Mudra, The Touch of Focus

Mudras (usually thought of as body or hand positions) are also used to activate sexual energy, bringing our body, mind, and spirit in focus during meditation. This can be done with the hands, body, tongue, during solo practice, or during sexual union. *Mudra* also refers to the state of deep, orgasmic intercourse and the final state of orgasm. This *Mahamudra,* the great orgasm, occurs when we become one with the Universe.

Simply placing fingers, limbs or the body in certain postures is not enough. We make hand gestures unconsciously with no effects. Unless we have had the training to give, receive and recognize energy (as in healing), hand and body positions are just that--hand and body positions with no Shakti. However, when one works with energy in a comprehensive manner, the sensitive nerveways have a charge and thus, have the ability to ignite and activate a corresponding energy point by mere touch. This can happen during healing, dancing, and sexual union.

In sexual *mudras,* ideally the couple will be equally dedicated to spiritual practices and have experience working with and handling energy. They may both become powerful givers and delightful receivers of this remarkable energy when they have the ability to generate electricity, literally.

A few of the *mudras* commonly used in meditation and Tantric meditation are as follows:

Chin Mudra--The index finger is kept at the root of the thumb; the last three fingers are unfolded, and hands rest softly on the knees, palms down, when the meditator is seated on the floor in a cross-legged position. This mudra keeps the energy within the body.

Khechari Mudra--Touch the roof of the tongue as far back in the throat as possible. This stimulates the anal sphincter muscle and the Kundalini Shakti, trapping negative and positive forces in the head (the yin and yang), uniting Shiva and Shakti. In some traditions, *Khechari* mudra is considered *Mamsa,* eating of meat, and for advanced practitioners it implies a sexual act.

Vajroli Mudra--The thunderbolt, or *vajra,* exercises the genitals. By squeezing the urethral sphincter muscles, we activate the second chakra, the *Svadhistan*. Squeezing the urethral sphincter muscles is experienced as stopping the flow of urine.

Begin by sitting in a comfortable position. Inhale through the nose, swallow, and draw the energy up to the third eye. Retain the breath and contract the urethral as many times as possible on the breath. On the last contraction exhale and feel the rush of energy go up the spine.

Aswini Mudra--The Gesture of the horse-contract the anal sphincter to activate the first chakra, at the *Muladhar*. Sit cross-legged on the floor with the heel (or a rolled up towel) pushing against the perineum. Inhale and fill the lungs about 1/3 full, contract and relax the anus rapidly as many times as you can do comfortably. Do not exhale, but inhale and fill the lungs another third, repeat the contractions and repeat the whole procedure once more. Hold the breath, pressing the neck against the chest, take a sniff of air, and exhale, releasing the tension and feeling the energy going up the spine.

Bandha, Energy Locks

In tantra, we also use *bandhas*, contractions, or locks, of the pelvic region and other areas, to awaken and contain energy in the body. The action of contracting and then releasing the lock, releases hormone rich blood. The hormones produced from these glands and sub-glands control every propensity of the human mind. Each of these propensities is represented in our subtle body as chakras, or lotuses. Each petal of the lotus represents one letter of the Sanskrit alphabet, which represents the propensities of the individual.

To control any of these propensities we must control the glands through meditation, repeating the mantra and activating and controlling the particular chakra that controls that particular propensity.

For example, if you are having difficulty communicating, that concerns the fifth chakra, so you could focus on practices to activate and stimulate the throat area:

Jalandhara--Neck Lock or Chin Lock-is done in *Siddhasana* pose and used during chanting meditations and *pranayam* (breathing exercises). Lift the chest and sternum upward and stretch the back of the neck by pulling the chin in towards the neck. There should be some tension in the back and sides of the neck. The chin rests in the notch between the collarbones and the head stays level without tilting forward, straightening the cervical vertebrae, and allowing the free flow of prana to the brain.

This lock puts pressure on the thyroid and parathyroid to enable their secretions, and in turn, activate the pituitary. Without this lock, *pranayam* can cause uncomfortable pressure in eyes, ears, and heart. It will also prevent dizziness caused by rapid changes in blood pressure that can occur when *nadis*, channels of pranic flow, are unblocked. *Jalandhara* focuses on the throat chakra.

For premature ejaculation, stronger vaginal walls, and improved orgasm capabilities we would use the root lock:

Mulabandha--Root Lock- "*mul*" meaning root or base, is the most frequently applied lock. Sometimes spelled "Moola Bandha", this bandha relates mainly to the muscles of the anus, penis and the muscles located nearby. It is best done in *Siddhasana*. The concentration is on the first chakra, the *Muladhar*. It is performed in three steps (quickly & smoothly with practice) by first contracting the anal sphincter, drawing it in and up (as if trying to hold back a bowel movement), then drawing up the sex organ (so that the urethral tract is contracted).

Lastly, pull the navel point by drawing the lower abdomen back towards the spine. This is applied with breath held (in or out), and helps unite the two major energy flows, prana, and apana, generating psychic heat that triggers the release of Kundalini energy, and often ends an asana or exercise.

Parshnibhagen sampeedya yonimakunchayet gudam
Apanmurdhwamakrushya mulbandhobhidhiyate
The heel should press the penis; the muscles of the anus should be
contracted and the apan vayu, gas, should be lifted upwards.
…Hathapradeepika 3:61

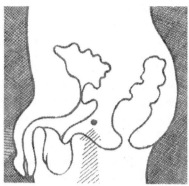

Epicenter of Moolam
- Midway between testes and anis
- 2 inches from floor when in sugasanam

Mulabandha-male

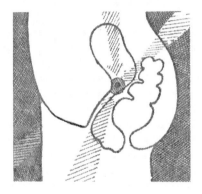

Epicenter of Moolam
- 2 inches inside body
- 2 inches from floor when in sugasana

- Includes contractions of vaginal muscles

Mulabandha-female

To move and transform *pranic* energy up to the neck region, stimulate the hypothalmic-pituitary-adrenal axis in the brain and develop a sense of compassion practice the diaphragm lock. This bandha can give new youthfulness to the entire body.

Uddiyana--Diaphragm Lock- is applied by sitting in *Siddhasana* posture, lifting the diaphragm high up into the thorax while pulling the upper abdominal muscles back towards the spine, creating a cavity, and giving a gentle massage to the heart muscles. It is normally applied with the breath held out. This exercise focuses on the *Manipur* chakra. The *Hathapradeepika* states that this bandha eliminates old age and death.

Mahabandha--This is the chin lock, abdominal lock and root lock done simultaneously to control the movement of the pranic energy.

Aside from the health benefits, mastery of these locks will develop the pelvic thrust ability in Shiva, and penile gripping power in Shakti. This should not be practiced by anyone who has blood pressure problems. If in doubt, consult a physician.

Pranayam

Pranayam is the yogic science of breath retention, control, and altering breath patterns. It has been used to alleviate depression, relieving stress, and eating disorders.

Yogic breathing patterns activate certain bodily responses. Rapid breathing activates the Vagus nerve, which connects with the diaphragm and some of the organs, such as the heart and the brain. Because of this stimulation, messages are sent along three different pathways that tell the body to shut off areas of worry, while awakening areas that control feelings of happiness in the brain.

One pathway leads to the frontal cortex of the brain and shuts down areas controlling excess worries and depressions. Another pathway shuts off anxiety parts of the brain, and a third wakes up the limbic system, which controls positive emotions. At the same time, hormones are released that encourage connectedness in mammals. One such hormone, called the "Cuddle" hormone (related to the peptide hormone), released during sexual activity, encourages bonding, says Dr. Richard P. Brown, a senior psychiatrist at Columbia University in New York. He adds, "Doctors need to understand that there is a scientific basis to this and it is not just a suggestion."[12]

In *pranayam,* we are mindful of the breath. We do not control the breath; instead, we allow it to occur in its natural cadence and depth. While breathing, we can focus on the flow of air as it goes past the tips of the nostrils, the insides of the nostrils, the throat, or the lungs. When we breathe, we must be aware of:

---

[12] Pranayam Has Scientific Basis, by Kalpahna JaianTimes News Network, Sunday, March 03, 2002

1. The abdomen's movement (inward and outward)

2. The sound of the breath

3. The state during the pause after each exhalation. The state of silence, with no thoughts. The quality of the air (perhaps its coolness or its scent)

4. The spontaneous rhythm of the exhalations and inhalations

5. The uniqueness of each breath, (the speed and depth and other characteristics)

6. The various sensations throughout the torso as the lungs expand and contract.

7. The unity with the breath process. We might feel that we are "being breathed" (instead of being a separate witness of the process).

As there are several breath techniques, *pranayam* is best learned through a qualified teacher; the point is we should make it a regular part of our *sadhana*.

Nadi Shodana, The Breath of Union

Anyone who has high blood pressure can do this exercise *without* holding the breath. This is one of the most powerful breaths there is.

Nadi Shodana, the Breath of Union, balances the *ida* and *pingala* energies. This is a very calming exercise, which also helps to get rid of impurities in the finer nerve channels.

First, place the right index finger on the forehead, between the brows. Put the right thumb over the right nostril. Inhale to two counts from the left nostril, visualizing the energy rising from the *Muladhar* chakra up the left side of the spine. Hold the breath for eight counts while shutting the left nostril with the right middle finger. Then lift the right thumb from the right nostril and exhale to the count of four, feeling the energy rushing down the right side of the spine.

Do this a few times, and sit quietly in meditation for a few minutes. Do not abruptly break this "state" to answer a phone call, or dash out of the house to run an errand.

Yoga Asana, Disciplined Bodily Positions

You cannot do yoga. Yoga is your natural state.
What you can do are yoga exercises,
which may reveal to you
where you are resisting your natural state.
...Sharon Gannon

Sexual energy is activated through the opening of the chakras through hatha yoga asanas, which is why hatha yoga is said to be a tantric practice. Yoga is highly recommended for a great workout, finding stillness, disciplining your mind and body, for building strength and stamina, exercising not only the external body, but the internal organs as well.

Blessed are the flexible, for they shall not be bent out of shape.
...Anonymous

The *Devi Gita,* which is from the Seventh *Skanda* of the *Shri Devi Bhagavatam,* is one of the texts that describe the best yoga asanas for the meditator.

Padmasana --Full Lotus Position: Place the right foot on the left thigh and the left foot on the right thigh, with the soles upward, and place the hands on the thighs, with the palms upwards. The yogis say that *Padmasana* is effective for all diseases.

Siddhasana

Siddhasana--Accomplished Position: Press firmly the heel of the left foot against the perineum, and the right heel above the genitals. With the chin pressing on the chest, sit calmly, having restrained the senses, and gaze steadily on the space between the eyebrows. This is the opener to the door of freedom. It is said many saints acquired super natural powers by sitting in this asana; thus, this position has been called "Siddhi", meaning supernatural power.

Yogasana

Yogasana--Yoga Position: Sit in cross-legged sitting position on a blanket on the floor. Put both hands behind the back and grip the left wrist with the right hand. Inhale and slowly drop the torso until the forehead and nose touch the floor. Exhale and lower the head. Keep the head on the floor for about eight seconds, expelling or holding the breath. Then rise up slowly, breathing in and returning to the initial position, and then exhale.

Ardhakurmakasana

Ardhakurmakasana--Half-Tortoise Pose: Get down on both knees, sitting down on the heels. While inhaling, extend both hands upward so that the arms touch the ears, and then join the palms together above the head. Then while exhaling, gradually bow down forward and touch the floor with the forehead and nose. Remain in this position, while holding the breath for eight seconds. Rise slowly while inhaling, back to the original sitting position with hands and arms pointing upward, arms touching the ears with palms joined. Strive to keep both arms straight and the buttocks on the heels all the time. Then lower the arms to each side while exhaling. Provides maximum relaxation, recommended for indigestion, constipation, and flatulence. Stretches lower part of the lungs. This is a recommended position for asthmatics and diabetics.

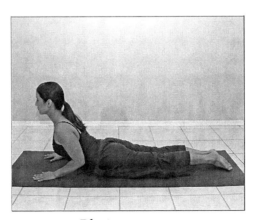

Bhujaungasana

Bhujaungasana --Cobra Pose: Lie down on the stomach and chest, and put forehead on the floor. Slide arms and hands, palms down, to each side of your shoulders. Tuck the elbows to the sides, keeping feet together. While inhaling, raise chest off the floor, supporting the weight on the palms, and roll head and neck back and up, looking up toward the ceiling as if attempting to look behind at your feet. Hold breath and remain in that position for eight seconds. Reverse the whole procedure while going down - i.e. lower chest, neck, and head as while breathing out and exhale slowly, coming down to the original position. Stretches the spine, strengthens the back and arms, opens the chest and heart. Relaxes discomfort in lower back.

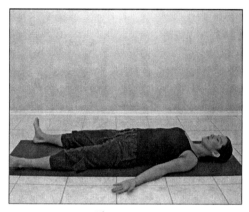

Shavasana

Shavasana --Corpse Pose: Lie on back, spreading legs and hands a comfortable distance from body with palms facing upward. Feel completely relaxed, free of tension, as if the life force has left the body making it a corpse. Relax and take a few long deep breaths. Relaxes and refreshes the body and mind, relieves stress and anxiety, quiets the mind.

Salutations to the Sun

Surya (sun) is the Soul, both of the moving and unmoving beings.
... The Rig Veda

The sun throughout history has been associated with energy and life force. *Surya* was an important God in Hinduism who was worshipped as the source of warmth and light, spiritual consciousness and awareness.

This combination of exercises is comprised of 12 yoga prostrations designed to increase flexibility, stamina and mental focus. They benefit cardiovascular functions, open up the rib cage, assist in digestion and elimination, and are often recommended for weight loss and obesity.

The Salutation to the Sun is a moving meditation, which is traditionally done facing east at sunrise, although you can do it anytime that is convenient for you, such as mid-day or sunset. It is even more relaxing if you can do them at the beach, on a mountaintop, breathing in the fresh air. If practiced with a partner, face each other or face the direction of the sun.

The Salutation utilizes most of the practices involved in yoga: visualization: mantra, mudra, asana, pranayam, bandha, and meditation, so it is a complete sadhana in itself.

There are several variations of the salutation to the sun. This is one version.

Standing Upright

1. Keep feet shoulder width apart. Hold chest high, and pull in the abdomen. Visualize the sun. This posture is great for grounding

and stabilizing the root chakra, affecting the *Muladhar* and *Anahat* Chakras.

Crescent Moon Pose

2. Crescent Moon Pose. Raise arms overhead and arch back as far back as possible, while inhaling. *Visshuda* Chakra is stimulated.

Head to Knees

3. Head to Knees: Exhale and bend forward with arms extended and drop head to the knees. Bend knees if necessary. This pose activates the *Svadhistan* Chakra.

Lunge Pose

4. Lunge Pose. Inhale and step back with the right foot. Lift chin and roll eyes up as if gazing at the sun. This opens the *Ajna* Chakra.

Plank Pose

5. Plank Pose. Exhale and bring the left foot back in line with the right foot. Hold and inhale. *Ajna* chakra opens.

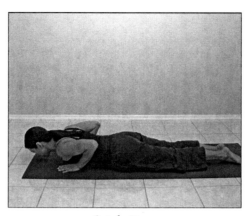

Stick Pose

6. Stick Pose. Exhale and lower body to the floor, holding body up using both hands and feet, as in a push-up. The *Manipur* Chakra is activated here.

Cobra Pose

7. Cobra Pose. Inhale and lift torso with the arms. Lift up so that only the tops of the feet and hands touch the floor. *Svadhistan* and *Visshuda* Chakras get stimulated.

Downward Facing Dog Pose

8. Downward Facing Dog (Mountain Pose). Exhale and lift the hips up high keeping head facing down. Performing the *Mahabandha* activates *Manipur, Svadhistan,* and *Visshuda* Chakras.

Lunge

9. Lunge Pose. (Step #4) step forward with the left foot. Bring right foot in line with the right foot. Inhale.

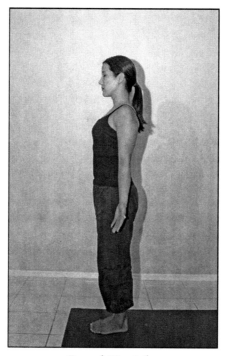

Stand Upright

10. Stand upright. Exhale. Opens *Ajna* Chakra.

Bending Pose

11. Bending Pose. Exhale and bring left foot forward.

Head to Knees

12. Bring head to your knees. *Svadhistan* Chakra is activated.

Straighten Body

13. Slowly straighten the body.

Crescent Moon Pose 2

14. Crescent Moon Pose. (Repeat step #7). Bring both hands up, inhale, and stretch arms over head. Then arch back and lean back as far as comfortable. *Visshuda* Chakra is activated.

Repeat (step #3) but on the lunge pose (#4) step back with the left foot, and on the plank pose (#5) bring the right foot to the back. On the next lunge pose (#9) step forward with the left foot, and bring the right foot forward to meet the left leg and stand upright.

When first starting to do these, try one or two every day, gradually increasing the number of sequences as strength increases. At first, the movements might not be so fluid, but when comfortable with this sequence, they can be done without any hesitation between each pose, flowing smoothly from one position to the next. The entire sequence can be done in a continual, graceful flow, like a dance.

At that point, add the *Khechari* mudra, with the tongue pressed against the roof of the mouth, and repeat a mantra, such as *Om* or the *Gayatri*, before and after each sequence, or select any mantra of choice.

Ayurveda

Only that person is healthy, whose doshas, dhatumal and agni (elements and energy streams) are balanced and free from all defects and disorders and whose mind and soul are in perfect harmony.

Ayurveda is a healing system, which, like tantra, was invented by Lord Shiva in India more than 6000 years ago, prior to the Rig Veda. The term *Ayurveda* comes from two Sanskrit words, "*ayu*" meaning life and "*veda*", or knowledge. *Ayurveda* takes a holistic approach to health care. Unlike the practice of medicine in the west, which tends to treat the body as an entity apart from the mind and spirit, the *Ayurvedic* system consists of treating and balancing the body, mind, senses, and the spirit.

Good for the body is the work of the body,
good for the soul the work of the soul,
and good for either the work of the other.
…Henry David Thoreau

This is a holistic science based on the concept that the body is made of five elements: earth, water, fire, air and ether. These elements combine and create three major physiological functions in our body. This *tridosha,* which governs our metabolism, is known as *Vata, Pitta* and *Kapha.*

While all three *doshas* are present in each of us, one will be predominant in our constitution, and therefore we work to balance this to benefit our well-being. The *tridosha* affects our physical health, appearance, immune system, our finances, temperament, dreams and so on.

For instance, *Vata* predominant people are creative and enthusiastic. Their constitution consists of ether and air. They are nervous and high strung, predisposed to anxiety, insomnia and constipation

Pittas are focused and intellectual, ambitious, articulate, judgmental. The elements of pitta are fire and water.

Kaphas, from water and earth, have a tendency to gain weight. They have a slow metabolism and can be lethargic, so they need to exercise. They are caring and grounded.

The science of *Ayurveda* involves following a nutritious diet, including herbs, having a regular meditation practice, sufficient sleep, proper breathing, fasting, and yoga for exercise. A concerted effort is made to avoid contaminants within and without.

Just as tantra is about having a perfect balance between sex, meditation and spiritual practices, *Ayurveda* is about balancing our metabolism through nutrition for rejuvenation, health, vitality and energy. *Ayurveda* makes it possible to live a long life with purpose and quality.

Tantra is an ever-evolving spiritual practice, a lifestyle that takes us from the mundane to the sublime. Tantra takes the best and makes it better. Tantra enhances every corner of our lives, bringing light and life to everything we do, through practices such as *Jyotish* and *Ayurveda*.

Jyotish, Vedic Astrology

The Sanskrit term *"Jyotish"* is derived from the root *"joti"* meaning "light" and *"isha"* meaning "god". Thus, it means the science of light--the light within each of us that is a microcosm of the light of the universe. It is the study and practice of the planets, the rulers of the planets and their positioning at the precise moment or our birth.

This science of light was divinely revealed to the *rishis,* or sages, ten to twenty thousand years ago--from Brahma to his son, *Narada,* to the sage, *Parasara.*

Like all ancient teachings, it was passed on orally for generations. Later they were finally transcribed and became an important limb of what has been called the world's oldest scripture, the Vedas. The study of *Jyotish* is an integral component of tantric practices, along with repetition of the mantra, worship of the Goddess and the initiation by the Guru.

Jyotish is the marriage of science and art, the union of heaven and earth as represented through the stars and planets and the *jiva,* or individual.

Jyotish is the science of self-realization through which everything becomes known. While Western astrology is extremely beneficial for analyzing character and personality, the Vedic system is an amazingly accurate and predictive science that reveals everything imaginable, from mundane to spiritual, from sexual to cerebral, from past lives to future incarnations.

The *Jyotish* chart is a blueprint of our karma resulting from our past lives, showing how that karma affects our current life. It reveals to us our tendencies and talents, our weaknesses and strengths, our abilities and attachments, everything that affects our body, mind and spirit, and when, where, and how events are likely to occur. More importantly, *Jyotish* offers remedial measures, such as gems and mantras, not only to minimize or to improve the negative aspects of our charts, but also to rectify and even alleviate any adverse planetary influences. Vedic astrology provides us with tools to confront our demons and also indicates the best times to successfully undertake our pursuits.

A professional *Jyotisha* can give you very powerful insights and predictions based on your birthdate, birthtime and birthplace. If you are unsure of the time you were born, he can rectify and determine the moment of your birth based on events in your life. He can determine in detail the compatibility of couples and point out the strengths and weaknesses of their relationship.

Tantra is a holistic art that weaves many threads of knowledge into a vibrant tapestry. The tantra aspirant would benefit by having some knowledge of Vedic Astrology. This is a blessed gift to us from the ancient *rishis* and the Universe.

Puja and Rituals

Tantric practices consist of several components, including mantras, yantras, mudras, yoga, and meditation. Provoking these powerful forces can be threatening if practiced recklessly without proper preparation. As our chakras open we become increasingly sensitive to energy. Therefore, it is necessary to keep our inner and outer environment as clean and pure as possible. With the awakened energy comes increased power. Increased power demands the highest attention and an exalted responsibility. And responsibility includes the protection of that God-given-power.

Protection from what you may ask? What is negativity? Negativity is any behavior or thought that is in opposition to our interests. Negativity can be self-perpetuated, or through the thoughts and actions of others, consciously or otherwise. Is it the same as evil?

Evil can be viewed as anything which inflicts pain or death, or which obstructs life's freedom, expression, or the resources needed for its sustenance. Some extreme forms of evil include murder, war, poverty, famine, terrorism, and obstruction of human rights, rape, racism, sexism, crime, violence, sexual molestation, emotional and verbal abuse, and cruelty.

There is "moral evil" and "natural evil". Moral evil is commonly called the human act of "sin". Natural evil includes death and illness, and "acts of nature" such as tornadoes, hurricanes, drought, and volcanoes, and floods.

One viewpoint is that evil is merely the absence of good. Buddhism and Hinduism refer to this fundamental condition of the universe as "duality"; good does not exist except in relation to evil, just as the word "up" has no meaning without the notion of the word "down".

Taoism offers the idea that the Tao is a balanced state in which neither good nor evil exist; it is only when we become aware of "good" that we must also simultaneously become aware of "evil". They are one and the same.

Buddhism approaches this issue with the idea that evil is actually "unskillful action" resulting from ignorance; in that example, the killer was unskillful in his or her attempt to establish self-esteem. (Plato, too, said that evil arises from ignorance.) Distortions can be detected in many so-called sins; lust might be considered a distortion of love or interpersonal attraction, and greed is a distortion of the drive to acquire the necessary materials for life. The concepts of unskillfulness and ignorance (rather than sinfulness) grant us an opportunity to try again without an undue sense of guilt.

Evil occurrences are the result of our karma. For most people, this position is difficult to accept, because it states that we are responsible for every unpleasant situation in our lives. However, the concept of karma is useful in explaining the apparently unjust suffering that results from "random violence" (such as natural disasters, crimes against the innocent, babies born with birth defects etc.) If we accept the concept of karma, all of life's fortunes and misfortunes can be attributed to *Sanchita Karma,* the accumulated karma of this lifetime and previous lifetimes that affects us in this incarnation.

However, it must be stressed that if we interfere in situations where the people do need to experience the trials, we literally "take on their karma", and we will be put into a situation where we must go through the same ordeal that we took from them. (See section on karma.)

If we take the attitude that evil is the work of the devil, and then in this scenario, evil is a religious problem, not one that can be confronted effectively solved through psychology, social reform, or political action. We are dealing with a conscious entity that exists outside of the human realm and is therefore distanced from any human effort to stop evil at its source.

Evil and good are a matter of degree. Everything contains some good and some bad; this truth is depicted in the *yin/yang* symbol that contains a spot of white within the black area, and a spot of black within the white area. (See section on yin/yang.)

In the theory that evil is the result of spiritual ignorance; evil acts would no longer be committed when a person gains a sense of spiritual oneness, in which a harmful action would be seen as an action against oneself, and spiritual love, in which we experience the underlying force of the universe as one which grants love to all.

As we start opening our chakra centers we will become exceedingly sensitive to energy. We may find ourselves becoming clairvoyant, clairsentient, and clairaudient. Seekers on the path may find themselves needing to protect themselves from negative energies, theirs or others'. While there is no such thing as law of intrusion, it is a fact that we create our own reality through our thoughts, feelings and actions. Thus, we draw to ourselves situations and people that allow us to experience what we have been creating with our mind and our emotions.

Therefore, we submit that we can manage and protect ourselves by the careful selection of not just the company we keep, but also the music we listen to, the books we read and movies and television we watch. We should be mindful of our body temple—that it is not contaminated by all the negativity around us, and we should manage negativity that is supported by ordinary people, who have no concept of mindfulness.

This doesn't mean that we have to be ignorant. We can watch the news or listen to a friend's drama from a state of detachment. Not indifference—but detachment. That is, we can witness the event rather than get drawn into it emotionally or mentally. When we get angry, upset or fearful, we will just attract to ourselves more of the same.

This entire universe is a play of consciousness, so if we remain the witness and maintain a state of equipoise, negativity (low, dark, and slow energy) cannot invade our space.

There are *siddhis* for eliminating calamities perpetuated by others, or by our own ignorance. Tantic practitioners often use rituals, called *puja,* to assist in creating a more positive atmosphere and purifying our inner and outer environment.

A serious problem may require the services of a Brahmin. Formal rituals and pujas are practices best left to experience and knowledge for best results.

Puja is an act of outer worship, a display of reverence honoring the deities. Brahmins can conduct these formal ceremonies for just about any desire. This is done through ancient fire rituals called *homas, (homams), yagnas,* at yearly festivals and celebrations that may include prayers, singing, dancing, meditation, and fasting in order to propitiate favorable circumstances and successful outcomes.

Yagnas are an ancient Vedic practice of offering prayers to the Lord of Fire, *Agni.* These are performed for many purposes, such as prosperity, peace, happiness, health, to cure diseases, salvation of the departed souls, spiritual enhancement, protection, for business, career, profession, to nullify evil effects of stars, planets or black magic, for world peace and so on.

Like other yogic practices, these must be performed with complete devotion, dedication, determination, regularity and patience for a considerably long period of time.

Yagnas, like other tantric practices, deliver results only after constant practice, true faith, devotion, dedication, determination and patience.

The intention of the devotee is to establish a connection with the Supreme through objects that are held to be in favor by the deities. The focus of the worship could be a photo, a statue, a vessel, or something from nature, such as a shell or coconut.

This Vedic technology extracts favors from the planets and deities, removes karma, converts negative forces into positive energy, bestows blessings, and alters one's life.

The energies of the planets, and rulers of the planets are stronger at certain times, therefore, worship is usually deemed more powerful if conducted at specific times.

HOUR   DAYS

From/To	Sunday	Monday	Tuesday	Wednesday	Thursday	Friday	Saturday
6-7 am	Sun	Moon	Mars	Mercury	Jupiter	Venus	Saturn
7-8	Venus	Saturn	Sun	Moon	Mars	Mercury	Jupiter
8-9	Mercury	Jupiter	Venus	Saturn	Sun	Moon	Mars
9-10	Moon	Mars	Mercury	Jupiter	Venus	Saturn	Sun
10-11	Saturn	Sun	Moon	Mars	Mercury	Jupiter	Venus
11-12pm	Jupiter	Venus	Saturn	Sun	Moon	Mars	Mercury
12-1	Mars	Mercury	Jupiter	Venus	Saturn	Sun	Moon
1-2	Sun	Moon	Mars	Mercury	Jupiter	Venus	Saturn
2-3	Venus	Saturn	Sun	Moon	Mars	Mercury	Jupiter
3-4	Mercury	Jupiter	Venus	Saturn	Sun	Moon	Mars
4-5	Moon	Mars	Mercury	Jupiter	Venus	Saturn	Sun
5-6	Saturn	Sun	Moon	Mars	Mercury	Jupiter	Venus
6-7	Jupiter	Venus	Saturn	Sun	Moon	Mars	Mercury
7-8	Mars	Mercury	Jupiter	Venus	Saturn	Sun	Moon
8-9	Sun	Moon	Mars	Mercury	Jupiter	Venus	Saturn
9-10	Venus	Saturn	Sun	Moon	Mars	Mercury	Jupiter
10-11	Mercury	Jupiter	Venus	Saturn	Sun	Moon	Mars
11-12	Moon	Mars	Mercury	Jupiter	Venus	Saturn	Sun
12-1 am	Saturn	Sun	Moon	Mars	Mercury	Jupiter	Venus
1-2	Jupiter	Venus	Saturn	Sun	Moon	Mars	Mercury
2-3	Mars	Mercury	Jupiter	Venus	Saturn	Sun	Moon
3-4	Sun	Moon	Mars	Mercury	Jupiter	Venus	Saturn
4-5	Venus	Saturn	Sun	Moon	Mars	Mercury	Jupiter
5-6	Mercury	Jupiter	Venus	Saturn	Sun	Moon	Mars

....
PRACTICE
....

Challenge For Her:

1. Perform the locks throughout the day, when you are driving, sitting at your desk, cooking, or eating. If you have difficulty doing this, you may want to purchase a crystal egg and insert it in your *yoni,* following the directions that come with it.

2. Repeat a simple activity for a period of five minutes. You can select action that is so easy that you would ordinarily become bored (and mindless) while doing it. For example, sit at a table with your arms resting on the table. Now, very slowly, reach several inches to pick up a pen. Raise it a few inches and then set it down. Move your hand back to its original position of rest. While you repeat this action throughout the time-period, experience each repetition with freshness, as though you have never done it before. You can direct your attention toward different aspects of the movement: watching your hand, or feeling the muscles contracting. You can even close your eyes and concentrate on your sense of touch, sliding your hand across the table toward the pen, and being aware of the different textures and pressures. (With eyes closed, a variation is to dwell on the sounds that are created by the sliding and your movement of the pen.)

3. Listen to some enjoyable, peaceful music. Each time you become distracted by a thought, write a brief note about the content of that thought. After five minutes, read the notes. What types of thoughts pulled your attention away from the music? Why did those particular thoughts attract you? Were they derived from charged elements in an archetypal field?

Challenge For Him:

1. Practice *Vajroli* exercise daily. Sit in a comfortable position with one heel under the perineum. If this is too awkward at first, roll up a towel and sit on that. Inhale through the nose, swallow, and draw the energy up to the third eye. Retain the breath and contract the urethral

as many times as possible on the breath. On the last contraction, exhale and feel the rush of energy go up the spine. This exercise stimulates the second chakra.

2. Watch a movie or television program while maintaining mindfulness. Our habit--and the producers' goal--is to lose ourselves in an emotional involvement. Try different types of programs: sitcoms, news reports, dramas, soap operas, etc. Write down the details of an activity after you have performed it mindfully. This activity can be a short walk or a household chore. Then repeat the activity, and notice the many details which you did not recall the first time.

3. Do a familiar activity as if this is your first time. Say to yourself, "I have never done this before". In Zen, this viewpoint is called "the beginner's mind" Be fascinated and surprised by each step of the process; you do not know what to expect next, so the activity is fresh and exciting and even ecstatic.

Practice For Couples:

1. The male can help his partner locate the "love muscle" by inserting his finger in her yoni and having her squeeze his finger.

2. Another practice is to sit in yab-yum, (without intercourse) coordinate your breathing, perform the locks on the inhale. Maintain eye contact and meditate together for at least five minutes.

3. Meditation and recitation of mantras is usually done while sitting on the floor. If you have trouble sitting cross-legged, this exercise may help. Sit on a chair and slowly lift one leg straight in front of you. Holding one leg up with both hands, make circles with this foot. Keep the back straight. Repeat with the other leg. Do this exercise for five minutes. If you have difficulty, have your partner sit in front of you so that you can use his or her lap to "support" your leg.

4. When the previous exercise can be done comfortably, add another. Lift the right leg in front of and bend it at the knees. Now pull this bent leg as close to the body as you can. Rest it on the opposite thigh. Gently push the knee down with one hand to stretch the inner thigh. Repeat with the other leg. Your partner can assist you with this stretch.

5. Sit on the floor with the back straight. With the soles of the feet together, push down on the knees gently. As you get more flexible, you may choose to bring both feet in closer to the groin without bouncing the knees, gently push down on them. A variation of this is to lie on the back and put the soles of the feet together. Keep the eyes closed and relax, be conscious of the breath and remain in that position for a short time, gradually increasing the length of time. This asana is wonderful during intercourse, with Shakti on her back, soles of the feet together in mid air as Shiva enters.

6. During sexual intercourse, mantras can be a very effective method of connecting two people at every chakra. A highly potent mantra that a couple can recite during coitus is the Buddhist, *"Om Mani Padme Hum"*, which means the "jewel" in the "lotus", or man within woman. As the couple chants this mantra, they can visualize the Shakti rising from the *Muladhar* chakra slowly to the *Sahasrar.*

//om//

Part Two

Iccha. The Burning Desire

Iccha--desire and will--is the magnetic attraction toward something, the possession of which is expected to create a personal benefit. It might be want for material gain, a pleasurable sensation, experience or a feeling. It is the energetic bond between two material objects; the subject (physical body or ego) desiring an object or a circumstance that we feel is lacking, something we hope will improve our lives and create happiness.

Desire alone is not sufficient to manifest our dreams into reality. What is needed is a strong will and abominable spirit to forge ahead in spite of any setbacks. Passion can actuate our desires if it has enough fuel to ignite.

What are our objectives? What do we desire? Most of us desire love, sexual satisfaction, and confidence; concurrently we want to eliminate needless guilt, fear, and unproductive habits from our lives. These objectives are universally sought after, but not easily obtained. The power of our intention is the tool that can give us more of what we want, and less of what we do not want.

Chapter Three:

The Objective

Humans have many needs and desires. Peace of mind, love, joy, good health and abundance, experiencing full-bodied orgasms and prolonging the sex act. Tantra is one remedy for erectile dysfunction, prostate problems, inability to achieve orgasms and more.

How do we achieve our goals, especially our sexual goals? What can we do to be more effective in life? Implementing changes in our life, especially in our sex life, involves altering our thought patterns and abandoning our old habits.

To do that, we must learn methods to release blocks that inhibit our true essence through a variety of practices, including making love and dancing. We learn to enable and develop passion and enthusiasm for everything that we do in life because when we lose our focus, our life energy dissipates into many different directions, and we are unable to achieve our goals, find our purpose or find fulfillment.

We can learn to become masters of our destiny when we acquire tenacity, determination, discipline, self-effort, and intention. But it is the fire of inspiration that propels us to take action.

In this chapter, we will concentrate on some of the subjects and issues that persistently block our energy, preventing us from manifesting our dreams and living in bliss. We can overcome our self-defeating patterns by eliminating unhealthy projections of our dark side unto our partner. When we cast aside fear, we invite our desires, such as love, to enter our inner abode.

Here's a Quick Tantra Tip:

How to find love:

Meditate for five minutes on these words from Swami Muktananda: "To experience love, we must go inside. When you experience real love you get into a state that is beyond words. You are filled with a joy that goes beyond all emotions. True love is the love of the inner Self."

To find love, we must cultivate love.

Desire

Desire is the starting point of all achievement,
not a hope, not a wish,
but a keen pulsating desire which transcends everything.
...Napoleon Hill

Desire is a magnetic attraction toward something, the possession of which is expected to create a personal benefit, e.g., a material gain, or a pleasurable sensation or feeling. This energy is a dynamic bond between the object, the subject and the energetic charge that bonds the object with the subject.

Desire, far from being a barrier to spirituality, is the mechanism by which soul sets into motion the circumstances in which it gains its spiritual education in the material worlds.

Desire, however, is denounced by most religions. Among the many impulses that lead us toward action, desire is the one that is most often condemned by eastern religions; it has a similar dynamic to that of another spurned phenomenon, attachment.

Desire focuses our attention on materiality. While our religion might be telling us to seek only God, desires pull us into the material world. Our thoughts and physical actions are directed toward the objects' acquisition, retention, and maintenance. And when we develop obsessive a-field constellations regarding possessions, we tend to cultivate attributes such as greed, lust, and envy, which might not be evil in themselves but they are distractions from the other activities that we could be engaging in the wholeness of our life, and they lead us to unbalanced behaviors such as lying, defrauding, stealing, and fighting (and they also give cause for the emotion of *fear* that we might not acquire the object of desire, and the emotion of *anger* that someone might be trying to take the object from us). Even when we are trying to be spiritual, desire might be present as spiritual materialism, the craving for mystical experiences and for religious personal traits as though they are trophies.

This dynamic can be condemned only if we believe that materiality is contrary to spirituality. However, tantriks believe that God created this material world for a reason: to give us a realm in which we could learn about life (i.e., spirit) through spirit's material manifestations of archetypes. If we have any spiritual purpose for being in this world, we are foolish to hate the world's material substance and our natural desire-filled response to it. And if we honor our human self, we respect the gene-based survival instinct that guides us to create a life of material safety, physiological comfort, and the other commodities that allow us to function during our time on earth.

While our religion might be telling us to seek oneness, desire is a reminder of our duality (i.e., the person who desires, and the object of desire). Even the noble goal of desiring to experience God is commonly recognized as an impediment to the experience itself; the desire can lead us to use the spiritual practices which bring us close to the experience, but finally the desire itself must be dropped as we enter the experience of oneness with our own essence (i.e., spirit, which is not God itself but rather the essence of God such that we do not become one with God but rather we become one with this essence which God and soul have in common).

Desire is a continual function; it ceases only at the moment of acquisition of the desired object, but then it immediately points toward new objects of desire and toward a repetition of current pleasures. (The Chandi Path refers to this inner enemy as "seeds of desire" that keep sprouting like weeds.) The perpetual presence of desire assures that we are never satisfied except during the instant of acquisition; during that instant, our joy is not due to the object itself, or to the appropriation of it, but instead it is due, in part, to the transient awareness of soul's divine wholeness and the opportunity to experience life and energy through our interaction with this object. In addition to other motivations, including the pragmatic drive to acquire the goods that we need in our life, one motivation in our desire for objects is our craving for that spiritual experience when the two halves of a duality come together.

Desire is an agent of our spiritual drive toward wisdom, love, and completion. As is the case with other psychological and macrocosmic dynamics that are condemned only because we misunderstand them and thus misuse them and, further, are pained by them, desire has a beneficial purpose in our life.

Desire is the enemy only when we create religious values that are contrary to the stimulation of life itself. If we are trying to control the mind when it seeks instead to fantasize about a desired object, perhaps we need to question the validity of our religious goal, which apparently has less vitality that does the fantasized object of our desire, and instead contemplate the nature and content of our desires; we might discover that these desires are showing us what we truly want and value, in contrast to whatever our religion, or another belief system says *should* be important to us. If we still want to develop the traits of discipline and control for their own sake, we can exercise them in the course of our everyday life; for example, instead of trying to discipline ourselves not to want money, we can discipline ourselves in the *pursuit* of money. Of course, sometimes we do need to attend to duties that are less exciting than our desire-driven fantasies; at those times, we can use transcendence.

We can accept the existence of desire as a part of life. It is part of our nature; it is part of the dynamics of this world. But we can have more than this fatalistic view; we can see desire as a stimulating adventure by which soul explores itself and eventually realizes its spiritual oneness with the objects of desire.

By becoming more aware of our desires, we develop our cognizance of our intuition as a source of inner guidance, we also note the *other* factors that are suggesting courses of action; desires are among the voices which are telling us what to do. We need to be conscious of our desires in order to distinguish them from our intuition; however, the intuition's suggestions are not *contrary* to our desires but instead they are holistic considerations of *all* of our needs, including those that are expressed by desires.

By allowing ourselves to pursue our desires, in the long run, perhaps *all* of our desires must be fulfilled, to allow soul to learn all about itself, although this would require many lifetimes. The people whom we admire for their wisdom and stability are usually those who were impetuous during their youth--following their desires, their passions, their heart, and their impulses, such that they acquired a vast range of experience; then, when they finished sowing their wild oats, they settled down. We might disapprove of the wildness, but we revere its final products: wisdom and stability.

If our desires are so powerful and persistent that our lives seem to be nothing but the meaningless acquisition of objects which we do not have time to enjoy, we are probably out-of-balance with the regard to the cycle of laboring and savoring. Our desires cannot be satisfied by mere ownership or by superficial interaction, because satisfaction doesn't come from the object itself but rather it comes from soulful, interactive savoring whereby we share the energy and information for which the object has come into our life. If we spend quality time with what we already have, we can explore more of its facets and dimensions, and we might discover that some of our desires can be satiated with these current belongings.

For example, if we strive to learn more about our marriage partner's many dimensions by which we can satisfy our desires, the marriage stays fresh with excitement and adventure and we do not crave affairs that promise to quench our myriad desires through shallow encounters with a variety of people. Savoring gives us two benefits:

1. We gain an enriching experience with the object, giving to it, receiving from it, learning from it

2. We do not waste our time and money in the pointless stockpiling of untended, unloved goods. We can enhance our savoring by setting aside some time to indulge the natural emotional qualities of acceptance and enjoyment and warmth and gratitude and appreciation toward the objects that we own. Love for

material goods is not the disparaged materialism; it is love.

The *troublesome* kind of materialism is in the acquisition of *symbolic* wealth (i.e., big numbers in a bank account, or an extravagant home merely to impress people or perhaps to compensate for thoughts of inadequacy in our Ego archetypal field); that type of wealth is useless, dead, burdensome, and unfulfilling to our desires.

Many contemporary spiritual teachers have rejected the ideal of the holy ascetic; they say instead that we can have any amount of material goods because what is important is not what we own but rather our *relationship* to what we own--a relationship which is founded on vitality and purposefulness in our life at this moment.

Love

Marriage is a recognition of a spiritual identity.
...Joseph Campbell

The unfettered flow of energy is what we call loving; its nature is to nourish, and to share, and to express, not in a self-conscious effort to display ideas of spirituality, but instead like the water of the Tao whose swirls and twists just naturally carry moisture and nutrients to all in its path.

Love is the essence of humanity that binds us together. It is all that is good, noble, and divine. Like the sun that shines, the warmth of love nourishes and nurtures our souls.

Although scientific instruments cannot measure love, it is a universal desire. The survival of the human race is dependent upon falling in love, and making love.

We do not need to *learn* to love; love is our natural state because of the perpetual current of life-energy from spirit--through soul, mind, emotions, and physical body. As we attend to this flow, as we feel the pleasure and joy that are created when life surges through us, we discover that the pleasure and joy are increased when we clear away the obstacles. Those obstacles are the inappropriate elements of archetypal fields; they are the thoughts and images which judge particular objects to be damned and not loved, and so we try to shut off (i.e., dam) the movement of life-energy to those objects.

Love is patient; love is kind
Love does not envy
Is not boastful; is not conceited;
Does not act improperly;
Is not selfish; is not provoked;
Does not keep a record of wrongs;
Finds not joy in unrighteousness,
But rejoices in the truth;
Bears all things, believes all things,
Hopes all things, endures all things
Love never ends.
…13 Corinthians

Love is the strength and tenderness that keeps us balanced even in painful circumstances. It is the condition of infinite devotion that includes more than passion and lust; it creates mutual intimacy and concern, unselfish motivation, vulnerability and friendship.

Our survival depends on the healing power of love, intimacy, and relationships. Love is the essential need at the center of our being, enabling us to excel. We learned loving behavior from our parents and friends, who taught us how to treat others and ourselves. Deprived of love, we become crippled physically, emotionally, mentally and spiritually. Love is a universal need that knows no boundaries, transcends time and space, race and nationality. Love is what motivates all of us--kings or paupers, young or old, male or female. It is what makes life worthwhile and fulfills our purpose. Love, in some form, is the most important objective of desire for most of us.

In romantic love, we have a combination of passion with intimacy, intense emotional and sexual desire. Love, however, is not limited to romantic love, but includes love for family, friends, country, mankind, humanity, and our own self.

The physical self is the ship of our soul carrying us thru this journey of life. Most of us think that we are only this body, but we are so much more. The body is the facade of our soul. All the great saints have said that God is within this body; "God dwells within you as you," "my Father and I are One".

How do we love our physical self? We love it by keeping it uncontaminated by intoxicants and poisons (such as cigarettes, alcohol and drugs), and showing respect and love through proper nutrition, exercise, and sleep. We make an effort to maintain its flexibility, health, and appearance.

The mental self is where our sense of conscience resides. Not to be confused with the brain (an organ that is measurable by scientific instruments); the mind is an energy field that vibrates at a higher frequency than the brain, giving us insight, imagination, and creativity. It has the ability to reason and store information, and gives us the ability to process this information resulting in our beliefs and the decisions we make; which in turn, results in our life's experiences.

Our mind is responsible for every manifestation, good and bad, in our lives. Every manifestation begins with a thought. Simply put, what we think about is what we become.

To invite more love into our lives, we must eliminate the destructive and negative thoughts that undermine our happiness. The more love we give, the more love we will receive.

Most of us believe that the feeling of love comes first, then we do acts that express love. In the beginning of a relationship that is true, however, a long and loving relationship requires a more mature understanding. Love is the result of actions we choose everyday. So, to create a strong marriage, first we must choose loving actions, and then feelings will follow.

The best way to change how you feel is to change what you do.

In other words, create your feelings through your actions. Honor, respect, worship, uninhibited lovemaking and passion--these are the laws of love. Many go from partner to partner on an empty search for fulfillment, but the answer does not lie in searching for the right person.

The secret to success is learning to love the person you have.

This is the way you "make" love. Love is cause and effect, action and reaction, with very predictable results.

O love, O pure deep love, be here, be now
Be all; worlds dissolve into your stainless endless radiance,
Frail living leaves burn with you brighter than cold stars:
Make me your servant, your breath, your core.
...Rumi

Love involves the emotional self as the way in which the physical body expresses itself. It is what colors the fabric of our experience. Our emotional quotient (EQ) is the measurement of our feelings and the way we process life's experiences, such as joy, disappointment, or pain.

EQ is described as having the capacity to accurately perceive emotions, the ability to use emotions to facilitate thinking, and the capacity to understand and manage emotional meanings.

Daniel Coleman, founder of the Emotional Intelligence Consortium, correlated success with EQ, rather than intelligence quotient (IQ). His research found that people who had a high EQ had better coping skills, were happier, more successful and more productive than those with a high IQ (intelligence quotient).

Love also involves the spiritual self. This is the transcended self, that part of us that connects us with all of nature and life. It is the knowing that we are part of the universe, beyond duality, transcending space and time.

To find that divineness within, we accept our wholeness with humility and gratitude, knowing that we are perfect. As we learn to love others and ourselves on each of these four levels, we will transcend maya and all the limitations that keep us from experiencing ourselves as the gods and goddesses that we are.

Mastery of the tantric arts improves our chances of finding happiness with our beloved. Sex is transformed to love, and love is transformed to "prayer", or meditation. When meditation happens with another soul, a deep accord of two bodies function as one. The popular concept of "soul mates" is secondary to the phenomena of "twin souls", which only occurs when there is a cosmic consummation of the One dividing itself into two separate entities, only to become One again. This state of Oneness is the closest approximation we may experience to the state of liberation.

There is a misconception as to who is a soul mate or twin soul. Most people believe that it is someone who has had the same painful past as you had (so you have a lot "in common"), when actually a soul mate/twin soul is one who you are bonded with, not in pain, hurt and anger, but in spiritual love and consciousness.

Love is composed of a single soul inhabiting two bodies.
...Aristotle

The conversion of ordinary sex into something "supernatural" is a gift we receive through the grace of God with our own self-effort.

Love grows when you trust that the Universe is on your side
... Rumi

Love is often confused with "romantic love". Romantic love is an oxymoron; it is romance, but it is not love in its fullest sense. We go through the motions of love--the attentiveness, the sharing, and the caring, but can differentiate romance from love as we examine romance's other characteristics. Romance can have a delightful place in dating and in a loving relationship, but we can avoid some of its pain if we understand romance's nature, and we do not mistake romantic infatuation for love.

What are the characteristics of romantic love? Romantic love is characterized by intensity. We experience intense passion, intense pleasure, and intense emotional and sexual desire. But we might also experience intense *negativity*, in the form of jealousy, anger, frustration, loneliness, longing, and other types of emotional suffering--during the relationship, and after it ends.

Romantic love is based on fantasy. We are in love with an ideal, a "dream." We imagine that this person has every wonderful trait. One reason for this idealizing is that we are projecting the anima or animus of our own psyche, and so we see that perfect male or female superimposed onto the person. In some cases, this fantasy occurs because the person is unattainable (and is therefore not present to dispel the fantasy) because of a geographical distance, or a social prohibition (as in the case of the feuding families of Romeo and Juliet), or a mysterious personality.

Romantic love breaks down healthy barriers. We become so focused on the other person and the relationship that we sacrifice our own identity. Because we have relinquished ourselves, we are excessively reliant on the other person for our happiness and the fulfillment of our needs and goals.

Romantic love is temporary. Because it is based on fantasy, it cannot continue when we learn more about the person, and we realize that the person's actual traits differ from those that we have projected in our fantasy. When we experience this "disillusionment", we have a choice:

1. We can terminate the relationship, and then seek a new person upon whom we can project our unreasonable ideals.

2. We can try to build a mature relationship with this real person who has real faults.

Intimacy

Love seeketh not itself to please,
nor for itself hath any care,
but for another gives its ease,
and builds a Heaven in Hell's despair.
…William Blake

Most of us "love" on a shallow level and yet we expect great rewards from our relationships. We are afraid to give of ourselves wholly in body, mind or spirit. We maintain some reservation about revealing who we really are. We are even stingy about giving our partner certain things, but we want our partner to give us everything that we think will make us feel good. Thus, we find we are never truly satisfied with our love life. Our partners, friends and acquaintances only know the parts of us that we wish to reveal.

We crave deep intimacy with our beloved. We want to have the feeling of security and stability, but we are afraid of those very things.

In order to receive a level of deep intimacy, we have to open up our body, our heart, our soul, and be brave enough to let go of the veil, the covering that envelops our real self. We hide behind this invisible armor just as a warrior yields his shield to protect himself from harm and danger.

But if we are to experience true intimacy with our beloved, we have to become fearless, transparent and vulnerable, courageous and confident.

Intimacy is the deep core connection of one being with another. Intimacy is a privilege we share with someone we love. We extend an invitation to this person to enter our sacred space, to share, play, learn and love together in an honest and genuine fashion. In intimacy, there is no room for fear. Fear prohibits intimacy.

Tantra gives us the tools to discover our true selves and the depths of our being, while exploring the profoundness of our partner. Intimacy is the tool that permits us to peel away layers of our ego, revealing our heart and soul. For this heart connection, the couple must be willing to surrender their egos, become vulnerable, and to give in to love.

Sexually, the opposite forces of Shiva/Shakti draw a couple closer and deeper. By allowing this natural force to develop, the two energies converge, and become One. We learn more about ourselves through the other. We see our image reflected back to us through their words, their look, their thoughts, and their actions. As our partner mirrors us, we learn, we discover, we change, we develop, we grow, and we learn to love ourselves and accept ourselves, just as much as we accept our partner.

On a mental level, deep intimacy gives us a sanctuary of inner peace, a refuge of comfort, and a safe haven where delight and ecstasy await. Our mind learns to stop the constant chatter; we become more creative and intuitive. We are able to communicate with our partner telepathically, psychically and beyond normal means of communication.

On a spiritual level, intimacy releases us from chains of suffering and sorrow, and replaces it with lightness, freedom and the bliss of union. The diamond scepter is the *lingam* in union with the soul of the lotus *yoni.*

On a mystical level, when we accept the union with mindfulness, what we feel and experience is deliberate and authentic. It is at this level where the *lingam* of the male becomes the *lingam* of Shiva, and the *yoni* of the woman becomes the goddess, not metaphorically, but in reality. This is the ultimate intimacy, the *Mahamudra*.

Is this level of intimacy obtainable? Yes, it is no different from learning any skill, like playing tennis or golf. If the knowledge and desire is there, all that is required is practice, study, direction, hard work, self-effort and mindfulness.

This is how we can create a level of intimacy beyond what we have ever experienced in the past.

Anima and Animus

anima - the inner self (not the external persona) that is in touch with the unconscious.

Carl Jung said, "The anima is a personification of all feminine tendencies in a man's psyche"; thus, the animus is the personification of all masculine tendencies in a woman. Beginning in childhood, we create our gender identity and roles, consciously or unconsciously, by enhancing the qualities that characterize our gender, and repressing or suppressing the qualities that characterize the other gender. But those repressed or suppressed qualities are still within us--the feminine qualities within the man and the masculine within the woman. This sorting-out process is similar to the one by which we create our ego through the enhancement of particular qualities while putting the opposite qualities into our shadow.

We are androgynous. Androgynous means that we have both male and female traits. As a Life Principle, the substance of which both the energies are composed is androgynous, in the sense that it contains all opposites, including male and female. Thus, soul can incarnate into either a male body or a female body. Even in the biological realm, we are somewhat androgynous; Jung noted that men contain some female genes, and women contain some male genes.

It differs from the masculine and feminine stereotypes. Society has created those stereotypes arbitrarily, by encouraging men and women to have different behaviors, attire, occupations, etc. However, Jung presented the concept of the anima/us not in the sense of those stereotypes but as the archetypes of Eros and Logos, (Eve and Adam, Shakti and Shiva, Energy and Consciousness). Eros, the female, is associated with human relationships, earthiness, receptivity, creativity, and passivity. Logos, the male, is identified with power, abstraction, and action. We do not experience the Logos and Eros as archetypes; we experience them in their manifested forms which have the peculiarities of our culture and of the people whom we have known of the opposite gender--particularly our father or mother.

It has contrary qualities. Just as the anima and animus are opposites of one another, they have opposite traits within themselves.

The male's anima has positive traits. When the anima is allowed to express her self through a man's psyche, she brings the attributes of feelings, emotions, tenderness, relatedness, commitment and fidelity, friendship, love and compassion, imagination, gentleness, romance, creativity, intuition, and a sense of aesthetics.

The male's anima also has negative traits. If the anima is rejected, her traits are deformed: feelings and emotions are replaced by moodiness, sentimentality, hysteria, or bitchiness; fidelity becomes possessiveness; aesthetics become sensuality; tenderness becomes effeminacy; imagination becomes mere fantasizing (particularly of sexual adventures); love and romance are twisted into a series of turbulent relationships or the man's withdrawal from his wife and family. The spurned anima does more than thrust her own feminine qualities into expression (however warped); she also disturbs the man's masculinity by, for example, degrading his thinking into the weak opinionating.

The female's animus has positive traits. The animus can endow a woman with assertiveness, courage, analytical thought, strength, vitality, decisiveness, a focused attentiveness, and a desire for achievement.

The female's animus also has negative traits. If the animus must push his way past the woman's resistance, his qualities are corrupted: assertiveness becomes aggression and ruthlessness; analytical thought becomes argumentativeness; focus becomes mechanistic behavior.

When we allow the anima/us to express itself, it enhances our lives. However, when we deny it (i.e., repress it), or we are unaware of it, it forces itself into manifestation anyway, with unpleasant results. We are refusing the balancing input from our anima/us, so our gender identification becomes a caricature. The man might become a macho, power-hungry, overly competitive brute. The woman could become a fluffy, passive, Marilyn Monroe-type figure with a vague ego and persona.

We experience the same problems that occur whenever we repress, or when we mismanage our shadow. For example, if a man has repressed his anima, he cannot use its qualities, e.g., tenderness when a situation requires tenderness.

It becomes more apparent at midlife. During midlife, our repressed qualities become more persistent in their demands for expression. Ideally, our ego has been developed and defined, and so the ego's antitheses can emerge, the shadow and the anima/us. Until we have sufficiently strengthened our sense of self, including our gender identity, we do well to retain the anima/us in the shadow, allowing it to express only as much as our ego can tolerate without being overwhelmed. At mid-life, many people acknowledge their anima/us qualities; we often see post-midlife couples in which the formerly dominant husband has accepted a passive, contemplative role (in the marriage and in society) while his wife has become the invigorated businesswoman or community leader.

If we do not claim the anima/us as an active part of our lives, it is projected, as we would do with any other psychological force which we do not claim and use; this is like the projection of a picture onto a movie screen. As in all types of projection, an anima/us projection is not indiscriminate; it is hooked to particular people. It is a person who closely matches our image that we took from our earlier experiences with people of that gender. For example, if a woman's personal image of the animus were based on her father's aggressiveness, she would project her animus upon an aggressive man.

Or, a woman who has cultivated her animus might be drawn to a man who displays intellectual power rather than a man who displays brute physical strength. We choose a person whose level of refinement matches that of our anima/us.

Many of our relationships are based on projections of it. We project the anima/us onto a suitable person of the opposite gender. The projection contains more than just an image; it is contains a highly charged energy.

We are attracted to this image and energy, perhaps more so than to the person. In some cases, the energy is intoxicating; thus, we experience the phenomenon of falling in love--the emotional, sexually charged, fantasy-filled, head-over-heels, mythologized, quasi-spiritual, electrifying, larger-than-life, you-make-me-feel-alive-and-whole, idealized fascination toward someone.

However, in truth, we are falling in love with our own anima/us; i.e., we are falling in love with ourselves.

Although anima/us projection causes an unintentional deception, leading us to believe that we adore the person when we actually adore the anima/us, the projection is a useful mechanism. It creates enough attraction toward the opposite gender to sustain us through the difficulties of a relationship. We are able to learn about the anima/us through our interactions with that person.

The projections cause problems in our relationship. A projection distorts our image of the person. When we are with that person, we are talking primarily to the projection, and we are interpreting the person's words as if they came from the projection, and we are expecting the person to fulfill the role that has been cast onto him or her. Thus, we might experience confusion, unfounded hopes, strife, disappointments, and anger.

We are offering an incomplete person to our partner, because we have projected out the qualities of our anima/us; thus we are missing the parts that we could otherwise contribute to the relationship, e.g., our power, our vitality, and our flexibility and range of potential behaviors. Ideally, we could use the full spectrum of our capabilities, for our own happiness and for the well being of the relationship; each person could add his or her own talents, without regard to stereotyped gender roles.

We can lose our identity in co-dependency and a participation mystique. We can become merely a spouse rather than a full person. We place a burden onto our partner to be the things that we refuse to be. For example, an overly feminized woman might expect the man to express his own strength and also to express the strength of the woman's projected anima; although some domineering men enjoy this situation, the task is tiring, and it is inherently frustrating, because a woman's power and perspectives can accomplish tasks which a man cannot accomplish. Ignorance of this fact, and the resulting failure to utilize the resources of women, has been one of the tragic errors of patriarchal societies.

We might feel dissatisfaction and envy as we see our own qualities in our partner. For example, the man needs to express his feelings, as a natural part of communication and self-expression, but, because he has relinquished that part of himself to his partner, he can no longer articulate the feelings himself; thus he envies his wife who does have this capability.

The negative side of the anima/us must be confronted. As explained earlier, the anima/us has both a positive and a negative side; the unpleasant side is almost certain to appear occasionally, in our mate and in our own self. If we are not aware of the dynamics of the anima/us, we will mistakenly try to deal with an unhappy anima/us as simply the person's bad mood rather than as a valid complaint of an archetype.

One way to respond to our mate's antagonistic anima/us is with a natural, poised strength; for example, when a woman's male animus arises, her husband can reply calmly with his male vitality to soothe both his own anima and his wife's animus. The woman's anima might have become quarrelsome for the specific purpose of provoking the man's masculine response in a case where the man has been too passive; following that masculine response, the man, woman, anima, and animus can return to their proper, constructive roles.

The anima/us imposes its own moods into the relationship, complicating our circumstances with the person, because we are actually dealing with four individuals: the other person, our anima/us, the other person's anima/us, and ourselves.

The projections fail eventually. During the "falling in love" stage, the individual might enjoy receiving the energy-charged projection, and being treated like the consummate man or woman. However, no one can live up to the expectations; eventually we notice that the person's behavior doesn't completely match our picture of the anima/us, and the person becomes uncomfortable in the realization that we are in love with an image rather than the individual.

At that point, we have two choices.

1. We can try, consciously or unconsciously, to change the anima/us and hope our partner will comply with the image. The manipulation will cause stress that can lead to the failure of the relationship. We

can look for someone else to fulfill the image. If we select this option, we will probably experience a series of brief relationships, in a futile attempt to find someone to be our anima/us. If we want to cease the destructiveness and unintentional dishonesty that have been caused by the projections, we proceed to the next stage.

2. We can withdraw the anima/us projections, and we can create a relationship between two human beings who each take responsibility for their own anima/us. We can accomplish this feat by learning about the anima/us within our partner and within ourselves. We can become aware of the anima/us by noticing the impulses that are contrary to our gender stereotyping: the man observes his moments of tenderness and other anima qualities; the woman recognizes her animus' desire to achieve. Then, instead of squelching these impulses, we accept them as usable resources that will broaden and enrich our life.

We can experiment with the traits that are generally associated with the opposite gender; for example, a passive woman can use the as-if principle to "try on" the behavior of male-like assertiveness. Our anima/us and our partner are of the same gender, so our understanding of our anima/us helps us to understand our partner; conversely, our understanding of our partner helps us to understand our anima/us.

We can seek a balanced relationship with the anima/us, allow its expression, but we retain our gender identity so that the anima/us will not overwhelm us (thus, creating a macho woman or an effeminate man).

We can learn about the anima/us within our partner. We look for the presence of the anima/us, to see how it influences our partner and our relationship. Because we are the same gender as our partner's anima/us, we can be a role model to help our partner in expressing this contrary part of him or herself.

Learning about our partner can enable us to dismiss the archetypal projection with its universal qualities; instead, we discern the individual's unique qualities, the unique needs, quirks, history, and personality. We discover this individuality by listening carefully to the person's statements, and closely observing his or her behavior. This is not an archetype; this is a human being.

The projection process becomes less active. The reason the projection occurred initially was because we weren't utilizing the anima/us inside. The energy and image had to be projected outwards in order to be recognized at all. But now we see the anima/us within us. Our outer relationships, to an extent, have been mere substitutes for the relationship that we needed with the anima/us.

We continue to need relationships with both our anima/us and with people of the opposite gender; some contemporary women are trying to become free and strong by creating a relationship with their animus instead of a relationship with a man. However, this can lead to problems internally and externally. The woman might experience an over-development of the animus, and a disturbance in relationships with men. Some projection will continue to occur, because we are never fully aware of all aspects of the anima/us.

Fear

Fear defeats more people than any other one thing in the world.
…Ralph Waldo Emerson

Osho said that people had three basic fears, which he described as
1. The fear of going "crazy"
2. The fear of "orgasm"
3. The fear of death

"Crazy" not in the literal sense but in the fear of being alone. All our lives we have been controlled by society and our culture, and as long as we remain within those confines, no one will think we are crazy. We are so dependent on the need to be accepted by our peers so we do not allow our intuition to develop, and we do not trust our feelings or our thoughts. All this pre-conditioning from religion, family and peers, prevents us from realizing our inherent goodness. This group mentality of "staying with the herd" can weaken us so much that we sacrifice any dreams we may have of following our heart.

The fear of "orgasm" is also the fear of "bliss". Ejaculation is not the same thing as an orgasm. To ejaculate is to cast out. In orgasm, when the person disappears the ego is no more. There is an experiencing, but the experiencer is no more. Ejaculation, however, is localized; but a real orgasm is experienced at every level of our being. Experiencing a full-bodied orgasm is having an experience with all of existence. It is making love to God. This is sacred sex, *Mahamudra,* when meditation occurs and transformation happens with every orgasm. This is the transformation leading to bliss; therefore, it is important to know how to have real orgasms and to have them often. This guilt about sex has forged fear, generating the suppression of movements, produced premature ejaculation (which is more of a psychological problem), and has manufactured the inability to genuine orgasm. To feel guilty about the bliss of touch is to condemn and repress both our spontaneity, the natural impulses of our life and honesty, our respect for the reality of our psyche.

All life exists because of sex. God wanted to guarantee the continuance of life; therefore, he had to make sex a pleasurable experience.

Ironically, religion had something else in mind. Instead of elevating the status of sex as a creation of God, religion has, for the most part condemned it, associating it with guilt and sin. This guilt is the root cause for sexual dysfunction, and all the perversion that exists in our culture. Sexual gratification is frowned upon, and climax is just a knee-jerk reflex. Real orgasm, we are saying throughout this whole book, is quite a different matter. Because of the guilt associated with pleasure, people are in a great hurry to get it over with, instead of savoring every moment of it.

This is a dilemma for humankind; whose biological nature is driven by sex, yet the mind condemns it. So as man and woman make love, they rush through it because it is "bad", they feel overwhelmed with guilt because it actually feels pretty darn good. Thus, we end up in a society where sex is a hurried process that leaves no time for orgasm or pleasure.

This repression is responsible for sexual dysfunction, personality disorders, sexual perversions, pornography, addictions and obsessions. When we deny the natural performance of sex and go against our natural state, we close the authentic expression of our sexuality and resort of deviant obsessive behaviors. To someone who is sexually satisfied, pornography is absurd and a wretched substitute for the real thing.

The fear of dying is the third fear. When we master the fear of going crazy and the fear of orgasm, the fear of death disappears, and we can experience life's bliss.

> *Bliss lives on the other side of fear. Love is the way.*
> *Fear stops love. Love stops fear.*
> *...J. Ram Sivananda*

Guilt

> *Although the most acute judges of the witches and even the witches themselves,*
> *were convinced of the guilt of witchery,*
> *the guilt nevertheless was non-existent.*
> *It is thus with all guilt.*
> *...Friedrich Nietzsche*

Guilt is an alarm mechanism by which we become aware that we have violated our values. It serves the purpose of human survival. The pain guides us away from behavior that threatens that survival; i.e., it threatens the fulfillment of our values that ideally are supportive to our life. Rather than being a "negative" experience, it is a constructive advisor that directs us toward social harmony, accountability, and our ideals of self and community. It is allied with our conscience--and our ethics and morality, which are the organization of the standards of the personal conscience.

Guilt encourages us to study our motivations and values, prodding us to investigate our *religious* standards. In the West, guilt says that humans are not gods, that we are never perfect; this reminder is the basis of a realistic humility, a knowledge of our human boundaries-- and the strategic decision to rely on a source of power and guidance that is greater than our own, such as the church.

> *The tragedy is when you've got sex in the head*
> *instead of down where it belongs.*
> *…D.H. Lawrence*

Where did fear and guilt about sex come from? The origin of man, (according to the Book of Genesis), began with the appearance of Adam and Eve, who lived in the beautiful Garden of Eden. They were held in God's grace, and life on earth was perfect. Fragrant flowers of every hue speckled the landscape, and fruit was in abundance. One day, at the urging of the serpent, Adam and Eve took a nice, juicy bite of the apple. When they did so, they were immediately whirled into the world of *maya*. They were aroused when they looked at each other's naked bodies and were overwhelmed with sexual desire. After their lust for each other had been consummated, they felt remorse, guilt, and shame.

The original couple had fallen from the Lord's grace; they were now "sinners". According to the Christian belief, the whole human race was contained in Adam, making all humans sinners.

St. Augustine devised a theory called the "original sin". He said that this "original sin" was propagated by sexual intercourse, from one generation to another in a lineage beginning with Adam

The Council of Trent (1543-1563) authorized the notion of the "original sin", denying that "sin" was committed by "imitation" (copying other people). They preferred to put the blame directly on sex.

Till today, even educated Christians believe in the Biblical version of the creation of man, renouncing the scientific evidence of evolution. Is it any wonder that ever since Adam and Eve committed the original sin, man has created enormous guilt and fear about his sexuality?

It is hard to imagine that intercourse was performed only in the missionary position, with the male on top. Ashamed of their body, people kept their clothes on, even during sex, and to avoid seeing each other's nakedness, they only had sex in the dark. Feeling enormous guilt, men rushed to ejaculation, getting it over with as soon as possible, (perhaps before it started to feel too good, which would make them feel even more guilty). Conversely, the "respectable" wife dared not to show any pleasure. Sexual contact was a duty and obligation that was not to be enjoyed.

Guilty feelings about sex prevent us from realizing our true divine nature. Instead of being the uninhibited dance between two lovers, it has become a clumsy and awkward effort, or an obligatory activity. Guilt and fear arises from archaic religious beliefs.

We might still carry unwarranted feelings of guilt from our childhood when our parents or church used it as a way to control our behavior. As adults, we can question these standards and decide whether or not they are working for us. In the individuation process, we develop a personal conscience, and we can do this only by challenging the values that have been imposed by other people. When this conscience becomes a sincere expression of our deliberated values, it does not need to be justified to anyone.

Guilt arises when our values are violated, such as through sexual molestation. We feel inappropriate guilt that is caused by idealistic perfectionism (personal or religious), and an inflated sense of responsibility (in which we have taken on the blame and burden of the perpetuator). We may still be suffering from the conflicting emotions of the shame caused by the molestation, and the temporary pleasure that was felt.

The most we can do is to forgive the perpetrator and realize that the action we took was the best that we could have done at the time. No matter what we did, it seemed like the best approach then, considering our view of the options, our skills in managing such a circumstance, our emotional state, and other psychological and situational factors. We could not have done anything other than what we did. This is neither an excuse, nor a release from the obligation of reparation; it is a realistically compassionate acknowledgment of our imperfect humanity. We are always doing the best we can, however indelicately.

When we blame ourselves for any act against us, we are likely to play out this role by continuing the behavior, subconsciously punishing our partners. We compound our guilt and our self-esteem is further injured.

To dwell on feelings of guilt is a denial of grace, thus to regain our self-esteem, self-realized masters recommend meditation.

The Criteria of Truth

A lie can travel half way around the world
while the truth is putting on its shoes.
...Mark Twain

How do we know if something is "true"? How do we discriminate between the false and the truth? Consciousness cannot be perceived since Consciousness alone perceives Consciousness. There are, however five criteria which must be met in order to be "true". They are direct perception, inductive reasoning, deductive logic, testimony and intuitive experience.

If we take Christopher Columbus' belief as an example: The world is round. Entire populations believed that the earth was flat for hundreds of years because it appeared flat when they looked out into the horizon and that's what they were told. They accepted what everyone else believed without question. Columbus however, did not believe this simply because everyone else did. He had enough courage to go against the accepted, common belief system of the time and was thought to be crazy.

1. Direct Perception--When Christopher Columbus watched the ships sail, he observed that the hull went out of sight slowly, leaving the mast to gradually disappear on the horizon as it moved away.

2. Inductive Reasoning--The hull went out of sight slowly, leaving the mast to gradually disappear on the horizon as it moved away, so Columbus reasoned that the world could not be flat. Inductively he inferred therefore, that the earth had to be round.

3. Deductive Logic--Christopher Columbus saw the world wasn't flat because the hull disappeared first. And slowly the mast disappeared. He knew that if the earth were flat then the ship would only diminish in size as it moved away due to perspective.

4. Testimony--He talked to the sailors who sailed over the horizon.

5. Intuitive experience--He knew the earth was round and was spinning on its axis through his direct perception, inductive reasoning, testimony and deductive reasoning. He concluded that the entire world was wrong and that their belief system that the world was flat was not

true, even though they had been told for centuries that that was the truth. All the evidence and his common sense showed him how wrong everyone was.

Spiritual Truth and knowledge also requires faith. Faith has many productive aspects. Faith can help us to make a "leap" into a consideration of new possibilities when we have created illusory limitations through our misinterpretation of input from the intellect, feelings, or intuition. Faith can help us to disregard other types of faulty input, e.g., public opinion (when the public is incorrect). Faith helps to diminish mental and emotional distractions, such as doubt, fear, anxiety, etc.

We are continually exposed to uncertainties; therefore, it is our faith in the possible goodness of life that allows us to proceed. If we lived in a state of total doubt regarding everything, we would hardly be able to interact with life at all. Faith might invoke the assistance of a supernatural force. Some religions say that our faith in a deity is an essential part of the relationship with that deity, and that the faith enhances the deity's willingness and ability to assist us.

However, if we rely on "blind faith" we are discouraged from learning, questioning, exploring and using our intellect, intuition, and personal power altogether. We believe in outer authorities and their mostly inaccurate dogma, because faith is a state that exists in the absence of experience or knowledge. A glorification of "blind faith" is a glorification of inexperience and ignorance; we are "blessed" for "not knowing".

Intuition can tell us whether something is worthy of faith. It can warn us when something is going to betray our faith. We need to cultivate courage, because we are venturing into new areas, perhaps in contradiction to our reasoning and our experience, but we should also be willing to accept changes. We change as we learn more about the object of faith. For example, as we learn about a deity, we are essentially having faith in a different thing. The thing is essentially the same, but our perception of it changes, and so our experience of it changes.

We discern worthiness through our intuition, our experiences with them, and other people's experiences with them. We can test the truth of anything by subscribing to the criteria of truth.

Muktananda said, "Have faith, but don't have blind faith. Have faith with knowledge."

We should not blindly follow the belief system of our peers. We have been brainwashed for centuries in believing that sex is bad, that we are all sinners. It is time to change that.

Dogma and Intellectual Slavery

Religion is the brainchild of fear, and fear is the parent of cruelty.
The greatest evils inflicted on humankind are perpetrated not by pleasure-seekers
self-seeking opportunists, or those who are merely amoral,
but by fervent devotees of religion.
...Emmanuel Kofi Mensah

There is no reason to change your religion when you study meditation, or yoga, including Tantra. However, there is good reason to change some of your old beliefs and ideals perpetuated by family, teachers, church, media, and politics. The fact that you have purchased this book is indicative that you are already trying to find answers to questions that have never been adequately answered for you.

There are some basic differences in the ways the East and the West approach God, life, sex and death.

Established institutions, such as governments and organized religions, find ways to empower themselves through controlling the individual's mind and will. It is done quite insidiously with tools of propaganda to control the masses. By limiting a person's ability to freely find the truth, many churches and governments can control the minds and wills of their followers through repetition. Organized religion tends to imprison the minds of the masses into a fixed form of beliefs. (There are spiritual paths, like Buddhism, that are individualistic.)

Religion without science is blind.
... Albert Einstein

The relationship between the Divine and the individual exists in the temple of our soul. It does not lie in a building, church, synagogue or mosque where we are told exactly what to do and what and how to think. Talk radio, television, newspapers and magazines all have a bias to "convert" the thoughts of the populace to their particular dogma.

Intellectual slavery can occur anytime we don't develop a keen and unbiased sense of truth, *viveka*. If we use the five criteria in the previous chapter, (intuitive experience, direct perception, inductive reasoning, testimony, deductive reasoning) to help us determine the truth, we can evaluate and conclude for ourselves what is true, and what is propaganda.

Numerous times in our history, the truth and traditional beliefs have been challenged and controlled by politicians, governments, the church and the media. This is intellectual slavery and our minds are still being enslaved today.

Dogma exists when the church or government tells you black is white and that we should accept it and believe in it because of faith; for instance, the concept of creation. Many educated people still believe that the world was created in seven days. Phenomenologically and scientifically this is not possible, yet amazingly, many people believe it.

This is my simple religion. There is no need for temples;
no need for complicated philosophy.
Our own brain, our own heart is our temple; the philosophy is kindness.
… Dalai Lama

Religion creates dogma,
dogma creates fundamentalism,
and fundamentalism creates terrorism.
…Swami Satyananda Saraswati

History has a clear record of humanity's struggle with science and the truth and knowledge that clearly advances humanity and improves our quality of life and awareness of everything.

> *Science is not only compatible with spirituality; it is a profound source of spirituality.*
> *…Carl Sagan*

A good example is the story of Archimedes, the famous mathematician, the father of geometry and modern calculus. This man was at least two thousand years ahead of his time. The Romans killed him senselessly about 300 A.D. but he left an amazing manuscript of his work, methods and discoveries. The monks of the religious order of the time, who thought it had no value, washed the ink from the pages and re-wrote a prayer book over the master's work.

This was lost for 2000 years and recently there was a great effort to recover and restore the manuscript. If we had some of the knowledge during the flowering of the renaissance, mankind and society might be further along than we are.

> *The losses in science were monumental.*
> *In some cases the Christian church's burning of books*
> *and repression of intellectual pursuit set*
> *humanity back as much as two millennia in its scientific understanding.*
> *…Helen Ellerbe*

This is just one example of the conventional wisdom of the day. Dogma and religion invariably stand in the way of brilliance, advancement and enrichment of our culture. It is all about power instead of truth and knowledge.

The church persecuted many other great scientists and philosophers, like Galileo, who believed that the earth was not the center of the universe and that the earth was round instead of flat. He was considered a heretic for challenging the church and not agreeing with their dogma.

> *Scientists were rated as great heretics by the church,*
> *but they were truly religious men*
> *because of their faith in the orderliness of the universe.*
> *…Albert Einstein*

Throughout history, great men were persecuted and destroyed for thinking outside of the box. Great saints, such as Jesus, were routinely condemned and persecuted. Christ's guru, John the Baptist, was beheaded, and many saints and leaders throughout history have been condemned, ridiculed, ostracized, shunned and killed for their views. During the Reagan years the enlightened master, Osho, was banned from many countries, including his own India. He was imprisoned for his unconventional teachings about sex, and for his criticism about church and governments. Many believe that his untimely death was a conspiracy of the government.

It is dangerous to be right when the government is wrong.
...Voltaire

Truth knows no boundaries, has no dogma. Truth remains the same regardless of time or place. On the other hand, religion is man-made and subject to change, subject to interpretation, and subject to editing. Rules are created to control the followers. The congregation is repeatedly told that they are sinners, that they are wretched souls, that they are bad and need to be "saved". They are told that they are unworthy and God is separate from them--that he is outside of them.

Truth says, "You were created in the image of God, so you are perfect being." You just don't recognize it yet. Your magnificence is there. The challenge and the lesson in life is to reconnect with it. Seek the light within. It is not separate from us. Saints and sages, including Jesus and *Tukaram Maharaj,* a saint from Maharastra, India, said, "My Father and I are One".

We are what we think we are.

The following chart will illustrate many of the differences between Western thought and Eastern teachings. Can you relate to any of them?

In the West:	In the East:
You are a sinner	You are divine
God is separate from you	God is within you
Go to church on Sunday.	There is no place or time god is not
When you die you go to heaven	Heaven is here and now
Allows for misbehavior by asking for forgiveness from an external source	Behavior is self-regulated, self-modified and comes from individual mindfulness
External order of law and punishment	Internal order of cause and effect (karma)
Worships culture of youth	Reverence for gurus, elders
Instant gratification	Allows gradual unfoldment
Sex is bad	Sex is natural
Instills fear	Instills love
Emphasizes guilt and shame about enjoying sex	Guilt and shame non-existent
God is patriarchal, usually angry	God and Goddess are loving and benevolent

Artificial appearance, sexuality and expression are worshipped.	Teaches you to be genuine and natural
Good sex belongs to youth	Sex gets better with age
Imitates sex by watching movies and pornography (artificial)	Sex should be real, healthy, natural
Heart is "closed" for protection	Open heart is the way to God
Act your age	Child like innocence, honesty is valued
My god is better than yours	There is only one God
I kill in the name of my God.	I love in the name of all gods
You are bad, god will punish you	You were created in the image of God, God loves you
Do not worship "idols" (referring to images)	God exists in idols and pictures of the deities, as well as within each individual. The "idols" to avoid are alcohol, drugs, promiscuity and things that take you away from your divinity
Money and sex are not spiritual	Pursuit of money, enjoying sex, having desires is natural and good for survival. Balance them with spiritual knowledge.
Death is final	Accepts reincarnation

Sex is for having babies, not to be enjoyed, get it over with as soon as possible	Prolonged, conscious sex is the key to bliss and ecstasy
I can't believe you are asking me to do that	I am honored to worship your body
I refuse to give up my power	Surrender makes you more powerful
Condemns others belonging to a different path	Recognizes that all paths lead to the same goal

Addictions, Substitutes for Love

After half a century in psychiatric practice,
I know without a doubt that the source of addiction is spiritual deficiency.
Irrespective of whether we are religious or atheist,
all human beings are spiritual by nature
and spirituality is the cornerstone of our recovery.
...Abraham Twerski

There is a huge epidemic in Americ, and that is the epidemic of addictions to food, alcohol, drugs, sex, cigarettes, anger and others. There has been a surge of programs to combat this problem.

Any addiction is a gradual process that may have taken years to evolve. Addictions are a result of feeling a void in our lives. So we develop unhealthy habits to fill the emptiness, yet we still feel empty.

Treating the symptoms of any addiction, rather than the cause is not the answer. We have to consider not just what we are addicted to, but also why.

Many people with addiction problems use substances as substitutes for love. More specifically, these substitutes are a desperate need for touch, and for sexual love. Clearly, any addiction is s a self-esteem problem, depression masking itself in the craving for unwholesome habits. There may have been some early childhood or sexual abuse issues that have not been resolved or some other recent traumatic experience that triggered the low self-esteem and addiction.

Adopting a spiritual practice is the first step. Doing physical exercises, such as in this book will build skills and confidence. Mastering the tantra exercise regime and meditation will make a marked improvement in the way we look and feel. When we feel good inside, we look good on the outside. Beauty begins from within.

Developing the ability to control our thoughts is essential for change. Practicing mindfulness, visualization methods, seeing in our mind's eye the way we want to look and feel, and carrying this vision can gradually reduce our feelings of inadequacy or unworthiness.

To love oneself is the beginning of a lifelong romance.
...Oscar Wilde

We can start the process of loving ourselves by looking in the mirror and talking to ourselves, acknowledging our worth by praising our attributes, talents, gifts, and accomplishments. We need to say it aloud as we look in the mirror. This may feel really stupid or silly, but we need to do it anyway. Realize that it is the ego that wants to sabotage our best interests. We can also write down all our positive character traits. Every day we can list at least twenty things that are positive, such as "I am kind", "I am honest", and "I love my family". Then we can read our entries several times during the day, upon awakening, and before retiring in the evening. We must be as obsessed about making changes as we were about the addiction.

When we are on the road to any kind of recovery, we must be selective of the company we keep. If our friends are not willing to make any changes along with us, they will actually reinforce our addictions. We really do not have much choice but to cut off the sources of negativity.

How do we break our old patterns of behavior? The answer is through meditation and being ever mindful of our thoughts and actions. We should meditate for at least five minutes in the beginning, then every five days or so increase our sitting time another five minutes, until we can sit still for an hour. It may take four to six weeks, but have patience. As we sit in meditation, we may add one of the mantras in this book to center our mind. All these methods are designed to focus our mind on something positive. Whenever we feel the urge to repeat any of our bad habits, we can instead, repeat a mantra and/or meditate till the urge passes.

Some people refuse to love themselves because they do not differentiate between self-love and other states such as vanity or narcissism.

Self-Love

If your leaders say to you,
"Look, the kingdom is in the sky,"
then the birds of the sky will precede you.
If they say to you,
"It is in the sea,"
then the fish will precede you.
Rather, the kingdom is inside of you, and it is outside of you.
When you come to know yourselves, then you will become known,
and you will realize that it is you who are the sons of the living Father.
But if you will not know yourselves, you dwell in poverty,
and it is you who are that poverty.
…Jesus Christ, Gospel of Thomas

Self-love is similar to some destructive states. Some people refuse to love themselves because they do not differentiate between self-love and other states such as vanity or narcissism.

Vanity is the belief that we deserve love on the basis of our fulfillment of ideals; for example, we believe that we should be loved because we are exceptionally intelligent or beautiful. Vanity is not self-love. Vanity is based on conditions (e.g., our supposed fulfillment of an ideal). In contrast, love is unconditional. Ideals are unattainable by humans. Thus, in order to believe that we have attained an ideal upon which we base our vanity, we must repress our awareness of the occasions when we do not attain the ideal; for example, we would deny or hate the pimple on our otherwise beautiful face. When we are in denial or hatred toward any aspect of ourselves, we do not love ourselves.

Narcissism is an obsession with ourselves, to the exclusion of other people--both their needs, and their gifts that they want to share with us. Narcissism is not self-love. Narcissism ignores the aspects of our selves that are fulfilled only through interaction with other people--giving to them, and receiving from them. If we love ourselves, we love the social aspects of ourselves, and so we reach out to people in a manner such that they will respond with the love which we require; we know that we must give love to get love. If we give something other than love, we get something other than love.

Narcissism is ineffective in nourishing the aspects of our selves that are fulfilled only through self-love. There is a type of nourishment that comes only from our selves to ourselves. But narcissism is mere infatuation; it does not nourish us, and so we spend an inordinate amount of time with a focus on ourselves, in a futile attempt to satisfy ourselves with this infatuation.

In contrast, if we have self-love, we do achieve the satisfaction, and then we can turn our attention to other aspects of our lives, including other people. In this way we can eliminate selfishness, or greed.

*You, yourself, as much as anybody in the entire universe,
deserve your love and affection.
...Buddha*

We love ourselves, not to please our egos, but to learn to accept our own Divinity. We are receiving our own love--self-love--for it is true that we can only love another to the extent that we love ourselves.

Passion and Enthusiasm

*Nothing great was ever achieved without enthusiasm.
... Ralph Waldo Emerson*

Passion is the *joie de vivre*, the joy of living. This is the only way we should approach life. We can be very passionate in that we engage totally in whatever we do. Passion should be part of what makes us breathe, what makes us get up in the morning. Passion is the juice of our existence, what makes us feel alive, what makes us embrace life. If we are passionless we become like couch potatoes. We become neutered. We have no motivation and no inspiration. Passion makes us embrace our partner and embrace everything in this world.

Passion is a learned behavior. When we are encouraged to do things we love we develop more passion for them. Sometimes we are discouraged, we are not rewarded, and so we never develop a strong sense of passion. Even with our lovemaking, we are never encouraged or totally fulfilled. We are not given the right tools or techniques so we do not develop this fire that is the heat of creativity. It is the passion that is released when the creative juices start flowing through us. It is what makes us either live life robustly and completely or makes us squeak through life with no fire at all, so that we are almost cold and dead.

The wonderful thing about tantra is that we can learn the techniques that set us on fire and awaken the kundalini. This fuels our passion, not just for sex, but for all of life. Whatever we do, we should do it with enjoyment. Zen, the Japanese Buddhist meditation tells us to approach life with a hundred percent passion. Passion is the juice of our existence. It is what makes us feel alive, what makes us embrace life. Whether we are mopping the floor, washing dishes or cooking, we do not consider is a chore. We do it with gratitude for all we are able to do. If we cannot find passion in what we do, then it would not be beneficial for our inner state. In general we are a passionless society. We learn to contract or undermine our passion to the point where we do things begrudgingly. It may seem normal because everyone else shares this emptiness and this commonness. In reality it is not normal.

Passion is having intense enthusiasm for life, connecting with our Inner Spirit. We feel most intensely alive during these moments. Our inner voice whispers, "This is the real me."

The famous poet and author, Samuel Ullman said, "Age may wrinkle the face, but the lack of enthusiasm wrinkles the soul." Imagine the leathery, shriveled souls of apathetic people. One of the first things we will find is if we make the practices of tantra a routine part of our life, then all of life can be an active meditation. It puts us in a semi-trance, yet we remain surprisingly alert. It is similar to what meditation does, except it is a "body" trance and it lets us reconnect with that life energy--that inner fire that is within us all--that which we need to find again.

And one of the things that happens is that we will feel like a child again as we remove that guilt. Enthusiasm, from the Greek *enthousia,* literally means, being possessed of God. Enthusiasm, passion and love are key drivers in living a successful life.

Passion is of the most important emotions we can have. If we are passionless, all we have is emptiness; there is no fire inside. All of life's experiences can be pleasant or may wound our soul. They hurt us and they create emptiness inside. We have to find ways to heal those wounds, to heal that inner soul in order to feel whole again.

Passion is awakened when we start remembering ourselves with our passion energy. It is not as rational as we are used to things being. We have done a lot of substituting. We have substituted faith for trust, fear for excitability, and compassion for passion. We have taken these awakened states and reduced them in a way that can be controlled.

We've demonized our sex; we've demonized our passion.

Passion and love are affairs of the heart, not the head. We are not rational creatures. Realizing we have deviated from the love of the natural life processes in our culture, we must make an effort to open up our hearts. We are where we're most in love.

We should allow passion and *joie de vivre.* Religious writers generally describe detachment as a passionless state. But passion is the flow of life-energy in its full expression of physical activity, emotions, energy, imagination, creativity, and soulfulness; our passion for life guides us to that which is highly charged, that which allows us to give and receive the greatest amount of this flow. Because of this craving for life itself, we spontaneously create the field-elements which facilitate this flow, and, because we are here for the liveliness rather than for the object itself, we easily release (i.e., detach from) objects which are reaching the end of their cycle (and are therefore exuding a diminishing amount of energy), and we eagerly seek whatever new object is charged to intermingle with us.

Passion is not founded on materialism, although it expresses itself toward material objects; it is founded on the living spirit that we experience when we are engaged with the particular objects that are charged for us at this moment.

Ironically, in a religious, *passionless* type of detachment, we are creating attachments that block the flow of life; we are attached to the limited and stifling assortment of behaviors and perspectives and thoughts and self-images that seem to exemplify detachment.

The Virgin Heart

Rama, the Lord has possessed me.
Hari, the beloved Lord, has enchanted me.
All my doubts have flown like birds migrating in winter.
When I was mad with pride
The Beloved did not speak to me.
But when I became as humble as ashes,
The Master opened my inner eye,
Dyeing in every pore of my being in the color of love.
Drinking nectar from the cup of my emptied heart,
I slept in his abode in divine ecstasy.
The devotee meets the Lord like gold merging with its luster.
My Lord loves a pure heart.
...Kabir

The heart has been associated with everything good and loving. We hear about someone who has a "heart of gold", or is "young at heart", a "sweetheart", "big heart", "light hearted", "lion hearted", " heart is in the right place", "won our hearts", "heartfelt", "from the heart".

On the other hand, the mind is usually associated with negative things, "poison the mind", "lose the mind", "weak minded", "simple minded", "make up your mind", "out of your mind".

Only a mind that has been purified only through awareness will lead us right to the heart state. There are many ways to purify and quiet the mind, such as chanting, meditation, reciting mantras, seva, contemplation, breathing, asanas and studying the scriptures.

The virgin heart is the state of innocence and purity--the childlike state of Goddess *Kumari,* the Ever Pure One, open, free, unblemished, loving, clear, uninhibited. A heart state that is steadfast and pure is only achieved by complete devotion and surrender to the supreme,

Lord Shiva, and through the grace of our Guru. We all want an "open" heart, but it is a boon that has to be deserved and earned. When our heart becomes contracted and encrusted with our negative thoughts and deeds, we remain in ignorance and need the guidance of a Guru or an advanced teacher to help us to purge away the impurities and replace our thoughts with pure love.

The heart is where the Truth resides. Truth cannot be known though intellect alone. The intellect must be purified before wisdom can arise from the space of the heart.

Great hearts steadily send forth the secret forces that incessantly draw great events.
...Ralph Waldo Emerson

How can one liberate the heart from its prison? Through devotion, understanding, action, and knowledge, we can loosen the knots and tangles of the heart woven by illusion. By repeating a mantra such as "*So' Ham*" or "*Om Namaha Shivaya*" we can find the One who resides within.

The constant chatter of the ego mind has to be subdued for the heart to open. The virgin heart is the heart free from blemishes; it is the first transcendent state where we transcend the limits of our ego and ourselves.

Christ said we have to become like children again to enter the kingdom of heaven, maintaining that respectful innocence and purity of heart would admit us into Bliss Absolute.

The Self

The Self has been described in various ways. It is a transcendent, unchanging part of us, in contrast to the ever-varying ego, shadow, complexes, etc.

This western definition of the "Self" has its roots in psychology.

It is a "God-image" within the psyche. Although Carl Jung was criticized for allegedly implying that the Self is God, he stressed that the

Self is not God itself but rather only an image of God, a representation of God as it would be depicted within the psyche (although he did call the Self the "God within us" in "Psychology and Religion" on page 334). An encounter with the Self feels like a "religious experience" with God. Jung said that the occurrence leaves us vitalized and enriched. In addition to being a symbol of God in the psyche, the Self could also be considered a symbol of what the religions call the soul.

When we encounter the Self, we re-evaluate the ego. Some people mistakenly think that when they encounter the Self, they are simply discovering a greater view of their ego. This erroneous thinking can cause the people to inflate their ideas regarding themselves (believing that the God-like luminosity of the Self is their own personal magnificence).

Ideally, in our meeting with the larger Self, we retain the sense of the ego self as a still-valid part of ourselves. The ego is no longer our only center of identity; thus its importance downsizes to being simply one element of many in the psyche, still powerful and important as a manager, but it is not the big boss.

The Self grants new perspectives. When we can look at the ego from the viewpoint of the Self, we gain an objective understanding of the nature of the ego and its claim to be our identity. We sense its distinction and preeminence over the psyche's other functions, its preferences and tastes, its quests for personal growth and mastery, and its self-centered perspective.

When we meet the Self, we realize that we have previously assigned some of the Self's functions to the ego simply because we did not know the Self, and the ego seemed to be the only part of us which could fill these roles. Now we can transfer some the ego's functions back to that Self. For example, instead of allowing the ego to devise our goals, we accept the Self's goals, which are aligned toward the actualization of its life-purpose. Our ego, without the wise, balancing influence of the Self, tends to select goals that are no more than ego-symbols, such as an audacious home.

When we realize that the Self has knowledge and power that are superior to that of the ego, we sensibly, strategically submit to this greater entity, and allow the ego to receive direction from it, direction which might be contrary to the ego's short-sighted preferences.

Because the Self's inclusiveness allows a full spectrum from which to select behaviors and identity components, we become more obviously unique and individual. Our individualism is charged with vitality and realness because we develop ourselves on the lines of the Self's destiny and life-plan instead of self-consciously creating ourselves from the ego's ideas of its own enhancement (primarily through material symbols of success).

We cannot know the Self intellectually. Although we can make certain observations about the Self we cannot study the Self in the same manner in which a scientist would examine an amoeba under a microscope. Because the Self is the entirety of us, any viewpoint (such as the ego's viewpoint of the Self) would have a limiting blind spot, as in the situation of an eyeball trying to look at itself. We would be separating ourselves as observer and observed when in fact the Self is both.

Intellectually the Self is no more than a psychological concept,
a construct that serves to express an unknowable essence
that we cannot grasp as such, since by definition
it transcends our powers of comprehension.
…Carl Jung

We can meet the Self in other ways. To the extent that the Self is comprehensible, we can become familiar with it through the sheer experience of it. We might also meet the Self in a dream's symbolic images, such as those of mandalas or crystals.

We truly become acquainted with the Self during midlife. Life is a cycle; in youth, we need to concentrate on the development the ego and its external manifestations -- home, career, our place in the world, our persona, our differentiation from other people, etc. Midlife is triggered by our relative completion of this ego development. At midlife, we have finished the first part of our life, and now we turn to the next task in the cycle of life, which is to re-integrate that which we needed to separate out during the ego-building stage; we meet our shadow, the anima or animus, and other previously ignored material. As we become familiar with those parts of ourselves, and we gain a view of the totality of us, we awaken to the synergism of these parts: they are not just separate elements, but they are also part of an overall system that has a great consciousness of its own.

The New Age movement often refers to the Self at the "Higher Self".That would seem to imply that there is a "lower" Self, or "another" Self. In fact, there is only one Self. It is just that that we have forgotten who we are, and we do spiritual practices solely for the purpose of remembering that we are--Divine, Perfect, Whole, Loving, Harmonious, and Powerful.

The Tantric Secret to Manifestation

Before God manifested Himself,
When all things were still hidden in Him...
He began by forming an imperceptible point;
That was His own thought.
With this thought
He then began to contruct a mysterious and holy form...
The Universe.
...Albert Pike

When "The Secret" came out in 2006, many people said that adopting a new mindset created wonders in their lives, while others complained, "It doesn't work".

Two things should be understood. The first is karma. For some people a shift in their thinking was all it took to create the change they wanted in their lives. For others, it still did not work. Why? It's all about karma. (We would urge the reader to please re-read the section on karma). And if it is karma, can it be changed? The answer is yes; but it takes diligence, commitment and a strong will.

It is also imperative to understand that there is a connection and an advanced spiritual component to "The Secret" which was not covered in the video or book. We will attempt to identify the parallels between the ancient Hindu scriptures and teachings of contemporary teachers. These teachings of the ancients, in the form of slokas and mantras are often undecipherable and hidden.

The principles of existence, *tattvas,* while understandable on an intellectual level, have been especially difficult to grasp intuitively. We have been making a comparative analysis of different authors and masters for some time. The mind accepted it; but longed for a deep *experience* of the knowledge, which can never come from just reading the words of sages past or present.

The Law of Attraction is not different from the *tattva* Principles of Truth in Tantra. The *tattvas* are just an elaboration of the Law of Attraction; or, we could say that the Law of Attraction has its basis on the *tattvas.* This is not surprising, since throughout history, philosophers, scientists, writers and others have always imbibed Eastern spiritual principles and experienced these Truths as their personal reality.

In the cycle of consciousness, the Supreme expresses itself through the individual and manifests as you and me.

Our purpose in life is to reclaim our Divinity and return to our true nature. The Supreme travels down from the heavenly sphere to experience an earthbound reality. Once that is accomplished, it yearns to return back to its home and seeks out various ways to reclaim that state of bliss--through religion, drugs (that create a state that feels good initially), prayer, meditation, sex, etc.

Our body lives through the thoughts we allow. If our thoughts are on default, we experience struggles, suffering, chaos and other unpleasant things. Why? Because our body is the result of our thoughts. What is seen on the outside is a perfect reflection of what is on the inside.

If you look at the illustration on page 206 you see that the driver (thoughts) literally drives the chariot (body) on its journey of this lifetime. The driver actually controls the emotions, symbolized by the reins. So the driver directs the horses (the actions and experiences) on a certain path it wishes to experience, as perceived through the senses, organs of action, including the bodily functions, and elements.

In the west, the manifestation basically ends here. To feel, think, and receive, or ask and receive--all with thanks and gratitude is a wonderful and joyous way to live. Ordinary becomes extraordinary. Commonplace becomes exceptional. Normal becomes genius. It takes a great deal of work and effort to maintain and control thoughts and emotions that feel good. This is the ultimate goal for most of us, and it is ideal and enough for many.

This is the basic law of attraction and manifestation.

But--suppose we *also* have an urge for *spiritual* fulfillment? Eastern tantric teachings continue to move forward for the perfection of the soul. In preparation for Union with the Divine, yogis, past and present, practiced meditation and yoga--having control of the *ahamkara* (ego), *citta* (knowledge), *buddhi* (intellect) and *manas* (mind). Tantra accentuates the union of nature with consciousness, defying *maya,* limitations and illusion of time, karma, space and destiny. Through self-effort and guidance by a self-realized master, tantriks strive to see beyond the *kanchutas* (covering or veils) that limit perception, vision and awareness.

Mastering the body, mind and soul is the key to opening the door of knowledge of the Truth, taking one from the dark oblivion of sleep to the awakened light of consciousness.

Tantra includes everything in "The Secret", that new movement inspired by that famous DVD, and it goes even further and deeper. The teachers on the DVD reveal that the age-old secret to manifestation is the Law of Attraction, which operates on principles of how our thoughts and emotions create our life's experiences.

The secret to tantra is beyond "The Secret". While "The Secret" operates on the mental body, Tantra involves the causal body as well.

It's true that thoughts create your reality. But it is the passion and energy of those thoughts that correspond and influence your life's circumstances. If you are lukewarm about your intention, the universe is likewise lukewarm, and you get lukewarm results.

We are a microcosm of the Formless Substance. When we impress our thoughts on this Substance, supported with love and gratitude, we too, have the ability to create our own little world.

We can open our divine potentialities by awakening the sleeping serpent at the base of our spine. As you recall, throughout this book, we have been focusing on this Tantric awakening beginning at the first chakra and purifying each chakra as it ascends up the spine. If you have been doing all the practices we have been describing, you can most definitely connect with Infinite Power. Our objective thoughts are the inspiration upon which that the subjective (sub-conscious) takes its cues and creates exactly what we ask for.

This matter of how thoughts create our reality is highly involved and evolves under certain conditions and applications that we have total control of. It is a study that is beyond the scope of this chapter, and we will, nethertheless attempt to give the reader a summary and glimpse of the vibrational power of thoughts.

As we awaken each chakra, we become aware of the potentialities of each lotus. We recognize our propensities for both positive and negative states, and one day we reach the *Sahasrar,* the seventh chakra, where the Divine Union takes place. Shakti joins Shiva in the Supreme Dance of Bliss, joined in absolute harmony.

It is this union of the Infinite becoming Finite, and the individual merging with the Divine, where manifestation takes place. The Supreme expresses itself through the individual, and it gives us whatever we think about, be it good, or not so good.

So manifestation through Tantric sex begins at the first chakra, the *Muladhar,* where physical union is taking place through the *lingam* and *yoni.* At this chakra, we store our *samskaras,* ideas, thoughts, and attitudes imposed upon us by others (parents, schools, religion) in this lifetime or previous lifetimes, at a time when we were either very young or too vulnerable to be able to discriminate fact from propaganda. These impressions have been deeply imprinted in our DNA and we really cannot do anything about the past. It is "what is". What we can do is learn to release our fears and demons and create a new reality for ourselves. A healthy first chakra is evident in our passion and commitment. We have faith and trust in our selves, our partner, and our dreams, and our co-Creator.

When the Shakti moves to the second chakra, the *Svadhistan,* we may feel excited and inspired, but it is only through concerted effort and spiritual applications that we have the ability to create our lives the way we envision it. Sexual energy is creative energy.

From thereon, the energy moves up the spine, striking each plexus, until it reaches the *Sahasrar.* This is the orderly sequence of Shakti as She ascends and unites with Shiva. Once joined, they descend chakra by chakra in reverse until they are back at the *Muladhar.*

The full spectrum of tantric practices brings us into a deeper awareness of our senses. We get feedback from our senses through our conscious mind. The conscious mind, or objective mind, is located at the brain center, the cerebro-spinal system. Manifestation occurs when our thoughts at this center travel down the spine through the vagus nerve.

So, mind has a thought at the *Sahasrar,* where anything is possible. This is *Jnana,* the knowledge stage of what you want, do not want, or think about all day long. It matters not; it will come to fruition, just by being entertained as thoughts in the mind.

> *A man is but the product of his thoughts, what he thinks, he becomes.*
> *...Mahatma Gandhi*

This thought has a "vision" though the *Ajna.* That is, we make an image of what it is we are thinking of through the sixth chakra, like a camera. We take a mental picture of what it is that we want or do not want.

This image travels to thorax where it expresses itself in the form of words at the *Visshuda.* Words are the audible expressions of our thought.

Thought is realized when accompanied by *bhakti,* intense emotion, which is located at the fourth heart chakra, the *Anahat. Iccha* is this desire stage.

The intensity of the feeling carries the thought to the ganglionic mass at the back of the stomach through the spine to the *Manipur,* the center of our being, or what is often referred to as our solar plexus.

The sun beams its energy to every part of our body without discrimination. Like the rays of the sun, the solar plexus, the sun of the body, dispatches our thoughts and transmits this data of thoughts throughout our body's nervous system, through the blood, cells, and nerves. This is the *kriya* stage, activity. It even radiates these messages outside of the body, affecting our immediate environment and circumstances. A person can have a "magnetic" personality when positive and strong energy is emitted from their solar plexus. Likewise, a person with slow or dark energy repels others with their state of negativity.

The so-called "lower" chakras do not actually participate in the manifesting. They have already done their work, initiating this entire process at the beginning.

We can manifest with or without a partner. How to manifest what we want rather than what we don't want requires effort, knowledge of the truth, genuine desire, and continuous application of the principles.

Any negative thought accompanied by intense emotion is not easily eradicated. The effects can remain in the system for years affecting our health, happiness, and well-being. With proper application and mindfulness, however, we can train ourselves to a new way of thinking. We can acquire new habits, and learn to control and manage our emotional states, thereby manifesting a wonderful life.

When we think in a new and different way, we invite peace to enter our abode. Then we truly can live in a state of perpetual orgasmic bliss.

The World of Tantra

What is the World of Tantra?

The World of Tantra is not just the external world of places to visit, but it includes your immediate world--your environment, your workplace, family, friends, your material world and your personal vehicle (your body matter) that transports the Self around.

So the world of Tantra is everything Without.

The world of Tantra is also everything Within.

The World Within is the dwelling place of the Self. It is the subtle body of the chakras; it is the abode of the mind, the world of manifestation and mysticism of the causal body.

For a pair of lovers, this also means that it is the world of everything that makes you *You*, in union with the World of everything that makes me *Me*.

With an understanding of the *tattvas* you can tap into the mysticism of the causal body of the *jiva*, in union with itself, and in union with all. This is a brief overview of the principles of life.

In the sixth chapter of the *Shrimad Devi Bhagavatam* it is stated:

The soul is known as the master of the chariot, and the body is the chariot.
The intellect is known as the driver, and the mind is the reins.
The organs of knowledge and action are the horses,
and all perceivable objects become concerns for attention.
When united with the organs of knowledge, action and the mind,
the soul becomes the enjoyer of all experience.
…Devi Gita, Chapter 6, Verse 35[15]

Chariot

1. The driver represents the mind. He is in control of his destiny. He decides where he wants to go and how to get there. The driver is the:

    a. *Ahamkara*--ego

    b. *Citti*--knowledge

    c. *Buddhi*--intellect

    d. *Manas*--mind, subconscious

2. But his emotions (the reins), which are under control of his mind, determine where his horses go (actions), and what he experiences. You could say that the four legs of the horse represent:

[15] Permission, Devi Mandir, © 1991, translated by Swami Satyananda Saraswati

a. *Karmendriyas*--Organs of Action

Arms, legs, tongue, sexual organs, anus

b. *Jnanendriyas*--Organs of Cognition

Eyes, nose, mouth, ears, feelings

c. *Mahabhutas*--Elements

Earth, water, fire, air, ether

d. *Tanmatras*--Organs of Perception

Sight, sound, smell, taste, touch

3. Having control of all your actions leads you to recognize your true nature:

a. *Prakriti*--individual body, nature

b. *Purusha*--individual soul, consciousness

4. Through your mastery of:

a. *Kalaa*--unlimited power to act

b. *Vidya*--unlimited knowledge of supreme consciousness

c. *Raga*--basic supreme will to create

d. *Nyati*-space, destiny, karma

e. *Kaula*-time

f. *Maya* (3 kinds of maya) and removal of the *kanchutas*--veils

5. With mastery of the mind and control of the emotions comes the realization of the Self:

a. *Suddha Vidya*--pure knowledge of creation, preservation, dissolution

b. *Ishvara*--I, aham

6. And Supreme Union with Divine Consciousness:

a. *Shakti*--Energy of *Jnana, Iccha, Kriya*

b. *Shiva*--Supreme Consciousness.

....

PRACTICE

....

Challenge For Her:

1. Repeat the mantra, Om Namah Shivaya 108 times. If you do not have a mala (rosary) get some beans or rice, count off 108 of them. You are honoring Lord Shiva, who is within you and your partner. Think of your partner as a manifestation of this great deity.

2. Look at your image in a mirror. See yourself as a manifestation of the goddess supreme. Honor your womanhood. The goddess is powerful, creative and strong, intelligent, beautiful and very feminine. There is no need to compete with a man; there is no need for penis envy. The sexes complement one another. Be the woman to his man. The masculine is consciousness, the feminine is creativity. Both are necessary for the continuation of life.

Challenge For Him:

1. See your partner as a manifestation of the Goddess. Treat her with dignity, honor and respect. When you are making love, have the awareness that you are making love to the goddess herself, and are privileged to do so.

2. Allow your "animal". You can honor and respect your partner, and still honor your primal instincts. Tantra lovemaking in no uncertain terms an airy-fairy, benign activity. On the contrary, it is an activity full of passion and fire, even when the couple is in "stillness". Tantra is about bringing together the animal with the divine, the higher consciousness with the animal, as in nature, the feminine with the masculine, the yin and yang. It is all about the union of opposite polarities. Tantra is organic.

Practice For Couples:

1. Repeat the mantra, "Om mane padme hum" (man within woman, the jewel in the lotus) during sex, and especially when it is close to orgasm.

2. Sleep on your sides, with the man behind the woman in a "spoon" position, with the lingam in the yoni. Sleep in the nude.

3. Eliminate fear from your life. Emerson said, "He who is not everyday conquering some fear has not learned the secret of life".

//om//

Part Three

Kriya, Taking Action

Kriya is spiritual action we undertake to accomplish our goals. In order to achieve our personal goals, we need three components. First, we learn everything we can. We obtain information and learn everything we can about the thing that we want. Next, we must have a burning desire to reach this goal. Third, we have to take action. We do everything to make it happen.

Like the three legs of a stool, all three legs need to be grounded and balanced. We must have the discipline to take right action if we are to manifest our desires.

Our actions become the expression of our desires. Actions become the interpretation of our knowledge.

On the following pages, we disclose several practices to embrace our being, and bring us to peak sexual experiences, which in turn, gives us the glimpse of authentic love, which manifests as eternal joy and bliss.

Chapter Four:

The Bliss

Refined, higher states of pleasure are available to all of us through the expansion and acceptance of our body and mind.

Tantra uses activity as a means to move sexual energy to the higher chakras, where bliss awaits. The rapture of extended orgasms is then carried on into our daily routine. As it becomes our way of life, we replace negativity with divinity. We strive to find joy in everything that we do.

Couples will find that deeper sexual experiences create a supreme connection and bonding that can not only withstand the greatest trials and challenges, but can bring them even closer. Being in-the-moment and being fully "present" is the secret to profound lovemaking and ecstasy.

The practices in this chapter prepare you for the art of honoring the temple of your soul-- your body and your partner's body.

Here's a Quick Tantra Tip:

How to appreciate the body:

Dance in front of a mirror for five minutes, simply observing the way the body is moving, the way it is feeling. Know that you are not the dancer, but the witness of the one being danced. Relax and flow. In calmness there should be activity; in activity there should be calmness.

Dance

Unless you can dance your way to god, you can never reach.
So this is what I would like to say to you: dance your way to god.
And dance comes by balance.
One cannot dance on one leg; both legs will be needed.
And one cannot dance by choosing the inward or the outward,
by becoming the introvert or the extrovert.
Dance will need continuous coming and going.
It is a movement. You have to reach others.
And it is helpful; it is not contrary to meditation.
…Osho

In India, dance flourished side by side with spiritual austerities, such as meditation, fasting, and chanting. Like other yogic practices, dance, like sex, was another method used to induce a trance state, and an ecstatic union with the Divine.

Beautiful South Indian bronzes dating from the tenth and twelfth centuries A.D. depict *Nataraj* (the dancing form of Shiva), within an arch of flames, in a vigorous dance called *anandatandava,* the Dance of Bliss.

Shiva performs his dance of ecstasy, in rhythm to the vibratory beat of universal time. Fiery activity contrasting his serene countenance simulates the union of the microcosm merging with the macrocosm in an unending dance of creation, maintenance, and destruction.

Thus, Shiva taught us that meditation can be celebratory and can be done during activity such as dancing, by remaining focused, keeping the heart open and moving energy consciously.

The temporal lobes are involved with processing and producing rhythms. Dancing is a type of meditation in which we use the rhythm, attentiveness, and an intuitive state that are typical qualities of many types of meditation. Any kind of dancing can be meditative, but there is also a classification of "sacred dancing", which is the use of dance to explore and express our identity as soul.

Dancing is a part of virtually all religions. Religious dancing is common in modern-day "primitive" cultures, and it was a part of ancient primitive cultures, guided by shamans entering a trance.

In nature-based societies and religions, like the Native Americans and the Polynesians, the rhythm of dancing was an imitation of the rhythm of nature (including the cycles of seasons); more than mere mimicry, dancing was an attempt to understand and unite oneself with those rhythms.

In some cases, religious dancing became secularized and it lost its original sacred meaning, as in the case of the familiar "Maypole" dance, which is now an innocent children's game but which originally symbolized the plunging of a huge phallus into the earth to fertilize the crops.

As our body becomes energized through movement, we discern more clearly the energy of the body and its relation to the energy of the surrounding worlds; the body becomes less of a solid mass and more of a sacred focal point of spiritual power within the physical world.

Dancing is a means of expression, a universal language that transcends cultures and boundaries, religions and words. Many mystics have said that words cannot communicate their visions and ecstasies. Some of those mystics have used dance to express those inner experiences and their devotion to a deity. A simple mudra can depict a revelation for which there are no words.

In a group, dancing is a means of ego-transcendence. We re-define the separate ego as we merge into the group's common activity, emotion- and rhythm. The rhythm induces a different state. Even if we are not specifically meditating on the dance's rhythm (in our body or in the accompanying music), rhythm influences the cadence of our heartbeat and breathing, which in turn affects our psychological state. Some yoga practitioners use the breath--in *pranayam* exercises--to experience other states of consciousness.

Dancing affects the functioning of our brain. For example, the repetitiveness and non-rationality of shamanic drumming causes the brain's left hemisphere to diminish its activity due to boredom and lack of meaningful input, thus allowing the right hemisphere to become dominant with its emphasis on emotion and intuition. We might notice the same shift to the right hemisphere in other repetitive activities as diverse as jogging, or marching, or staring hypnotically at the white lines on a highway, or sexual activity that establishes a physical rhythm.

One of the guidelines for dance meditation is to focus on the dance, not the ego. We are not distracted by a need to impress people who are watching us, or to dance in accordance with our self-image (as a "talented dancer" or a "klutz"), or to set standards for any qualities such as gracefulness or spirituality. Instead, we become immersed in our moment-to-moment expression of the feelings and revelations which emerge. We might say that we "become the dance," or we lose ourselves in the dancing, or we dance to a deity, or we surrender to the dance, or we let the dance happen through us. We allow ourselves to be whatever emerges.

We can be wild, silly, sweaty, strange, primitive, or ethereal. In order to achieve this unself-consciousness, we must either dance alone or in a group in which the people are accepting and non-judgmental. When we improvise, put aside the persona, and express the intimate aspects our selves, our spiritual devotion, unconscious impulses, and the feelings that seem to be too tender to be expressed in our daily life. We allow ourselves this freedom, and allow it in the other dancers, too.

When we dance, we can find the "dance energy" within ourselves. Our body is filled with life, and it is constantly generating energy. While dancing, part of the meditation is to perceive the subtle energies and feelings that emerge from inside of us. We can detect the various places from which the energy radiates most powerfully -- the heart, the digestive organs, the brain, the sexual organs, the *hara* (about 2" below the navel but in the center of the body), the chakras, and other locations.

Notice the movement of energy throughout our body, flowing upward from our feet, outward to our hands, etc. These energies propel our body in dance meditation. We sense the energy's uncompromising assertiveness and power. The best that we can do is to administer it respectfully and accurately as the thrust of our own life.

We can express those energies through our body by allowing the body to improvise its own movements and then we are surprised and perhaps thrilled by the mysterious vitality that moves in ways that we never would have imagined. As we gradually diminish our conscious intrusion, our body asserts its own life. The life is somehow coming directly from the soul and filtering through us until the entire body is such a perfect expression of the energy that the body becomes a light, vibrant entity that is virtually indistinguishable from the soul itself.

When we permit the body to express itself and to move in its own way, we are likely to feel a profoundly sensuous and exciting sensation streaming throughout us. This is the body coming to life. We allow ecstasy. This is the state in which the ego's dysfunctional elements no longer control us; they cannot demand that the body conform to any mental image, nor can they convince us that the body is nothing but a stupid machine which has meaning and direction only if guided by the analytical mind. This ecstasy-- wild, beautiful, bold-- is perhaps the body's natural state.

Forget the dancer, the center of the ego.
Become the dance.
That is the meditation
Dance so deeply that you forget completely that 'you' are dancing
and begin to feel that you are the dance.
The division must disappear.
Then it becomes a meditation.
If the division is there, then it is an exercise:
good, healthy, but it cannot be said to be spiritual.
It is just a simple dance.
Dance is good in itself.
As far as it goes, it is good.
After it, you will feel fresh, young.
But it is not meditation yet.
The dancer must go, until only the dance remains.
.... Osho

Shiva Nataraj

It is not necessary to be a "dancer" in order to "dance". As our body and mind become one-pointed in its focus, we can dance to the soul. This integration of body, mind, and spirit is the purpose of tantra. The depth of this journey is infinite. When we open our heart, we release any inhibitions or judgments we may have about ourselves. Remembering there is no right or wrong way to do this, we simply express and experience our own beauty and love.

During other sessions of dance, we can direct our attention throughout our body, to notice the parts that we generally ignore; for example, we are all aware of our hands (because we use them almost constantly), but now we have an opportunity to regard other parts, such as our individual toes, or our elbows, or the top of our head. Becoming aware of all parts of the body, we dance as though the world around us is our partner. As we move, we respond to the objects in the room, twirling around with a chair, stroking the wall, embracing a curtain, and dancing as though the air was dense enough to embrace. We notice the sensations in the body, we practice how to become more sensual, and we experience the energy that passes between other objects and ourselves.

Devi Dance

The Devi Dance is a term we invented to describe our dance of the Goddess, which is an eclectic blend of universal movements, Middle Eastern, South Pacific, and Asian, with the natural movements of the soul. The Devi Dance is our unique interpretation, involving isolation movements of the pelvis, abdomen, and joints, in concert with our five senses, the five elements, Consciousness, and Shakti. It is an activity for both men and women, where there are no strict rules of any kind, except to move the neglected pelvis area and enjoy the bodily sensations.

Nature is all around us, is a part of us. One way to touch nature is through Devi Dance. We start by contemplating how we are feeling, and we can select an element to reinforce our needs or counter any negative or undesirable feelings.

Many of us in the West have no concept of the impact that rhythm; chanting and dancing can have to our health. Dance has the ability to change our mood, relax our body, and bring a sense of satisfaction and completeness.

Element of Earth--Dancing enables our bodies to maintain a high frequency even in the midst of change. When we are feeling disjointed or aimless, the energy of mother earth can "ground" us and give us stability and solidity. We can select anything rhythmic, such as the cries of wild animals in the jungle or birds singing in the tropics. To become like the element of earth, we can mimic the nature of these animals, imagining we are as primal and wild as they are. As we become aware of interact with this force, our senses--sound, touch, scent, sight, taste, and intuition become enhanced substantially.

Element of Water--Water is a remarkable substance that forms the basis for all of life on planet earth. Its alchemical quality allows it to change states, from gas (vapor) to a solid (ice) or liquid. In its solid and liquid form, it conforms to the shape of whatever container it is in. It can be heated as well as frozen. Water constitutes approximately 80% of our body, and 70% of the earth is covered by water.

When we feel emotionally imbalanced, we may need to recall the energy of water, by first selecting music that conveys its essence, such as a soft rain, or a gurgling stream. We may need the tranquility of a placid lake beside a flowering meadow, or we can become like a river meandering along the countryside. Alternatively, we can imitate a tumultuous sea or become a drizzle. All that is needed is our imagination. When we invite spirit to take residence in our sweet space, we release all pre-conceived concepts, and allow ourselves some relief from our everyday stresses and tensions. Undulating like the waves of the sea, we can allow this dance to happen all by itself.

Element of Fire--When we are feeling tired and bored, we may want to invoke the element of fire to give us some "spark".

Our motions should reflect the dynamic energy of fire; the music we select should feel "hot", passionate, and dynamic. As we become mindful of every move, we should be able to feel the warmth spreading throughout our body. We can visualize this energy growing, moving, and burning away our *samskaras.* The effulgence of this inner sun expands beyond our body, radiating throughout the solar system. Following the drum impulses, we begin to transform our latent potential into actualization. We feel a "charge", a surgence of energy. Moving passionately to the dynamic pulsation of the drum, we can build a powerful electro-magnetic energy by all our movements.

Element of Air--When we feel "static" or "stuck" in a situation, we may wish to connect with the element of air to give us the lilt of a soft breeze, or we may need a "gust" of energy. We can select "airy", ethereal music with some woodwind instruments, or we may look for music with the wind force of a hurricane. We can use a prop as we soar through the atmosphere, such as a veil, swinging it over our head, or waving it to our sides, visualizing that we are in heavenly flight. (Even macho men will enjoy this exercise, since it gives them an opportunity to safely get in touch with their feminine side.)

Dancing teaches us about interacting with the forces of nature, because like nature, the body is in perpetual motion. Even when we sit or sleep, there is action in the heartbeat, the breathing, and the small adjustments of muscles. The slow movements create a calm mind, which is one of the goals of sitting meditation. The body makes its own movements, at its own pace, and we experience lightness, effortlessness, and softness.

We can bless, heal, and celebrate the wonder of our body, and give it thanks for serving us well. We can be mindful of the motion of muscles, our contact with external surfaces (such as objects or the floor), and the movement of energy within the body (and the interchange of that energy with the external world). We should respond to our body's natural responses to stimuli (such as the rhythm of music), the special position of individual body parts (particularly the spine), and sensations throughout the body (e.g., warmth, cold, pressure, pain, pleasure, etc.). Our breathing can be allowed to occur in synch with our movements, or independent of them. Let the body express its sexuality, through dance. Communicate the body's sexual longing, joy, pleasure, and assertiveness. Experience the body's sexuality, not the mind's concept of it.

Dancing is one of the most ecstatic ways we can learn to meditate. Life is a divine dance.

The Devi Dance honors the Goddess through sensual undulations and isolated movements, centered on the pelvis and belly. The pelvis is the very foundation of our body; therefore, it must remain flexible or strong in order to support the rest of the body properly. When the spine is not properly supported, the rising of the awakened Kundalini Shakti is impeded, and unnecessary stress is placed on our spine. It is no wonder that back pain and stiffness is a common complaint in our culture.

Every movement we make (walking, dancing, etc) strongly depends on the flexibility of the pelvis. (Most healing practitioners in the west, do not "adjust" the sacrum, while in Japan, it the gentle manipulation of the sacrum is a common practice.)

As the basis of all movement, the pelvis makes no distinction between acceptable and prohibited movements. It only speaks the language of stiffness or flexibility. It houses the genitals and should move without restriction, however, the hips cannot move freely when the pelvis is stiff. Our hips and pelvis are so "frozen" that it has created multitudes of problems in our back and spine, (which connects all our organs and connective tissue).

Unlike the Middle Eastern and Polynesian societies, in our culture there are no activities utilizing the pelvic area, so these specific movements have to be practiced. Thousands of years of religious conditioning has resulted in the loss of the "natural" feminine sensuality, and has created immense guilt and shame about the body. In the west, we avoid movement of the hips, belly, and the pelvis, (the "suggestive" areas), and instead, dancers utilize their entire limbs rather than the individual joints. Ballet, tap dancing, ballroom, and the River Dancers of Ireland, while all wonderful, are netheretheless, creations of this "limb" dancing. There are a lot of arms flailing, and legs kicking, but everything else barely moves. There are no joint, hip, torso, or belly movements, and the internal muscles do not get the exercise that they need to stay flexible and mobile.

Devi Dance consists of moving the joints in a sensual manner. Limb motions have its purpose, but our dancing should not be limited to moving just our limbs. We need to exercise our joints and our pelvic area.

Additionally, modern culture idealizes a flat and hard abdomen, and so we tend to pull our stomach in and up, so that the center of our body has now become the chest. This unnatural shifting of our center to the chest creates shallow breathing, which adversely affects our lungs, heart, and general health.

The natural center of gravity is our abdominal area. Proper breathing begins here and not in the chest. The lower abdomen does not need any tension, however, in our attempt to satisfy the ideals of modern "beauty", that is exactly what it gets. When we try to shift our center to an unnatural place, we sacrifice our spontaneity and mobility, since our movements are limited.

Rather than focusing on making our belly flat and hard, our focus should be on strengthening the muscles of our pelvic floor, the perineum. (See bandha section in chapter 3). By restricting the movements of our belly and pelvis, we create stiffness in our back that results in blockages of energy throughout our body. Instead of suppleness, our body becomes rigid. When our body is rigid, it also follows that our minds are rigid as well.

Society has forced women to "choose" between their feminine nature, and their yang nature (competitiveness and aggressiveness), but both are necessary to survive in today's world. Thus, many women have lost their true feminine essence. We cut our hair short; wear pants, which is all perfectly wonderful. But oftentimes, we emulate masculine behavior. In order to maintain a balance, woman must embrace her intuitive, feminine side, as well. By reclaiming her yin power through pelvic dance, she will feel much more balanced and complete.

The feminine pelvic dance is an ancient art that uses the body seductively to move and isolate the joints of the body without inhibition. Her center of gravity, the navel, is the *bindu* (the dot), the beginning, and continuity of all life. The best gift she can give herself is to claim back the beauty of her femininity, the openness of her heart, and the natural movement of her body.

The Devi teaches the dancer how to embrace her feminine beauty. She caresses her body with lavishing flowing silk scarves, dancing as if it were her lover. She wears jewels on her ears that hear the vibrations of her breath. Her eyes are mysteriously outlined in kohl, looking deep within the soul of her beloved. A diamond nose ring shines brilliantly, like the jewel of her soul. On her *Ajna* chakra, she places a jeweled *bindi* that opens her spiritual vision.

Her long tresses kiss her rouged cheeks. She leaves no part of her body unadorned. Atop her head is a bejeweled crown protecting her at the *Sahasrar* chakra. A garland of gold wraps around the *Visshuda*, whispers the secrets of life. On her arms, gold and silver bangles, tell a tale of love and devotion, opening her at the *Anahat* chakra. Her fingers display a gallery of the gems of the planets, and a wide band of gold circles her waist. Tinkling gold anklets announce the arrival of the Goddess.

Here are some basic moves for women and men to strengthen the pelvis and abdomen. Hardly any space is necessary to do these exercises; the body itself is the space.

Try doing these sitting on the floor, standing, moving, on a chair. When these moves begin to feel "natural", add a scarf, remembering to express through the eyes, hands, and mouth.

The belly, the *Manipur* chakra, is the gravity center of our being. To maintain a balanced state, roll the stomach muscles sensuously in a vertical manner, balancing the spiritual with the physical. Without moving any other part of the body, roll the belly around in a circle, then side to side, in and out, or flutter it rapidly.

Become aware of the back the entire time. The spine connects all the organs, and more importantly, it is the conduit for the kundalini Shakti to make its ascent.

Stand with the feet shoulder width apart, bending the knees slightly. Now without moving the torso, draw a large circle with the hip. Start at the right; the pelvis around to the front, then all the way to the left and around the back. Do this several times and reverse the circle. Do it in different tempos. This is a hula or Tahitian movement

Draw a figure eight by imagining there is a large "8" sideways on the floor. Trace over the lines using the hips as the paintbrush. Do not move the torso, and keep both knees slightly bent and relaxed.

Bend knees slightly and keep the torso still. Push the hip out to the right side with a soft "thrust". This movement requires controlling the action of the hip, keeping the bump "tight" and quick. Repeat on the left side.

Another thrust--this time thrust the pelvis forward as if throwing a ball to someone. Thrust in the opposite direction.

Facing straight ahead, isolate the upper torso and move it from side to side. Remember to keep the torso still. Dance in front of a mirror, and honor the wonder of the body and all it can be trained to do. When we are doing the pelvis moves correctly we will notice that the *Mulabandha* and *Uddiyana* lock will occur naturally. This strengthens the perineum, and the result is a more relaxed and flexible pelvis, which can move spontaneously, without restriction.

My beloved Vajra Guru,
Let me treat you to a preview of the Cosmic Dance of Love.
Behold her dainty feet, bejeweled with silver rings on crimson painted toes
and glimmering baubles on both ankles.
The earth energy surges through the Bubbling Spring,
moving up to her knees to her inner thighs,
already becoming moist as the morning dew.
Feel the contractions in the Muladhar as her pelvis rocks
forward and back, rhythmically... to the soft echoes of "oooo".
The wide circular movements of her hips tell her story.
The sensuous patterns, dynamic thrusts, and primal rhythms
invite you closer and closer to her roots. What secrets lie here?
As the Shakti moves to Svadhistan, she has full control of her sex center,
from the strong, slow contractions, pulling the silver-chained abdomen in,
breathing it out...to the rapid fluttering of a butterfly's wings
as her muscles contract and expand rapidly... in and out, in and out;
side to side, side to side...as she gazes deep into your eyes,
promising heavenly gifts, breathlessly murmuring, "uuuuuuh".
At Manipur, feel her power...and her will
as she isolates the rolling, circular movements of her solar center,
sparkling with gold dust...while her hips glide and slide.
Hypnotized by your presence, anticipating the power of your manliness,
she caresses herself...moaning "Ohhhhh".
Journey with her to Anahat.
Open your heart to the love and grace that reside here.
"Ahhhh"...
Surrender and unconditional love have long searched for you...
awaiting you here...between her firm, glistening breasts.
She holds the key to your heart...Her delicate and graceful hands,
shimmering with gems and golden bangles, move intentionally...
suggestively...
slowly and sensuously, over her jasmine scented body,
inviting you in... telling the story meant just for you...
At Visshuda, with total abandon, her sounds of love call out to you
alone...
her serpentine body undulates and reaches for you...
she cries for your touch...for your soul...her search of a lifetime now

coming to an end.
Intoxicated with bliss…she summons you to join her…
and opens wide the gates to her Divine Temple and calls for you--
to enter her abode of love.
…Chandi Devi to J. Ram Sivananda

Dervish Dance

When we were children, one of our first experiences with an altered state was to spin like a top until we became dizzy and fell to the ground. The *Sufi Mevlevi Order* (i.e., the "Whirling Dervishes") has institutionalized this activity into a style of group meditation; they are able to spin without becoming dizzy. Before we begin whirling, place cushions around to fall upon--and be certain that the stomach is empty, to minimize nausea.

Start by extending the right arm upward, with palm directed toward the ceiling (toward the sky), and the left arm downward, with palm directed toward the floor--toward the earth. A different technique is to start with arms across the chest and then slowly extend them to the side while spinning (with the right palm upward and left palm downward). Slowly begin to turn in a circle--most people turn counter-clockwise-- and keep both eyes open but not focused. While spinning, the Dervishes meditate upon spirit, and they chant a holy phrase (i.e., a "wazifa" or "zikr") such as "Allah Hu" or "There is no god but God"; we can use a different phrase or mantra. Feel centered in the quiet, motionless core of an energy vortex (like in the middle of a hurricane). Start slow, do not try to rush. After 20 minutes, we can begin to increase the speed.

The Dervishes continue to spin for hours, but we can do it for a shorter period. Eventually, we might fall to the ground; if this occurs, we should lie there for ten minutes or more, relaxing and grounding your energy with the earth beneath us.

Shamanic Trance Dance

One of the oldest Shamanic traditions was the use of trance dance. Trance dance gave them the opportunity to separate from their egos and their minds, and to reconnect with their soul. It was a method of connecting with spirit and healing illnesses and diseases. Trance was used to celebrate the natural forces of nature through rhythm, movement, and sound.

Tantra and Shamans have some common roots. They worshipped nature. The Shamanic perspective is God is the intelligence that is found in nature, and they worshipped that force. Trance brought them into a state of deep meditation, where they learned to ally themselves with animal spirits, believing the animals could heal them.

They ate of nature, and they imitated nature. They worshipped the elements of nature; dancing like the wind, moving like water, and soaring like an eagle. They healed themselves with herbs and prayer. They would dance the animal and adorn their bodies with parts of the animals, and mimicked how the animals functioned in life.

Trance is accompanied by drumming that replicates the beating of our hearts. This dynamic connection between the individual and the Supreme releases the ego and we find ourselves with deeper insight, calmer presence of mind and a higher state of awareness.

Life's traumas and experiences wound us, and through trance dance meditation, we reconnect with our soul, and learn to accept who we are. Through trance, we explore our microcosmic energy and connect with the macrocosmic forces of nature. We become one with it.

Trance dance, is a profound meditation that the ancients discovered thousands of years ago, which is still as effective as ever today.

Cathartic Dance

Like trance dance, cathartic dance is a method of releasing energy that we have not been able to express, such as anger, or some positive emotions, such as our longing for love.

A word of caution, if this exercise releases energy and emotions that are too intense, stop immediately.

For ten minutes, be totally wild. Jump, and roll, and twitch, and shake. Let your breath be erratic. Hit pillows. Allow your voice to scream and babble, if it wants to do so (and if you have privacy). Do not be self-conscious or disturbed by anything that you do; just express the chaos and repressions that you carry beneath the polite persona. Use these actions to express something real which is within you; they are not just random actions or an exhibition of your *concept* of wildness.

After this catharsis, walk around calmly, to gradually put yourself back together. Then do a sitting meditation, if you want to quiet yourself even further. Catharsis is not a long-term solution to any problems; the energy that is being released would have been better spent in direct mediation with those problems, but, because we do not always have the situations or skills with which we can fully express our energy, we might need to do some catharsis occasionally to release the remnants of that force.

Movement Meditation

Movement meditation is any type of meditation in which we are moving. Movement meditation includes a wide range of techniques, such as dance. Any movement can be performed as a meditation, if we apply mindfulness and a slow pace.

Movement meditation is ideal when we feel energetic. Some people are so vigorous or restless that they cannot use sitting meditation; thus, moving meditation is a productive alternative. In some monasteries and retreats, participants alternate between sitting meditation and moving meditation (usually walking meditation) in order to give the physical body some exercise and to release physical tension and stimulate blood circulation.

The body lives in a world that is free from concepts, so our observance of it automatically takes us to the non-conceptual state that is sought by practitioners of sitting meditation. Because the body is a part of the physical world, movement meditation helps us to understand the nature and sanctity of this world. The body is neither more nor less "defiled" or "illusory" than our mind and emotions. On the contrary, it too has a connection to our soul.

In some types of movement meditation, we focus on a particular part; for example, a yoga posture might be loosening the leg muscles so we would naturally be attentive to those muscles. While moving, we can shift our attention to every part, and appraise its state; for example, a part might be numb or even disliked, as in a belly which does not match the ideal which has been established by magazine centerfolds.

When we locate these disowned parts, we can offer them our love and acceptance and an invitation to re-join the "family" of our body. As we do this, we might feel a warm vitalization of that part, and its re-integration into the general functioning of the body.

To an extent, the body is not "our" body; it is a living organism in its own right, with its own needs, its own pleasures, and its own "consciousness." (Consider the fact that the cells, in their organic world, know nothing about our day-to-day life.) Enter the world of the body. Enter that world of bodily sensation, vitality, chemical processes, warmth, breathing, and moving (in contrast to our usual world of concepts). We can enter this world more easily if we do some of the techniques with our eyes closed (to block our sense of sight), or our hands over our ears (to block our sense of hearing).

Let the body move in its own manner. Try this motion: lean to the left while keeping the body rigid and the muscles tight. Now return to the upright position. This time, simply think about leaning, and initiate the motion, but let the body move into the leaning position in its own way and at its own speed--probably very slowly.

When the body controls this movement, we feel many individual adjustments in the muscles and internal tissues as the body leans.

There are rhythms and brief pauses in the movement. We feel a constant seeking of pleasure and comfort in each increment of the leaning. There are changes in our breathing in response to the slight exertion and the repositioning of the lungs.

We can feel the cooperation and feedback among the body parts as they coordinate their efforts in this engineering feat.

Move slowly. Slowness allow us to perceive more of the individual motions within a larger motion; for example, if we quickly raise an arm straight up, we probably notice only the single upward movement--but if we do it slowly, we perceive many separate events within the body.

Try that now; take approximately 30 seconds to move an arm into the straight-up position. Be aware of the contractions of various muscles, and the adjustments in the joints as they adapt to the changing positions. The constant physical balancing (through the shifts in weight and the muscular contractions in other parts of the body), the heat which is generated in the muscles, and the gentle stretching of tissue allows for the arm's movement.

Movement meditation is usually done slowly; for example, walking meditation might be only slightly slower than our regular pace, or we could spend an entire minute for each step.

While doing these individual techniques, we can use the guidelines, particularly the idea of moving slowly, and being attentive.

For five minutes, make every movement in synch with the breath. Breathe at the natural rate or at a slow, controlled speed. Put both palms against the belly. Slowly inhale, extend the arms outward in front of the body; exhale, let the arms return to the belly. While doing this, feel that the energy of the breath is projecting the arms outward and bringing them back.

From a sitting position, slowly stand up with a sense that the body is "lengthening" into the upright position. The neck extends upward, the back becomes longer, and gradually the entire body has lengthened into a standing position. Now walk forward, with that same sense of lengthening in the legs as each foot is put forward. Finally, sit down again in a lengthening motion.

While standing or sitting, move the spine and the rest of the body in subtle motions while seeking "perfect posture"--one that is thoroughly comfortable and relaxing for all parts the body. Scan the body for areas of discomfort and move to adjust their position, until it comes to rest in its ideal posture. Starting with one toe, spend about twenty seconds at each joint in the body, and let it move back-and-forth slowly. Feel the sensations in that joint as vividly as possible. Move in a rhythm that is synchronized with the heartbeat.

Experiment with different degrees of mental "supervision" in controlling the body's movements. We can find a new balance between the mind's willful control of the body, and the body's own preferences.

For example, try this in the movement of raising the arm slowly straight up. First, do it willfully, keeping the muscles tight.

Now raise the arm again--but this time, let the arm stay relaxed, and be aware of the feedback (e.g., comfort or discomfort). Respond to this feedback to move the arm in a more natural manner.

On the third time, simply intend that the arm should rise, and then, while maintaining a gentle will, let the arm slowly float upward. Let the arm be creative and playful as the upper arm, forearm, hand,

and fingers gradually find their way toward an upright position, while perhaps turning, twisting, and bending, like smoke rising on a delicate breeze.

If allowed, the body turns every movement into a graceful dance, but these subtle movements occur from the body's own expressiveness and sense of pleasure, not from self-consciousness, mentally conceived artistry.

We take for granted our ability to move our body. Now, while we very slowly open and close a fist, marvel at the ability of the mind to control the body. Our thoughts create motion. Many people are skeptical about the possibility of mind over matter or telekinesis (also called psycho kinesis), but our mind performs this feat every time we move the matter of our body. Try to sense the link between the thoughts and the moving hand.

Move in the rhythm of a mantra. Allow the body to move in that rhythm, expressing the feelings that accompany the words. Alternatively, let the body express a single concept, such as beauty, love, peacefulness, freedom, or spirit. Use all of the body, and make facial expressions. Another variation: Express these ideas with only one single part of the body, e.g., the hands.

While walking, be aware of the flexibility of the spine. Move as though the spine is a snake that bends and curves in every direction. Feel these snake-like wave-movements as they extend throughout the body. Notice the increase in energy in the spine and the rest of the body as this is done.

Slowly walk around the home, touching the objects--the chairs, the curtains, etc. While being observant of all movements, also notice the energy that passes from the hands into the objects. Experience this energy transfer as a part of the movement:

- Feel the energy which causes the arm to extend outward.

- Feel the energy traveling down the arms as we touch the object.

- Feel the energy flowing into the object.

- Feel some energy from the object flowing back into the hand.

In a standing position, slowly move the pelvis in various motions-
-left and right, front and back, circular clockwise or counterclockwise,
or in a figure eight. Be aware of the sensations.

As we lie on the floor, on our back, we can imagine that we are a
flower that is responding to the early-morning sunlight. Very slowly,
raise both arms as though they are being drawn upward by the sun.
Then gradually move to a standing position, constantly being aware of
the imagined sunlight and of the feelings that it creates.

In a standing position, we can become aware of gravity's influence
on our body. During a period of a few minutes, we allow it to draw
us very slowly from this position to a reclining position as we calmly
surrender our body's mass to the planet beneath us.

Shakti Shake

We were created from sex. We were created from the joining of two
cells, which multiplied and multiplied. When we shake our body, every
cell is meeting its opposite cell and energizes us. First, we learn to shake
our outer body, and then our inner body will shake on its own as we
learn to just let it go. Be natural, animalistic, and uninhibited. Shaking
allows us to meet with our "genuine" self, not the pretense that we
present to the world. Shaking releases us from our ego self, our self-
consciousness. When we can truly let go when no one is looking, and
then bring that state when we are with our partner is the beginning of
"real" sex.

A great energy activator, which is simple and fun to do, is a "Shakti
Shake". This is an exercise in being non-judgmental about our body.
It will begin the process of activating energy so that it can flow more
readily. This energy is directed to calm, heal, and rejuvenate us. Put
on some rhythmic music, such as tribal drumming, or anything that
is exciting. Let the body move-- loosen every part of it--let it interact
with the music. Lose all inhibitions; shake all parts of the body, scream,
shout, jump, and move.

Without being concerned about the way you look, just be wild,
free, and joyful. Life is a dance. When the music ends, be still for a few
minutes and observe any sensations or feelings that arise. It may take
weeks of practice before you really begin to feel any sensations. Listen

through the body, rather than the mind. Love and thank your body for its endless support.

This outward shaking is an exaggerated form of an inner vibration that will get more noticeable with time as it connects with the macrocosmic *spanda.* Your partner can feel this vibration during sex. It will just happen without any effort when individuals and the Cosmos are in union.

Isometrics from the Rishis

The sages, or *rishis*, who lived in the Himalayas, devised a set of exercises to improve their circulation. These exercises were also intended to raise the kundalini energy. They are easy, very powerful, and convenient; you can do them in a small area. We work one muscle against the other to create a dynamic tension instead of relaxing into a position as is done in Hatha Yoga. These exercises strengthen the sex muscles, especially the anal sphincter muscle. It is very meditative, helps us to focus, balance, and direct the sexual energy.

When we do the isometrics, always inhale through the nose, and exhale through the mouth. Notice where the most tension is felt. Squeezing the anal sphincter muscle and holding the tension will restrict the flow of blood; then when we relax, we will release a flow of oxygen-rich blood.

Having a fit and healthy body is a prerequisite for tantric practices. In the west, we tend to concern ourselves mainly with our outer muscles and physical strength, neglecting our internal muscularity. Tantra yoga focuses on maintaining and energizing our body, keeping our mind and spirit equally healthy and fit.

The following set of exercises is gentle, yet extremely powerful for activating energy. Do them at least three times a week. They take just a few minutes, and require very little space.

Of course, please consult a doctor or health practitioner before embarking on any exercise program.

It is preferable to use music whenever you do any kind of exercise, such as something rhythmic and sensual, a meditative instrumental.

First, stand with both feet shoulder--width apart. Slowly come up on the balls of the feet, the bubbling spring, while inhaling. Lift both arms out from the sides to above your head. With palms together, we push them against each other, and as we do so, we squeeze our anal sphincter muscle. Hold the tension, exhaling as we release the lock, bringing our arms back down to the starting position. Repeat three times. Be aware of the energy as it moves in the body. We simply observe our feelings, and if any part of the body is calling out for attention.

The second exercise. As in the previous exercise, slowly come up on the balls of the feet while inhaling. Clasping both thumbs together above the head, exhale and slowly bend the torso to the right side as far as possible. Stretch both arms as far to the side as possible and feel the pull on the opposite side of the body. Hold the position, feel the tension, squeeze the anal sphincter, and inhale to return to the upright position. Repeat three times. Repeat on the left side three times.

Third. With feet shoulder width apart, place the right foot forward. Clasp thumbs behind the back and exhale bending forward slowly, keeping the chin up. Lift arms behind as high as possible. Hold for a few seconds. Slowly come back to an upright position and inhale. Relax. Repeat three times, and then repeat on the left side. Observe the energy. How does it feel?

Fourth. With feet together and palms together stretch back, bend from the waist as and inhale. Arch the back like a crescent moon, and drop the head back. Hold the tension and squeeze the anal sphincter. Then exhale on the return to the starting position and continue to bend forward until the torso is parallel to the floor, both arms reaching out straight forward. Repeat twice. The third time, bend the torso forward until is parallel to the floor but this time, continue bending the torso until both arms touch the floor. Return to an upright position. Observe the breath and notice if there is any tingling or sensations anywhere in the body.

Play and Pleasure

Pleasure is the flower that passes;
remembrance, the lasting perfume.
…Jean de Boufflers

Pleasure is the sensation of being fully alive, with our senses alert and eager. Pleasure is our natural state; it happens when we allow ourselves to feel and function with a spontaneous, unaffected indulgence. We do not create it; we get out of its way and give it permission to radiate from inside of us.

Pleasure and play are important parts of a tantric life. They take us away from our daily concerns and connect us to a vigorous world of refreshment and physical sensations. They provide a safe environment in which to practice new behaviors and skills (including social skills). We concentrate more easily and learn more quickly in an atmosphere of entertainment and fun. They help to keep us healthy by lowering our blood pressure, reducing stress and tension, and aiding relaxation.

Everything we do is motivated by a desire for pleasure, *kama*. Whether we are pursuing love, a better job, a bigger home--or fudge ice cream--what we want is the pleasure that we believe will be generated by that item.

To enhance pleasure, we can enjoy play for its own sake. We are not "playing" if we have a serious intent; real play is neither the reward for past work, nor a recharge for future work. We get more physical and psychological benefits from play if we take it on its own terms and we relinquish control to the inner child who knows that play is not meant to be productive. Left-hemisphere goals would diminish the benefits of these right-hemisphere activities. Ironically, we attain the goals of recharging and refreshing only if we are not thinking about them or trying to make them happen.

The mind is in a world of images and concepts; the body's world is one of sensation. When the mind disregards the body's reality, it selects goals based on images that falsely represent pleasure to us, such as a high-paying job where the pressure is a burden (and perhaps a cause of ulcers and a heart attack). If we honor our need for pleasure and physical health, we might choose a position that brings less (but sufficient) money but more enjoyment. Just as the body works to serve the mind's goals, the mind needs to concede the body's right to pleasure (and to admit that some of its goals are inconsequential without the pleasure they might bring). This mutual acknowledgment permits a productive cooperation and an integration of mind and body.

Our bodies want to feel pleasurable sensations constantly--touching, breathing deeply, dancing, looking with curiosity, walking rhythmically, playing with objects, and so on.

Pleasure comes in many forms. We can set aside our notions of whatever "should" feel good--as well as the dreariness of the work ethic, deadening philosophies, and any feelings of guilt precipitated by frivolity--and let our whims guide us to new sources of delight.

Our capacity to "feel" includes the feelings of both pleasure and pain; if we numb our perception of pain, we are also numbing our perception of pleasure. To be fully alive, we must be sensitive to all sensations--enduring pain when it occurs so that we can experience pleasure during its time.

Pleasure is the result of a playful quality in any endeavor. Our enjoyment is increased when we seek the following principles in our activities. These principles are reciprocal; for example, when we are self-expressive, we experience pleasure--and when we are experiencing pleasure, we tend to express ourselves. We are expressing our feelings, thoughts, and personality. We are creative.

Play and pleasure keeps us interested, curious, open, amazed. We relish each detail. We "lose ourselves" in whatever we are doing. We have no self-criticism, perfectionism, or embarrassment. We enjoy the action for its own sake (and for the pleasure that is inherent in it); we have only secondary interest in goals, scores, and competition.

We enjoy fun, humor, and silliness. We become childlike. Even a frivolous game assumes significance that the child within us understands, but which cannot be explained to the intellect. Simple tasks become unique rituals.

Play keeps us young, passionate, and enthusiastic. We reach out to a new friend or a new adventure. We experiment. We try new activities. We become more aware of beauty in its many forms. Even if we are not creating "art" in the classical sense, we feel a quality of elegance in whatever we are doing. We want to move our bodies--giggling, wiggling, from head to toe.

Sensory Development

We use our senses in most types of meditation. Those types of meditation include mindfulness, concentration, movement, etc. However, we can also meditate on the senses themselves--their input and their means of perceiving "reality". As with mindfulness meditation, we can practice sensory awareness during our everyday life, but we will experience a greater depth and intensity if we set aside some time specifically to dwell on the senses.

We gain benefits from sensory awareness such as mindfulness meditation. We acquire more information; we perceive more accurately; we increase our understanding of the physical body; we learn to "live in the moment".

When we develop sensory awareness, our senses become more acute. We notice more details and nuances and the uniqueness of the individual objects around us. We experience more pleasure from the objects of perception and from the energized sense organs themselves (perhaps as a tingling sensation in the eyes or ears, for example).

There are several techniques for developing sensuality. One technique is to have a non-verbal experience. In many types of meditation, we enter a state in which we experience things directly and intimately rather than merely thinking about them. In sensory awareness, too, we perceive objects themselves rather than the labels that we would attach to them; to hear a sound is not the same as to think, "the chirping of a chickadee".

Our senses operate in a non-verbal world. In sensory awareness exercises, we enter that world as fascinated observers who are quietly exploring the lushness of perception-- without identifying, comparing, or using the other functions of the word-oriented analytical mind.

Much of our sensory "mindlessness" occurs because our actions are quick. At that pace, we are processing only superficial sensory data. For example, we pick up a pen to write, and we experience it simply as a utensil for a task. We must be in this state in order to concentrate on the task; a profound sensory experience, of pen in hand, would be a time-consuming distraction. However, during such activities, we can split our attention between the task itself and our sensory experience of it.

However, to develop sensory awareness to any depth, we must assign time solely for our senses. During this period, we move at the body's own pace and rhythm, and we allow the senses to regard their objects for as long as they are intrigued. When we permit the senses to explore in their own manner, they are likely to be enthralled with an object for a considerable period, continually discovering new minutia that they savor.

For an entire day (or perhaps just a few hours), be aware of as much sensory stimuli as possible, without labeling any of it or responding to it with thoughts. A variation is to devote this time to a single sense, such as the sense of smell or hearing; this might require us to keep our eyes closed so that our visual input will not distract us from the other senses.

The sense of smell--The nose is the most spiritual of all the senses. Memories are recalled through the sense of smell, a principle on which aromatherapy is based.

The anointing oils of the Bible activate the amygdale gland, which is the gateway to the frontal lobes and higher consciousness. The major anointing oils are frankincense, myrrh, and sandalwood. Frankincense is considered a holy anointing oil in the Middle East and has been used in religious ceremonies for thousands of years. It was well known during the time of Christ for its anointing and healing powers.

> *They presented unto him gifts, gold, frankincense, and myrrh.*
> *…Matthew 2:11*

Frankincense is now being researched and used therapeutically in European and American hospitals. It is used on all chakras, especially the first three, and the third eye. Sandalwood is high in sesquiterpenes and has been researched in Europe for its ability to oxygenate a part of the brain known as the pineal gland, the seat of our emotions.

The pineal gland is responsible for releasing melatonin, which enhances deep sleep. Sandalwood is similar to frankincense oil in its support of nerves and circulation. It was used traditionally for skin revitalization, yoga, and meditation. It is also used on all the chakras.

Amber and rose are the yin and yang of fragrances that help the aspirant on their path.

Ylang Ylang may be extremely effective in calming and bringing about a sense of relaxation. This native flower of Madagascar and the Reunion Islands is symbolic of love, and the fragrant, pale yellow petals are often strewn across the marriage bed. Its soft, floral scent is often used in men's fragrances as an alternative to the sweeter and more feminine rose. This is especially nice on the heart chakra.

Smell different fragrances: flowers of various kinds, incense, soap, perfume or cologne, foods and spices from the kitchen. As we smell a fragrance, notice whether it changes our mood or state. Smell something that would generally be considered unpleasant -- spoiled food, or garbage. Removing judgment from the experience, we simply investigate the scent. Walk throughout the home or backyard, with eyes closed. (Be careful not to stumble.) Notice the subtle odors in the different rooms.

The sense of taste--The tongue and mouth are perhaps the most sensuous of all the senses; without them, life could not exist. Drinks and foods nourish our body and give us a sense of deep satisfaction. In fact, when we feel bad, sad, or blue, we try to fill the void by "over" eating and drinking. This emptiness is a prime cause for our eating disorders and addictions.

When we eat on the run, or gobble everything down in a hurry, we deprive ourselves the pleasure of our most primal need of "suckling". By being conscious of every bite we take, we can learn to enjoy and explore the flavors.

We have four types of receptors in the mouth; each discerns only one quality in the food-- sweetness, bitterness, sourness, and saltiness. Eat different types of foods that predominate with one of these qualities.

The sense of sight--The eyes are the mirrors of the soul, reflecting out to the world what is within. The non-verbal communication always reveals the truth. The eyes are said to be masculine because it creates duality, i.e. it needs an object and a subject. Sight has dominated over all the other senses and should be balanced.

To develop "in sight", practice gazing in the mirror and looking deep within. Practice gazing into the eyes of others and see beyond the façade that veils their divinity.

Look into the eyes of animals and pets and observe the depth of their being as well.

While the masculine sees an object in front of him, he has difficulty seeing that same image in his mind's eye. To develop visualization abilities, gaze at an object without blinking for as long as possible, then shut the eyes and try to see the image in the "eye's mind".

Meditate with the sense of touch. Collect a variety of fabrics and objects. This might include velvet, nylon, fur, wood, steel, plastic, foods, etc. Select items with various qualities: smooth, rough, wet, slimy, and so on. Now touch each one, allowing the fingers to explore the texture. Do a household chore, being aware of the hands' contact with the objects that they encounter. Walk throughout the home, mindfully touching the furniture and other articles. Touch objects of different temperatures. This might include objects from the refrigerator and freezer, or tap water that varies from hot to cold. Touch the skin on numerous parts of the body, and notice the sense of touch through the hand that is touching and through the body part that is being touched. Be aware of such qualities as texture, temperature, oiliness, hairiness, and vitality.

Touch the body in various ways--tickling, scratching, rubbing, tapping, stroking. A variation is to explore the skin of a partner. Instead of touching objects only with the hands, touch them with other parts of the body--forearms, bare feet, head, etc.

The sense of sound--Sound is the gateway to the soul. Music, speech, and communication are all related to sound. While the sense of sight is said to be masculine, and the sense of sound is feminine.

Listen to music that has more than one instrument. Follow a single instrument throughout the entire piece. Alternatively, focus on a different aspect of the music-- noticing only the rhythm or the changes in pitch or volume. Do a household chore, perhaps sweeping or cleaning and listen to the sounds that are created.

Listen to music and feel the body's response to it. Do certain muscles relax or tighten? Is there a reaction in particular parts of the body, such as the gut or your head? Listen to two different types of music consecutively, and notice the differences in the body's response. Put a finger gently into each ear, and listen to the sounds within the body. We might hear our breathing, our heartbeat, and much else.

When we use our senses to connect more fully with our environment, we are establishing a warm, nourishing contact with our body, our human identity, and the physical world.

We can have physical contact with the world around us by moving meditation. During our daily routines, we are always in contact with physical objects-- touching, holding, grabbing, stroking, or merely sitting. For grounding, we can strive to have a feeling contact with these objects. We sense the warm energy flowing from our hands into the objects, and we allow our hands to hold the objects and savor them until we intuit that we have discharged the energy that was meant to pass into the objects. We might feel even more of this discharge if we lie outside on grass or dirt (or if we handle the dirt, as we do when we are gardening). Our excess energy will flow naturally into the earth. Our surplus energy can discharge through our feet, too, so we need to have our feet flat on the floor when sitting.

In the Tantric parlance, all perspectives are equally real and valid as part of soul's multi-faceted exploration. Since we are aware of karmic consequences, we can freely choose the perspective that is most appropriate, effective, loving and dharmic for our purpose in this moment. If our purpose is to balance ourselves, we can select the human viewpoint without worrying that we are sacrificing our spirituality; in fact, we can appreciate this opportunity to explore spirit as it expresses itself in the human world and the physical world. Spirituality is not separate from our human-ness. We are souls having a human experience.

....
PRACTICE
....

Challenge For Her:

1. When you urinate, stop flow, start again and continue this a few times. Do this exercise every time you urinate.

2. Strip for your partner. Use movement as an honest expression of who you are. Be genuine in what you are feeling and doing. Sexiness comes from within. *Feel it.* If you are between relationships, put some sexy music on and dance in front of a mirror. Remember, sexy is as sexy does. Sexy is not an artificial phenomenon. Sexy is not competitive, sexy is not bought. Sexy is honest, ego-free, a natural ability to express and create, completely void of fear, guilt, or shame.

Challenge For Him:

Stimulate yourself or have your partner help you manually or orally. When you are close to a "peak", say a mantra (Om Namah Shivaya is a good mantra to honor the God within) and do a transmutation breath, described in this book) to allow the lingam to relax, then continue to stimulate it again, and repeat this a few times.

Practice For Couples:

1. Do the rishi isometrics with your partner, facing each other, gazing in each other's eyes. On the third and fourth part (see section on Rishis) when you lean forward, touch your partner's forehead with your forehead. This is the called the "Tantric kiss".

2. Practice sensory exercises. Use tactile awareness to discover each other's erogenous zones. Make this a light and friendly encounter. Nowhere do the ancient sages suggest that lovemaking be serious or mechanical work.

//om//

Chapter Five:

The Art

When the exercises and skills described in this chapter are mastered, we become the artist. Our partner's body is the canvas upon which we paint a masterpiece. We create magic and ecstasy. Worship becomes an art.

When tantric sex is executed in a wholesome, honest and genuine manner, we shift the way we feel about our body and about sex. Guilt, taboos, limiting beliefs and blocks cannot exist where there is only love, honor, respect and an open heart.

Innate wisdom and proficiency of this art is the key to a joyous co-existence with your partner. In the East, tantra is taught only after intense preliminary spiritual studies, as it is a very advanced practice reserved for a few. In the West, it is the reverse. We start right off with sex, and the mystical experiences inspire a few fortunate ones to delve deeper into spiritual endeavors.

Here's a Quick Tantra Tip:

How to cultivate an attitude of gratitude and surrender in less than five minutes:

Put your palms together and bow to an image of a great saint. Also, put your partner on a "pedestal", figuratively, and bow in reverence to him/her. Verbalize your thanks to your partner. This may be a "stretch" for most of you, but there is no harm in doing this, and it is actually a practice that results in humbleness and humility. Even though this is an ego-buster, realize this does not make you "lesser" or "inferior" to the one you are paying respects to. This is a simple practice of surrender. It is a common practice in Eastern cultures to show respect and reverence toward others through *pranam* and thereby, showing respect and reverence to yourself. Can you do it?

Hint: If you feel silly or awkward, remember it is the ego feeling silly or awkward. It may help to set a "mood" if you both "play act", by dressing the part of the god and goddess.

Sexual Union

It is my duty to lift you up to the infinite heights of bliss and yours to take me down to the depths of your senses....
bringing together these extremes opens the doors out of this mortal dimension and stops time in order to feel the Infinite grace of the Universe......
... J. Ram Sivananda to Chandi Devi

When Shakti arouses Shiva, they travel together down the spine back to *Muladhar*, where her journey began. Now joined in perfect union they ascend to Supreme Consciousness together.

This is not just a metaphor for sexual intercourse. The sex act is a divine act in itself. Lovemaking between a man and woman, when entered into with complete awareness, is a gateway to both sexual and spiritual ecstasy. This is what is popularly known as "sacred sex".

Our journey begins with learning how to awaken the kundalini Shakti and free ourselves from the limitations of the mind. One way we can do this is by raising the energy during sexual union through the chakra system (the plexii), where the more mature delights manifest.

Tantra is the path of surrender and honoring of the *yoni* (vagina) and *lingam* (the Divine Phallus). When we surrender our ego we are free to honor and worship the *lingam* and *yoni* without inhibition.

Then we will see the divineness in our partner, in ourselves, and all of life itself.

The *lingam,* the thunderbolt of consciousness, is the male prime cause of the Universe, Shiva, who, until awakened by Shakti remains inert. The *yoni,* the container of energy, is the Goddess Mother of the Universe, the creator of life, who stirs Shiva and arouses him to join her in union. This is not only the union between two partners, but also ultimately, their merging into one Supreme Consciousness.

To activate the sexual energy during sexual union, we contract the muscles of our anus and thighs in a lock called the *Mahabandha* (described earlier in this book) and awaken kundalini at the first chakra, the *Muladhar,* at the base of the spine. Shiva, Lord of the Animals, *Pashupati,* reigns over our primal instincts and passions and we need to invoke his energy. The nerve chakra in the physical body is the sacro-coccygeal plexus.

Shiva and Shakti together can direct this *ojas* (primal vigor) energy up to the second chakra, *Svadhistan,* the fluidal plexus, and upward.

Through sacred lovemaking, we can merge the dual nature of our sexuality into an ecstatic union. Through this will come the harmonization of our own internal masculine and feminine polarities and a realization of the blissful nature of our true nature.

He felt now that he was not simply close to her,
but that he did not know where he ended and she began.
…Leo Tolstoy

Ritualistic sexual union is called *maithun.* It is the art of preparing the body, mind and spirit for joining the two partners in a union with each other and the Cosmos. Everything we have presented so far has been in preparation for the *maithun.*

The first effort should be learning the art of the kundalini awakening, learning to open all the chakras for a total experience with our opposite. It is not a joining of equals; it is a joining of *opposites* on an *equal* level.

The sexual experience of the *maithun* should awaken the kundalini and flood the chakra system from the first chakra on

247

up the spine, all the way to the crown. This art is not mastered overnight, but with intent and practice, the chakra vortexes will be awakened.

A first chakra connection will have both partners with a balanced amount of energy. At the second chakra, there will be similar levels of passion and desire. At the third chakra, both partners will have an equal amount of will to please one another. At the fourth level, there should be unconditional love for one another and an openness to express this love.

At the fifth chakra, the couple should both have the same level of communication to profess or exchange verbally the truth of the experience with one another. At the sixth level, there will be a mystical understanding of one's partner and the ability to intuit his or her needs.

At the seventh chakra, unity through duality is experienced with the couple entwining together and joining their souls. The complete joining of this entire chakra system with our partner takes practice. Start at the base of the experience. Start at the *Muladhar* and work up the spine.

This kind of "conscious" union is absent in western-style sex. Many men and women are very cerebral and disconnected from their bodies and senses. Moreover, the *maithun* is one method for developing passion into a relationship.

The best dance is the communion of souls, where the electrical current flows between both partners. When we are in a spiritual union with our beloved, the confines of duality ceases, and we can experience the bliss that awaits us.

The *maithun* rite can be very bonding for a couple that wishes to stay connected emotionally, spiritually, physically, and mentally. We believe that this process should involve our partner only. Inviting another person in the formula will dilute and contaminate the energy, and will eventually de-bond a couple. This is the unfortunate circumstance that has separated many couples. Once the sacredness of the *maithun* is undermined, it becomes more of an "un-bonding" process.

Just remember one thing:
never make love to a person you don't love.
That is a perversion -- because then you will remain obsessed with sex.
Make love to a person you really love, otherwise wait –
because when you love a person, the very love will pull the energy
upwards.
And once the energy has started moving towards love,
love is so satisfying that who bothers about sex?
Sex has never satisfied anybody.
It creates more and more dissatisfaction.
Sex has never fulfilled anybody -- it knows no fulfillment.
Have a sexual relationship only when you have a loving relationship,
so love and sex become associated.
And love is a greater center, a higher center.
Once sex is hitched to love, it starts moving upwards.
…Osho

Partner Selection

*One of the chief causes of this absurdity is that, at
this age, contemporary people in most cases lack the
corresponding type of the opposite sex necessary,
according to law, for the completion of their type,
which, from causes not dependent upon them but
ensuing, so to say, from Great Laws, is in itself a
"some-thing not complete". At this age, a person who
does not have near him a corresponding type of the
opposite sex for the completion of his incomplete
type, is nonetheless subject to the laws of nature and
so cannot remain without gratification of his sexual
needs. Coming in contact with a type not corresponding
to his own and, owing to the law of polarity, falling
in certain respects under the influence of this
non-corresponding type, he loses, involuntarily and
imperceptibly, almost all the typical manifestations
of his individuality. That is why it is absolutely
necessary for every person, in the process of his
responsible life, to have beside him a person of the
opposite sex of corresponding type for mutual
completion in every respect.*
…Gurdjieff

Sex is a natural phenomenon, an urge of union as a survival mechanism. To survive as a species, nature gifted us with this pleasurable biological process, which in its natural state is free from guilt and shame.

Sex is our biological nature, our leftover wiring from a time when we were animals, aspiring just to survive. In the animal kingdom, the dominant animal wins, and there is competition among the males to be "selected" by the female as her mate. The female determines the selection process, not the male. She has an innate ability to choose the most suitable and healthy partner to assure the continuity of her species.

Even today, the female species is actually the dominant creature. She selects the one she wants to mate with. The male attracts, but it is up to the female to make the choice. The male is not very choosy; he will usually go with any woman who "selects" him. For example, here is a scenario: he goes to a bar, and a woman gives him all the signals that she is willing and available, and he is flattered and delighted to have been "chosen" that he goes to bed with her, no problem.

We often find ourselves with someone based on sexual *convenience* and this could be very damaging to our inner peace and harmony. If we are careless, we may find out later that the one we thought was beautiful, handsome, gregarious, romantic, and successful is actually obsessive, depressed, neurotic, psychotic, angry and unbalanced. That's a hefty price to pay for sex.

Both women and men may deny their sexual needs, and replace it with work, success, and other ideals that they find fulfilling. Still, there is an underlying need for *something* or someone outside of them, or else there would be no need for popular dating sites, bars, clubs, etc.

There is also a great deal of "detached" sex, which is temporal and fine if a person has no desire to grow, or to develop. Most of us, however, whether we admit it or not, want to love and be loved. And we try to instigate love through sex. And it is true--for love to grow there must be optimum sex; but for optimum sex, there has to be love.

The pleasure of sex, food or drugs is caused by dopamine, a natural chemical being released in the body. In the brain, dopamine functions as a neurotransmitter, which is central to the reward system. This feeling of pleasure motivates us to proactively repeat the behavior in order to hold on to the feelings; this is normal.

Some of us seek this love by having sex with multiple partners. It is the syndrome of more is best. Many who practice polyamory, rationalize this lifestyle as "tantric". If the first chakra is dominant, the tendency will be to spread the seed (if a male), or invite anyone *in* (if a female) with hardly any discrimination. Although some polyamorists define a union as "intimate", the long-term effects of simultaneous multi-relationships, can have an opposite result; rather than inviting "more" love, it will actually result in "less" love and more distraction, the antithesis of intimacy, and everything that Tantra stands for.

T. is a male, aged 55, who has been on a spiritual path for over 30 years. He is a tantric adept with a strong sex drive and exceptional spiritual knowledge. He sincerely believes that his dharma is to initiate his female students into Tantra. The only problem is that most females don't share his intense drive for either sex or spirituality, and as a result, they experience much pain and either abandon him or sex altogether. Thus, he has an emotional/sexual need to keep looking for a willing sex partner. Perhaps he prefers living alone without the entanglements of an intimate relationship; he still has not found his sexual/spiritual match.

Tantric sex is about having an intimate relationship with yourself and your other. As we all know, it is a daunting task to *know*, and to *find*, our self. It is a full-time job--requiring a committed and tireless effort to learn who we are--to own and deal with our *asuras,* our karma, and the propensities of our mind. Even when we have a partner we love with all our heart, we still have to create a new formula: it is "us" plus *their* inner demons, plus *their* karma, plus the propensities of *their* mind. So even when we invite our beloved into our heart, to share our life, we willingly open ourselves to all sorts of uninvited psychological and karmic guests because of our love, and we work to attain higher states together.

Have relationships with multiple partners and you don't need much imagination to picture the chaos internally and externally for all involved.

We simply cannot focus or worship many partners at one time. Part time attention does not constitute worship or honor. One pointed attention is a requisite for success on any path, including the journey on the love boat. How can we reach our destination as we sail down the river of life if we have our left foot in one boat, and the right foot in another?

This is *not* implying that we must have just one sexual partner per *lifetime,* because as we are growing and expanding, we may outgrow our partner, and have several partners during our growth. The dating scene should be enjoyed, but carefully. Eventually, when we are ready, we will find our twin soul, the one who identifies and relates to the spiritual passion we possess.

Use *viveka* in the partner selection process. The random process of having sex with whomever is willing and/or available is playing sexual roulette. When we decide to have sex with someone, even if it's a one-night stand, we will have created karma, for better or worse, usually for worse. It is a gamble.

We so carefully select a job, the house we live in, and the car we drive. We weigh our options: how far do I have to drive to work, is the house in a good neighborhood, is it near schools, is this car good on gas, reliable, have good ratings, is this food good for me, should I buy this dress or that? We should be even more selective when it comes to selecting a partner. Selecting our partner could be the most important decision we will make.

When Rose, 50, married W., she knew they were like day and night. She is basically a quiet, shy, timid, tiny person, while W. is tall, husky, obsessive, controlling and unyielding. This is probably the most unfortunate of unions, because they are totally incompatible physically, sexually, emotionally, and mentally. Sadly, this mis-match has created three extremely dysfunctional children, and after over twenty years of marriage, they are finally divorcing, leaving a trail of five broken, angry people, with horrendous mental anguish.

We select our mates mostly by default or by unfortunate examples. If a mother continually belittles and scolds her husband, the male child thinks this is *normal*, and expects and attracts the same kind of woman. If the father is non-communicative or cold, the female child may attract men who display those same characteristics. Or, we think we can change someone, so we get involved, or we make our choices for the wrong reasons, for money, convenience, a reputation, prestige, a "trophy", a conquest, and so on.

P. is a beautiful woman in her 40's, whose only desire is to find a wealthy husband. Her attraction to money eliminates many other men who are probably more compatible with her spirit. The money factor that attracts her to certain men, unfortunately, also attracts other women, so she always seems involved with deceptive men who lie and cheat.

Spiritual practices help us in breaking this cycle of self-defeating choices, and discovering alternative ways of living and loving. Tantra helps us open and clear our chakras so that we can attract a more compatible spirit to join us in Divine Congress.

We mentioned in the chapter on the Guru Principle that the Guru awakens you, but then you must practice Tantra with someone who is your equal. When you take a class in martial arts, you have to practice with someone on your level, so that you both learn techniques and skills together. If you were a beginner, they would never pair you with a black belt. In boxing, they would never put a bantamweight against a heavyweight. They match two fighters with equal abilities. In Tantra, of course, you are not sparring, you are making love and making love is a skill requiring two equals, for the most promising results.

On a first level chakra, we should choose someone who has the same flow of sexual energy that we have and shares the same natural instincts we have, so that one is not highly sexual and the other asexual. We should look for pleasing traits and characteristics on the second chakra in selecting a compatible mate. Someone who is physically matched, has the ability to pleasure us the way we like to be pleasured is the ideal. At the third chakra, our partner should have a similar amount of will, ability and intelligence that we have. At the fourth chakra, he or she should have empathy and a genuine capacity to love and demonstrate love. Our partner should have the fifth chakra capacity to express and communicate feelings, thoughts and emotions, truthfully and effectively. We want a partner who shares some of our intellectual knowledge and intuition so that we can experience a true psychic connection at the sixth chakra. Finally, we share our spirit and a deep psychic connection of souls so that together, we can ascend in a selfless union to connect with the Cosmos.

To summarize, the partner we select should share our basic philosophy of life, possess interests, energy and passions similar to our own, and have a capacity for spiritual growth, mental expansion, and emotional development.

It is important to make a distinction between "judging" a potential partner and using *viveka* in determining if someone shares our energy and outlook, because a gross mis-match can have an outcome that is not beneficial for the health and happiness of all involved. The idea is to find *your* most compatible potential partner, fully acknowledging that there is someone for everyone, and what is perfect for one person may not be right for another. So, we are admonished not to *judge*, just be *aware* how someone's energy corresponds and balances with our own. And since everyone has "quirks", *sadhana* enables us to love unconditionally.

H., an intelligent, highly sexual male, at 35 married a conservative Christian woman, who did not enjoy sensual pleasures. Knowing this, he was sure that he could "fix" her, but after fifteen tumultuous, and practically celibate years, he finally had to abandon the marriage. Five years after his divorce, and after a few more mis-matches, he finally found his ideal partner.

Through unwavering commitment to our spiritual development, unconditional love and mindfulness, we can improve the relationship we are already in, regardless of its present condition; or if we not yet in a relationship, we can manifest the right partner by working on ourselves starting now.

Orgasm

*Orgasm is a natural state where your body vibrates like energy, electricity. It actually is an electric phenomenon. Physicists may say that there is no matter, that all matter is only appearance; but deep down, that which exists is electricity, not matter. You may actually see sparks of lightning and feel as though you've been struck by lightning for days after.
…Osho*

Without the guilt factor, a woman can experience frequent orgasms that benefit her health tremendously. However, as we have seen earlier, there is a vast difference in having an ordinary orgasm and having a tantric orgasm. Ordinary orgasms, which are the norm, are of short duration, isolated in the sex organs, and affect just the physical body. The after-effects of a tantric orgasm, remain hours or days. In actuality, orgasms may affect us for the rest of our lives. *Mahamudra,* the great orgasm, unites the body, mind and spirit with the Supreme.

Most people, Osho said, know sex only as a relief; they do not know its orgasmic quality. He said that people mistakenly think they are having an orgasm when it is actually just a "genital relief". To obtain the benefits of a real tantric orgasm, the Shakti must pierce each of the chakras, as it ascends the spinal cord. It must reach the brain's central nervous system and endocrine command center, the hypothalamus and pituitary gland to command the changes that will benefit our not only our sexual health, but our health in general.

Frequent orgasms increase the level of the orgasm hormone, oxytocin, which is linked to the personality, passion, social skills and emotional quotient (EQ), all of which determines our career, marriage, emotions and social life. Because frequent orgasms can empower our pituitary (brain function), they are very beneficial

Tantric sex can make great changes in our lives, not just on the physical level, but on the spiritual and emotional level as well. It is imperative that our sexual health be in optimum condition for the positive changes that we seek.

Osho describes orgasm as follows, "In orgasm, you reach this deepest layer of your body where matter no longer exists, just energy waves. You become a vibrating, dancing energy, pulsating with your partner. Tantric sexual orgasm needs time, the longer, and the better, because then it will go deeper into your being, into your mind, and into your soul. Spreading from the toe to the head, every fiber of your being will be throbbing with it. Your whole body will become an orchestra and it will come to a crescendo.

"However, if you are in a hurry, the so-called orgasm becomes just an ejaculation, it is no longer an orgasm. It is a localized, miniscule, meaningless experience. In fact you will feel tired, frustrated, depressed afterwards because you have lost precious energy and you have not been washed in a spiritual bath, so it is a mundane experience, a release and a relief, but not an orgasmic experience."

Lately there has been a lot of fascination with female ejaculation. A shooting ejaculation is a very yang phenomenon (sometimes with *genital* orgasm) that requires a degree of muscularity, however, urinary incontinence is often mistaken as female ejaculation. Female ejaculation is said to "age" a woman, since she is expelling vital life force, and therefore, it should not be a goal. Just as men should control their ejaculation, (to build and contain life force), women should also pull the energy up to the higher chakras and experience an internal orgasm, which is far more beneficial to her well being. Ejaculation located in the first chakra is not the same thing as having a full-bodied *Mahamudra,* which affects the entire body field, and has the ability to transform us on every level, taking us from ordinary to extraordinary.

A tantric orgasm that touches the physical, subtle and causal bodies (hence, the term "full-bodied") is the ideal. We do not recommend that early practitioners of tantra use any unnatural substances such a psychoactive drugs when having sex because it may actually take away from the senses. The whole idea is to be "present".

Osho goes on to say that religion suppresses sexual expression and the enjoyment of sex, even with a life partner. Religion has deprived its followers the enjoyment of a perfectly natural and organic phenomena, sex. This condemnation and guilt about sex has gone to the very roots of the body, to the core of our being.

He continues, "This hatred and condemnation of sex has to be changed, and that can be changed if you start developing a reverence for sex.

"There are three basic elements in sex that bring you to a blissful moment. First there is timelessness; you transcend time completely; time ceases for you. You are not in it. Second, in sex, for the first time you lose your ego. You become egoless. You are not, nor is there the other. You and your beloved are both lost into something else. And third, in sex you are natural for the first time. You are a part of nature, a part of trees, a part of the animals, a part of the stars - a part. You are immersed into something--the Cosmos, the Tao. These three things give you ecstasy."

The Taoists describe the stages of the female orgasmic response in nine steps, but this is not to be confused with the grand full-bodied orgasm that is described by Osho.

1. The woman sighs, breathes heavily and experiences sensory excitement.

2. The woman extends her tongue to the man while kissing him. She is extending her heart to him.

3. The woman grasps and holds the man tightly, welcoming him.

4. As the shakti begins to flow, the woman experiences a series of vaginal spasms as her secretions begin to flow.

5. The psychic fire is burning hot as the woman's joints loosen and she bites the man.

6. The woman undulates like a snake trying to wrap her arms and legs around the man. The kundalini energy is flowing powerfully now.

7. The woman's blood is boiling and she frantically touches the man everywhere. The shakti is boiling over.

8. The woman's muscles begin to relax and she bites even more. She becomes totally enveloped in bliss.

9. The woman collapses in a "little death" as she completely surrenders to the man and opens her heart. Time stops as she floats in a sea of total bliss.

Erection and Premature Ejaculation

A man should learn to control his ejaculation.
To be greedy for feminine beauty and emit beyond one's vigor
injures every vein, nerve, and organ in the body, and gives rise to every illness.
Correct practice of sexual intercourse can cure every ailment
and at the same time open the doors to Liberation.
…Yang Sheng Yao Chi

How can men maintain an erection? It is not necessary to resort to artificial methods to get an erection. Drugs can be used to make the lingam erect, but it is a localized sensation that still will not lead one to the experience of having a full-bodied internal orgasm. The key is to relax through meditation techniques, and give up the urge to control the *lingam* (the secret to *lingam* control is to relax the *mind*). One would think that it is easy to relax, but the fact is we are so conditioned to be in constant activity, whether it is the mind or body, that relaxing is something that has to be learned, and more importantly, it has to be practiced. There is no easy way. Just like building strength and muscles, it takes patience.

The good news is that meditation really does work, and the male absolutely can learn to meditate while having sex. It would also be most preferable that his partner has the same goals as he. When having sex with someone who does not share the same commitment to the practices and meditation, the sex may be okay, even good, but it will never have the depth that is only possible when two people are really yoked in all the chakras and not just at the genitals. (This is why practicing tantriks are neither fascinated nor allured by "casual" sex, a temptation perpetuated by ego. There simply is no *real* magic with multiple partners because there is no *accumulated storehouse* of Shakti, only a diluted version of it. Tantric sex is a "process", not a one-night deal.)

In addition, a couple's energy fields should parallel, in other words, a "high"(conscious), or "light"(illuminated) person should not be cavorting with someone who has "low" (unconscious) or "dark" (un-illuminated) energies. A person with "fast" (positive) energy should avoid a partner who has "slow" (negative) energy. All of the couple's chakras, should complement their physical, mental, psychic, and etheric bodies. Ideally, their genitals should also be somewhat similarly matched, because there are reflexology points within the *lingam,* that correspond to the reflexology points in the *yoni,* that when engaged, creates a spirited charge.   Males should not be so concerned with their erections, because in tantra, it is typical to go in "soft" and come out "hard", instead of the other way around. The "soft" *lingam* can take the place of a tongue, so there should be no pressure and effort to keep it "hard". Be natural.

Another matter of concern is the avoidance of premature ejaculation. When males feel the urge to expel, they should take a deep breath and repeat a mantra to themselves. (As mentioned elsewhere in this book, it could be *"Ee-Ah-Oh"*, *"Om"*, *"Om Mani Padme Hum"*, *"Om Namah Shivaya"*, or any chosen mantra.) At the same time, he puts his tongue in *khechari mudra*, as he continues to visualize the sexual energy flowing "upwards", rather than "outwards", having absolute control over the energy in his mind's eye. Everything takes practice, and the *sadhak* must be motivated enough to set aside a half an hour a day to meditate and do the exercises if he truly wants to master ejaculation control. When the urge has been transmuted, he may experience a very deep "internal" orgasm that is incomparable to an ordinary release.

Many men feel intimidated about their sexual performance, fearing that they will not meet the high expectations of women. They are terrified of women and this fear has injured their confidence and crippled their performance. Having the right partner can make all the difference in the world. Rather than "settle" for any partner to have sex with, it is best to be more selective. We are selective about the car we drive, the clothes we wear, the job we take, the house we live in. Why not the person whose energy and karma we will absorb? The aspirant may be wiser to do the practices alone, with the faith, expectation and intention that the right partner will show up at the right time. (Since tantra is a powerful mystical path that does not dissuade the material needs of its devotees, manifestations are not just a possibility, but also a probability.)

Men, acknowledging the Shiva within, should repeat *"Om Namah Shivaya"* as often as possible, while working, playing, resting, driving, studying and during sex. Women also can chant Lord Shiva's name to invoke his blessings during times of sadness, distress, or danger, and whenever there are positive feelings of appreciation, joy, and celebration.

In the beginning of this book is a tribute to Lord Ganesh, the elephant-headed God, the Lord of wisdom, and the remover of all obstacles. We can petition his blessings by the continuous repetition of his name *"Om Gam Ganapataye Namaha"*.

A Woman's Body

> *Women are heaven; women are dharma (truth);*
> *and women are the highest sacrament.*
> *Women are Buddha; women are the sangham (community);*
> *and women are the Perfection of Wisdom.*
> *...Candamaharosana Tantra*

A woman's body is a delicate, beautiful instrument that must be played like a musical instrument. In order to orchestrate the finest music, her partner must not only be a virtuoso, but the woman herself must be "tuned" correctly. If her instrument is not tuned correctly no great music can come from it no matter how much of a master the man is. The greatest maestro on earth cannot take a musician with minimum or no training and expect him to perform Beethoven's Fifth Symphony.

So it is with sexual union. The maestro, Shiva, needs a finely tuned instrument, if he is to command a high performance. The masculine and feminine must be equally prepared on all levels.

For example, the body temple must be in good health not only physically, but in the spiritual, emotional, and mental sense as well. The body must be fit and strong to enable it to generate and contain the power of the Shakti. The person should be as spiritual as he or she is sexual.

The tragedy of sexual intercourse is the perpetual virginity of the soul.
…William B. Yeats

A woman must have good control of her internal muscles. One method is to strengthen the kegel muscles, by using tools, such as an "egg" attached to a string, which is inserted into the vagina (like a tampon) and held while working or doing housework. Keeping the egg in and expelling it at will also strengthens this set of muscles. The woman should be able to hold the egg inside for at least eight or more hours, even when moving around and about, when urinating or having bowel movements. (Be careful not to let it fall into the toilet, or flush it by accident.)

Another method is to practice the *bandhas* (locks) regularly. The *mulabandha* lock will strengthen anal sphincter muscles, the wall of the vagina. Perform the *mulabandha* lock by squeezing the anal sphincter muscles as if holding back a bowel movement. The "cheeks" will tighten and contract when this is done correctly.

Strengthen the abdominal muscles by pulling it in towards the spine in an *uddiyana* lock, or doing simple sit-ups to strengthen these muscles.

Women should practice pelvic thrusts, and isolate the pelvis area without moving any other part of the body. With knees slightly bent, she can thrust the pelvis forward, as if throwing a ball to someone across the room, without moving any other part of the body. This should be practiced in front of a mirror.

Her body should be totally free from self-consciousness. (This is quite different from shallow exhibitionism, which is ego, an entirely different thing.) Being "free" means being free from the ego. Revealing breasts on the Jerry Springer Show is not "freedom". It is a cheap "thrill".

Real freedom is a state of psychological and spiritual state that enables a woman to fully communicate with her body and express herself without feeling guilt, shame, embarrassment or fear.

A man must not only have sensual skills, he must have control of his ejaculation, (see section on ejaculation), and he must also be master of his body. In this Supreme Shiva-Shakti, union there is no right and wrong because every act is an act of love. The body is the vehicle through which we attain our goals; it is the instrument of enlightenment. The mind must be fully illuminated and have knowledge and understanding of the tantric arts, such as mantras, yantras, meditation, chanting, and *maithun*. The mind must be able to recognize, observe and detect the ego and its' tricks. Through an egoless state, we surrender to our partner as a manifestation of the Divine, and witness the consummation of the marriage of the microcosm and macrocosm.

The mind must be devoid of ego-driven desires, expectations and behaviors. At the level of Godliness, there is an exalted responsibility of behavior in actions, and thoughts as well. The spirit or soul dwells in the physical, spiritual, emotional and mental body. It is never separate from us. In the spirit body, the Shakti moves in and throughout the vehicle and the *sadhak* is able to direct and control its movement. The couple must be spiritually mature, highly disciplined, and fully imbibed with awareness on the highest plane. Their hearts must be open and remain open even during crisis.

When a couple is in tune with each other on every level, they can experience the most profound lovemaking. However, playing with this sexual energy may bring to the surface all kinds of "stuff", that could be both wonderful and painful, but necessary for transformation.

As our energy level becomes elevated, it can become disconcerting, and sometimes, humorous. Too much energy can crash computers, stop clocks, cause lights to turn off and on. Things can move on their own, appliances and electronic devices may go haywire, and friends may ask the tantrik to stay away from their computers. On the other hand, people will be drawn to this mysterious energy; children and animals will be fascinated with one who has this "light". Practitioners may become very sensitive to cosmic energies; so enhanced clairvoyance (second sight or inner vision), clairaudience (psychic messages that are "heard"), and clairsentience (psychic touch) are not uncommon.

In the light of consciousness we can dance to our soul with our beloved, with our instrument tuned, orchestrated and conducted by none other than Shiva, Maestro of the Universe. Every note and chord that we bring to life through our discipline, and practice will bring us closer and closer to Cosmic Truth and Spiritual Knowledge.

Does Size Matter?

Women's Liberation is just a lot of foolishness.
It's the men who are discriminated against.
…Golda Meir

The size of the male's phallus has been of great significance to the media, the porn industry, and even sex therapists. In the west, the size and condition of the *yoni* is ignored, but in Eastern thought, it is of equal significance.

In tantric practices, it is preferable that the *lingam* and *yoni* have a perfect fit. In general, a small *lingam* in a generous *yoni* will not feel like much to either partner. A large *lingam* in a small *yoni* is not conducive to prolonged sexual encounters. So what to do? Ideally, we find the perfect match. The *lingam* and *yoni* have reflexology zones that correspond to each other, and when the zones in the *lingam* match up to in the *yoni,* (i.e. heart to heart, lung to lung, etc.) the experience is amazing.

It's not that easy to find our life partner who is also our equal sexual counterpart, but there are ways to minimize any discrepancy in our sizes (as well as the cultural or other differences we may have and learn to "adjust" to). We can "adjust" to the size of our partner through muscle control, mastery of techniques and certain sexual positions. However, it is important to stress that both men and women are equally responsible, because size *does* matter, *both* of their sizes.

Women can skillfully massage the *lingam* internally, by squeezing it with the *yoni* muscles. The *yoni* becomes the *lingam* in reverse. In fact,

---

[19] Author

the most gratifying experience is achieved when both partners remain relatively still, and work just the internal muscles

In tantra, ejaculation is not the goal; rather the male learns to control this ejaculation, so that he can pleasure the woman for any length of time, or he may not ejaculate for weeks. (The less a man ejaculates the more frequently he becomes interested and ready to have sex again).

Men learn to control their ejaculatory impulses in order to give their woman the prolonged depth of intimacy. A *lingam* that has a knee jerk reaction and ejaculates in a few seconds is hardly satisfying. Tantric men have "internal" orgasms, that is, sans ejaculations, which are far superior to the external orgasms in ordinary sex. Internal orgasms in a man or woman have been described as a powerful rush of energy beginning at the *lingam* (or *yoni*) moving all the way to the head; an energy that suffuses the entire body with incredible electrical force. This moment of ecstasy does not involve ejaculation, and men will attest that it is far superior to an ordinary orgasm. It is recommended that men ejaculate on a regular basis, however, whether it is every 10 times, weekly, or monthly. Some men ejaculate after every "session" of 2 to 4 hours. There is no rule, other than ejaculation is not the goal.

We believe that the most profound experience takes place only when we are fully present. What does being "present" mean? It means being fully absorbed in our partner, not thinking about other things, but listening to their every word, feeling their touch, being totally focused and having no distractions or interruptions. That is being "present", and "in the moment".

This natural "high" can be of such magnitude, that nothing can compare to it. And it is safe. Women may experience waves of bliss that spontaneously overlap and move simultaneously in perfect harmony with their partner, for hours if they choose. Opening their hearts in complete trust, they surrender fully to their magnificence and vulnerability. This is done by relaxing the body and mind and allowing the bliss. Do not hold back anything, and have no fear of being judged.

Couples should work together and coach each other, and practice this art. Climaxing is not the goal but sharing a loving space is. More importantly, this practice will result in a deeper intimacy as you open up to each other's needs, guiding, sharing and exploring ways to enhance your relationship. The whole idea is to enjoy, lighten up and not be so serious about making love. Be natural, relax, and have fun.

There is no place for inhibitions or uneasiness in any loving space of intimacy. Here there can only be trust, honor and respect. Lovemaking becomes a sacred haven.

Surrender

Your soul's temple offers sweet refuge to my soul,
Drawing me away from the conflict and drama of this world
into the sweet nectar of the sublime grace of the divine.
…J. Ram Sivananda[19]

The word "surrender" conjures up in our minds mental images of some sort of slavery where there is no free will, where we are resigned to a life of indenture to some lofty, manipulative character.

However, when we use that term in the context of spiritual practices, surrender means surrender of the ego; letting go of the chains that bind us. The truth is that when we surrender our ego, we actually become more empowered. Seems like a contradiction, but it is true. Surrender equals empowerment.

We all know we must surrender our ego if our soul is to experience lasting bliss, but it is not a simple task. Our ego, relentless and adamant in its resistance to change, uses cunning and trickery, flattery and ingenuity to insure its existence. It creeps up on us when we least expect it, morphing into different forms, invading our thoughts, on the pretense that it has our best interests at heart, while actually the whole agenda is to sabotage our efforts to find inner peace. The ego is quite creative and desperate because it wants to survive. (See more about ego in chapter one.)

In tantra, we also surrender to our partner. First, we should try to find someone who is our equal. If we are with an un-conscious (unaware) partner, it may be difficult, but still possible, to surrender to them. If this is the situation, we should detach from their faults if we continue to stay together, trying not to get involved in their drama. This means we could be supportive, and still "detach" from the situation. We become the witness, not the doer, observing our own actions, instead of judging our partner and we can say, "Thank you Lord, for appearing to me in this form."

If you aren't involved with anyone yet, you should try and get a partner who is on the same page with you, who shares the same energy barometer that you have. You don't want to be the victim of a "vampire" who sucks up all your energy, therefore, you should try to partner with one who is in total synch with you--your equal.

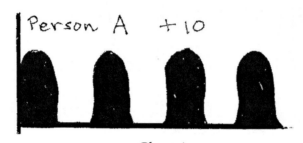

Chart A

In the figure 37, person A is a plus 10 in energy.

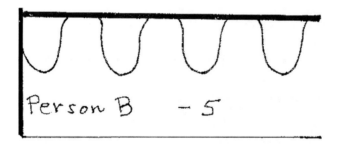

Chart B

Person B, in Fig.38 is a minus 5 in energy.

Chart C

Therefore, when they get together, Fig.39, person B (dotted line) will gain something from person A, (dark solid), but person A sacrifices 5 points in the process.

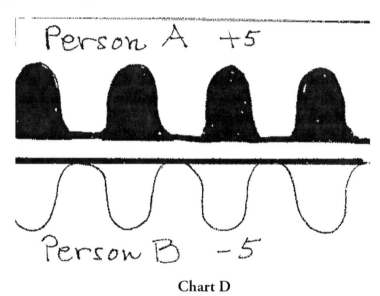

Chart D

In Fig. 40, person A is a plus 5, and person B is a minus 5, the net result is zero, they cancel each other out and both gain nothing, as in the algebra equation (+5) + (–5)=0

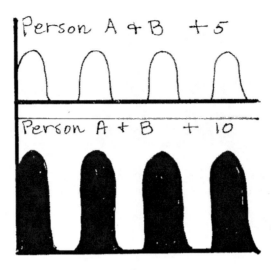

Chart E

If both A and B are synchronized, (both +5), both double their gain, fig. 41. For instance if A is a plus 5, and her partner is a plus 5, the result is that both become plus 10.

Surrender is not the same thing as "submission". Surrender means to "release" our own *ego,* while "submission" is being subservient, like a slave. Surrender is a voluntary action, but submission is succumbing to the wishes of another, whether or not we really want to.

To appreciate the benefits of ecstatic living, surrender is an absolute prerequisite. In tantra, that means that we leave our ego behind and develop a strong sense of Self, appreciating and accepting who we are. We discern the difference between Self and ego, becoming the witness of our lives. Anytime we feel embarrassed, ashamed, or self-conscious about our looks, and what our partner or others think of us, that is the ego doing what it does so well.

Surrender means we do not judge ourselves. It means that we are not chained to false notions about our body, and thus, we are free to find pleasure through our senses. It means we are can embrace our partner's body, and welcome the worship of ours.

Surrender is opening our heart fully without consequence to our partner, so when we are engaged in lovemaking, we employ all our senses, caressing our lover with our eyes, admiring every inch of their body, and exploring the texture their body with our hands and mouth.

We taste their essence, the sweetness of their lips and mouth, their jade stalk, or lotus blossom. We inhale the sweet fragrance of their skin, hair, and body, listen to the love sounds that they make, observe their breath and breathe together as one.

Surrender is losing our self-consciousness about the way we look, and stop worrying about what people think of us, (which means we will hold back our full expression and deny ourselves any pleasure). Surrender is having trust in our partner and in ourselves. In the West, surrender is the most difficult art to master. It is a necessary on the path of union with a partner. When we release the chains of bondage and surrender our arrogance to a higher consciousness, bliss will prevail.

In Tantra, surrender to the guru (see section on guru principle) is a basic tenet. In this tradition, the aspirant surrenders to the guru, in the same way that the guru surrendered to his teacher, in an unbroken lineage going back thousands of years. It is said, "Only one who follows can lead", and a qualified guru guided every great being. One method of showing our respect is by *pranam*, bowing, in front of the guru, an act of relinquishing our ego.

The Japanese, who are imbedded in a culture of respect, lower their heads in a bow, in greeting of courtesy, not only to an exalted being, but also, to their elders, friends, teachers, and others.

In an intimate scenario, a woman should surrender to her Shiva, and her mate should in turn surrender to his Goddess. This is not an act of submission, nor is it an act of dominance, but an act of mutual respect and an obligation to demonstrate character that is totally trustworthy and impeccable.

Worship

Throughout this book, we have been showing ways to prepare the inner temple. Now we will describe ways to prepare the outer temple.

First, we want to describe the state one must bring into worship. *Puja*, or worship, is an important element of tantra. It is a ritual combining certain elements and tools to honor our Guru, the Goddess and Shiva, who are not separate from the Self but held in the highest esteem. While we worship them externally through rituals, we know that they live within us. We worship our partner with the same reverence. External worship is one way to relinquish our ego.

Our state is important during a ritual. We enter this "altered state" when we sense a meaningfulness and depth, which induces our attentiveness, reverence, and passion. We feel an intense involvement of our whole being, beyond conscious actions or words. We already create rituals spontaneously, as a natural part of life, but when we want to create rituals intentionally-- for meditation, or for enhancing our daily activities, we can do a few things.

Intuitively, we understand the symbolism. For example, in tantra ceremony we prepare our inner and outer temple in a manner that expresses love and respect for each other.

Tantric couples excel in the art of worshipping each other. The husband becomes the Lord; his wife is his Goddess. In this way, they learn to become gurus to one another--teaching, surrendering, trusting, and worshipping each other. Their duty is to illuminate one another, and to perform *seva*, (doing things for the other without any expectations) as an expression of their pure love and devotion.

To love rightly is to love what is orderly and beautiful in an educated and disciplined way.
…Plato

Rituals are founded on actual dynamics. Although rituals might seem to be merely symbolic, they express and convey the energy that is represented by that symbolism. Every ritual possesses an energy that is as "real" as the physical activity that represents that energy, particularly if we consciously experience and direct the energy.

First, we need to set up an altar in the same vicinity where the worship will take place. It could be a small table or other flat surface in the bedroom, for instance.

The altar should be our own sacred place and every object placed on the altar should be an object of devotion and purpose. Cover the altar with a pretty fabric or scarf and place one or two candles on top of it. When buying a candle get something that can burn for a few hours and will not tip over easily. Unless one is allergic to scents, burn some incense or sage to purify the air. Fresh flowers bring aliveness to the altar. In addition, place a statue, sculpture, yantra, or photo of a god or master who is associated with tantra: Shiva, Babaji or the Goddesses, Saraswati, Lakshmi, Kali, or any other great being whose energy you want to invoke.

Ideally, an altar should be set-up where there will be no disturbances, an area where meditation can take place. The more you meditate in that space, the more the shakti will build at that spot. Have a special pillow or mat to sit on each time to collect the spiritual energy.

Next, get the bath ready. The bath is necessary to purify our body and mind. A sensual experience is to fill the bathtub with rose petals, bubble bath, bath oils etc, and arrange candles all around the tub. Invite your partner in the tub and proceed to wash each other by candlelight. If you plan to remain in the tub for a while it is nice to have music playing and perhaps something light to eat, like grapes. If you only have access to a shower, you can still create an ambience by having beautiful music, indirect lighting or candles, special soaps and wash sponges, bath brushes and luxurious towels.

Have spray bottles filled with essential oils, or essences, to spray your body and towels. Bath powders and fluffy powder puffs feel wonderful after every bath or shower.

One note of caution: If you have any pets, please take precautions, since any kind of aroma, odor, and incense can affect their well-being. It may be in their best interest to keep them in another room where it is safe and cozy for them.

When finished with the bath or shower, dry each other off with soft, fluffy towels and return to the special place, which presumably is in the bedroom, although it could be anywhere else.

Before continuing, make sure that there will be no distractions or interruptions such as phones ringing, television, alarms etc. Be totally prepared to devote this evening lavishing quality attention on your beloved. Prepare in advance some treats, such as a large bowl of fruit, like bananas, strawberries, or mangos, and have a little paring knife and napkins handy. You do not want to be running around getting things later. Chocolate is wonderfully seductive and sexy especially when it is placed in each other's mouths, or on the navel to nibble on. You can create a sacred feast of the bounty of the earth in honor of the Goddess and yourselves.

Two champagne glasses should be nearby with a bottle of chilled champagne, or alcohol-free champagne. (Note: Although the use of alcohol can be used in this ritual, we personally don't use any alcohol because muscle testing revealed to us that alcohol has a lower frequency of energy, although as we said earlier, a bona fide satguru has the ability, through ritual, to "purify" the alcohol). Have a lot of music ready. A CD player that holds a few CD's is best.

Again because the frequency of music varies, we suggest selecting music that is uplifting and positive. Instrumental is preferred because you do not want to listen to words and get into your heads. You want to remain in the heart. The exception is listening to music with Sanskrit lyrics, or mantras—they are empowering. We love to play music with a great deal of shakti, and songs sung by Gurus, seekers, and devotees. It can be dynamic music, or serene. Have a variety available and change your "dance of union" when the music changes. Let the shakti in the music drive the shakti within both of you.

The body deserves to be worshipped and adorned as a temple. The body is a wholesome abode for the indwelling of the Divine, which we worship by the food we eat, the clothes we place on it, the jewels we wear, the thoughts we have, the music we listen to, the books we read, the movies and programs we watch on television, and the company we keep.

Worship, when done with conscious effort and intent becomes a practice that builds *kama* in a wholesome, divine way. Adornments are added to draw energy to the worshipper. Adorning ourself is not something we do for our ego or vanity, but it is strictly to create a body temple. The intention and purpose is to worship, therefore it is Divine. The worship of your partner is a direct worship of the Divine.

Couples will find that wearing jewelry with a *sankalpa,* or purpose, will seal their intention and reflect their desires in a dazzling way.

Gems and metals are used as super conductors for channeling the Shakti, because they have the ability to open chakras, allowing for an increase and an abundant flow of erotic energy. Kings and queens wore gold crowns imbedded in jewels not only for virility (which ensured the continuation of their lineage), but also to give them mystical and psychic powers.

In *Jyotish*, gems, metals, flowers, scents and colors that correspond with the chakras are used to propitiate and appease any negative effects of the stars, planets and their rulers, as well as to negate the unconstructive propensities of our minds.

Hindu goddesses and gods are bedecked from head to toe in brilliant, colorful gems, flowers and jewels, lavished in gold and metals on every limb, and draped in radiant hues that suggest their Divine attributes. We too, are god and goddess manifest, and thus, are every bit as divine and worthy of worship. We can perform this worship and empower our partner and ourselves with pure energy, exclusive of the ego mind, vanity, or narcissism. (See section on Self-Love in Chapter 3).

The following chart is a quick guide to the appropriate gems and colors used in *Jyotish, Ayurveda* and Tantra.

The point is to become so enmeshed in the deities' energy, and take *kama* to a summit of ecstasy.

Planets	Attribute	Color	Gems	Finger
Sun	Spirit, energy	Red	Ruby, spinet, garnet	Ring, Index
Moon	Mind, emotions	White	Pearl, moonstone	Ring
Mars	Energy, ambition	Red	Coral, carnelian, bloodstone	Ring, Index
Mercury	Intellect, communication	Green	Emerald, peridot, tourmaline, aquamarine	Baby, Middle
Jupiter	Justice, wealth, fortune, expansion	Yellow	Sapphire, topaz, zircon, beryl, citrine	Index, Ring
Venus	Love, Beauty, Sexuality	White	Diamond, sapphire, zircon, quartz, coral	Baby, Middle
Saturn	Judgment, karma, malefic	Blue and purple	Sapphire, lapis lazuli, amethyst	Middle, Baby
Rahu	Expansion, Too much, takes us into the world	Orange/cinnamon	Zircon, hessonite, gold hessonite	Baby, Middle
Ketu	Wisdom, too little, takes us out of the world	multi	Cat's eye chrysoberyl, tiger eye	Baby, Middle

The Kama Sutra states, "When a wife approaches her husband in private, her dress should consist of many ornaments, various flowers, a wrap of different colors, and some sweet-smelling ointments or unguents." A woman reserves her best clothes for her husband and he should do likewise. Every woman who wishes to please and excite her partner should have a range of intimate clothing and should remember to dress up for her man, rather than reserve the "best" or most alluring clothes for when they go out socially, a habit women have in the West. In the East, women adorn themselves with special jewelry for the delight of their lovers, rather than for public show

In Tantra worship, Shiva (the male partner) could wear loose pants that have a drawstring waist, made of a sensuous fabric, such as silk, rayon, or velvet. (He may be lucky enough to find a pair of pajama pants that are made of a soft fabric, which has a nice pattern. He might wear a vest or be bare-chested.)

Shakti (the female partner) might wear a sexy belly-dancing outfit, exotic lingerie, a simple sarong, or tie a beautiful scarf around her hips with nothing underneath. The key is to be bold, and let the imagination run wild.

In addition, you may want to have a few other things handy: a fan, feathers, scented massage oil, plush pillows, anything that will feel sensual and add to the experience.

What is really fun and exciting is to create a "story" where both partners become the actors. This is a fun activity, for special occasions, like an anniversary, for instance. And it gives you something to reminisce and talk about for the next several years.

You can plan a "vacation" of say, ten days of uninterrupted lovemaking. This does not mean you are engaged in aerobic sex the entire time, but it does mean that you will be making "love" the entire time. You can eat, but make every meal an act of worship, make the bath an act of worship, and make sleep an act of worship. Do nothing else but give undivided attention to the one beside you.

Preparation and worship is important if you wish to have more joy in your life. However, you must make a serious effort in order to succeed. Therefore, when you want to create rituals and when you have a clear intent of what it is that you want (better meditation, or preparing for a magical event with your beloved) try the methods we have disclosed.

Worship your beloved. "See God in each other", said Muktananda. This is the greatest worship. This is the greatest gift you can give your partner. This is how to love.

Honor and Love

*I will cover you with love when next I see you, with caresses, with ecstasy. I want to gorge you with all the joys of the flesh, so that you faint and die. I want you to be amazed by me, and to confess to yourself that you had never even dreamed of such transports.... When you are old, I want you to recall those few hours, I want your dry bones to quiver with joy when you think of them.
...Gustave Flaubert, letter to wife Louise Colet, 15 August 1846*

How do we really honor and love our partner? Rituals are one way to do this. More explicitly, we could undress in front of each other, stand naked in each other's presence, and admire each other's bodies as a Divine manifestation of god's creation.

When you touch your partner, do not just touch their skin, but reach inside and touch his or her soul. The male *lingam* is a symbol of Shiva. When you touch his *lingam*, be reverent of it. This is his *vajra*, the thunderbolt of initiation.

The woman's *yoni* is temple of bliss and the origin of all life. All life has to pass between through those gates. Woman should take the *lingam* in her hand and pull the *lingam* into her body, enjoining her Shiva with her soul. By doing so, she is inviting the union of Shiva, Guru, and the Goddess.

*Take refuge in the yoni of an esteemed woman
...Candamaharosana Tantra*

Simply rubbing two sense organs together is not a sacred act, but accepting the union on all levels; the physical level, the spiritual level, and the mental level is.

One way to worship and honor one another is through a special witness dance done just for the other. In the witness dance you are not dancing, the dance is moving your body. You are not the doer. Your innermost thoughts can be communicated through dance, gazing deeply into your lover's eyes, and observing the circulation of energy that is being shared.

When your dance is over, rather that sitting down right away, remain standing, holding that space for as long as you feel comfortable. When ready, you can share whatever was experienced, perhaps an insight.

Another way to add to this "honor" exercise is to create costumes and play different roles. Applying special makeup and wearing jewelry stimulates our imagination and manifests the energies of the deities. You can create this ritual of love, making it a divine ceremony complete with sensual music, softly lit candles, and intoxicating scents.

Tantra Massage Meditation

See! the mountains kiss high heaven,
And the waves clasp one another;
No sister flower would be forgiven
If it disdained its brother;
And the sunlight clasps the earth,
And the moonbeams kiss the sea: -
What are all these kissings worth,
If thou kiss not me?
…Percy Bysshe Shelley

Tantra massage is a sensual technique to connect and bond with your partner. Where massage therapy uses systematic and scientific manipulation of the soft tissue to improve muscle tone, relax, repair and relieve the body from pain, tantra massage is a fully charged meditation experience for the Tantra couple, designed to build trust and intimacy, where each becomes the giver and receiver. Done in a spirit of love and worship, tantra massage meditation is an exquisite experience that can heal old wounds and improve emotional health by clearing any blocks in the chakras. It is a sensual, spiritual full-bodied experience involving surrender of the ego and being in the moment. It involves creating an ambient space where the couple can perform rituals of the Shiva *lingam* and the Goddess *yoni.*

The Tantra Massage is yet another way of making love without any expectations of having intercourse or orgasm, although if the urge is there, you always have the option to transcend the urge through the breath, or to release the urge with gratitude and awareness.

In order to fully benefit from tantra massage, it is important to let go of the ego and have an attitude of complete surrender and vulnerability, and trust in your partner.

Tantra Massage is the worship of Shiva and Shakti through the partner.

Along with Gopa, he experienced bliss.
By uniting the diamond scepter and lotus,
He attained the fruit of bliss.
Buddhahood is obtained from bliss, and
Apart from women there will not be bliss
The man [sees] the woman as a goddess
The woman [sees] the man as a god.
By joining the diamond scepter and lotus,
They should make offerings to each other.
There is no worship apart from this.
... Candamaharosana-tantra

Touch is the most fundamental intuitive communication experience that we have, a basic universal need that pre-dates language. Touch is primal, cuts thru all languages, and is the animal's language. We use touch to bond with others, and to express all emotions. Feelings such as tenderness and anger evoke energy from the body. Touch can be healing, exciting, provoking, and endearing. Touch is an extrasensory energy, creating an aura field around the body. It is an honest form of communication; an intuitive means of communicating which takes us out of our cognitive experience which western man is dependent upon. Touch is one way for us to give to our partner.

Tantra yoga is a spiritual practice combining the dual forces of Shiva and Shakti in "worship" to form a cohesive union, through duality. Tantra involves a daily practice of reverence and honor, built layer upon layer, by two people who share the same goals and dreams. Because tantra is all about sharing and absorbing energy fields and karma, be extra selective about your relationships and surroundings.

Tantra yoga is the divine yoking of two energies in a focused and premeditated manner. Massage is an intimate way of communicating love through deliberate touch. Tantra bonds us with our partner through this exquisite union.

The purpose of tantra massage is to open up the meridian channels in the body so that sexual energy can flow more freely. The awakened Kundalini can give us a glimpse of Cosmic Divineness, and give us a profound connectivity with our partner. It gives us a chance to worship our partner and subdue our ego.

The effects of this practice are cumulative and therefore inconsequential if one strays here and there, trying out different partners, or "wandering to and fro", one of the demons demolished by the Goddess in the "Chandi Path".

Sexual energy is the most fundamental energy in existence. Through tantric practices, including massage, the path of energy through the meridians move to clear any blockages in the body, resulting in better health and increased well-being. Tantric practices integrate all the aspects of the physical, subtle, and causal bodies with consciousness. The full-bodied orgasm is the most powerful method to achieve this union with the Universe.

Tantric massage circulates this dynamic energy freely in the body of the one who is receiving the massage and benefits the giver as well. This flow of energy circulates between both partners, as it does in sexual union.

There are a few basic hand positions that we use in massage. The first is percussion, where we use our hands like a drum on the receiver's body. Next, we can use the flat-hand method by keeping our palms flat and either with the fingers on the palms we can push and maneuver the energy on the receiver's body. There is the one-finger method where we use one finger and direct the *chi* from the hand into the body of the receiver. The fourth position is to use the fingers to pull the muscles.

The first thing we will do is to prepare ourselves for worship by setting up the sacred space, with music, candles, and bath. To explain this ritual, we will be assuming that the receiver is the woman and the giver is the male. Naturally, it could be the other way around.

To begin, Shiva will be seated at the head of the goddess and will close his eyes and take a few breaths. All thoughts should cease and the concentration should be on the present moment only. Shakti will lie on her back with a pillow under her head and under the knees. Her eyes will be shut and her body should be straight with legs slightly apart. Shiva will observe her breath and relax by coordinating his breath with hers.

When he is ready, he can open his eyes and begin. He will first rub the palms of his hands vigorously together to generate *chi*. Next he will place his hands on her temples and gently start to pull in an outward direction. He will continue this motion for a few minutes before moving his hands to the area of the chest, where he will stretch the flesh at both sides of the chest and pull away from the ribs. He will hold the position for a few minutes and close his eyes and meditate. He will continue the pull by moving to the upper abdomen and pulling the skin outwards, repeating this pull at the lower abdomen and finally at the side of the hips.

Now, very gently he will touch her scalp and rub the crown of her head with his fingers apart. He will massage her temples for a few minutes and move on to her forehead, and then to her eyelids, upper cheeks, nose, her lower cheeks and around her mouth. He will place both hands along the sides of her neck and knead them gently.

Now that the energy field is open, have her turn over and lie face down. He remains at the head of his partner. Using his pads of his fingers, he rolls his fingers on the vertebrae of her neck. Gently rocking the vertebrae back and forth, he gradually moves down the spine all the way to the sacrum.

He moves himself to her left side. He will lay his right hand on her sacrum and visualize heat emanating from his hand onto her body. With practice, both partners will be able to actually feel the heat. After about a minute of two, he moves himself between Shakti's legs. Starting at the sacrum, with a flat-hand, he crosses his thumbs, places them over her spine, and moves the *chi* slowly up her spine. When he reaches the medulla, he will pause, take a breath, and return his hands to the sacrum. He should repeat this three times.

Now instead of pushing the energy up her spine, he will gently blow on her spine, without touching her body with his lips, all the way up to the base of her neck and repeat this three times.

After this, Shiva can proceed to the *yoni* massage, or if the giver is Shakti, she will continue with the *lingam* worship.

Worship the Lingam

Shiva is without sign, without color, without taste, without odor,
beyond the reach of words or touch,
without qualities, immutable and immovable.
The distinctive sign by which one can recognize
the nature of something is therefore called lingam.
...Linga Purana

The Sanskrit word for the male sexual organ is *lingam* and is loosely translated as "Wand of Light". Its' meaning is different in intention from the typical Western view of the penis. The *lingam* is respectfully viewed and honored as a "Wand of Light" that channels creative energy and pleasure. The term *lingam,* in Sanskrit, means "sign". Shiva, as the Absolute, that which is unmanifest, can only be perceived by the means of his creation--the source of life from which the world is issued. This is the principle upon which the veneration of the phallus is based in Shaivite mysticism.

He who desires perfection of the soul must worship the lingam.
...Linga Purana

In some legends, the Shiva *lingam* "pierces" the three worlds or cities. In one version, it is related that the gods Brahma and Vishnu were debating which of the two of them was the "greater", when there appeared before them a vast column of light. Brahma, mounted on his swan, flew upwards to find its peak, while Vishnu, taking the form of a boar, descended to find its foundation. Although they searched for thousands of years, they could find neither peak nor foundation. Finally, they found a *Ketaki* flower that had fallen from the *lingam's* head. The flower told them that it had been falling for ten eons and that no one knew how much more time it would take it to reach the ground.

Thus the *lingam* as being a primordial axis mundi, a form of world-tree or shaman's ladder that passes through all of the known worlds. In the microcosm, the *lingam* springs forth from the *bindu* within the triangle formed by *Jnana-Iccha-Kriya* Shaktis and rises, piercing the chakras.

The *lingam* massage is a way to honor the Divine Phallus of Shiva, thus it is performed in an attitude of total surrender. Worship honors the God residing in every male. The male honors his own Shiva-ness and his partner surrenders her ego to Shiva when she worships him.

The *lingam* massage builds trust and intimacy between two people. The man must learn to receive. He can relax and receive expanded pleasure from his *lingam* while his partner, experiences the joy of facilitating and witnessing her man surrendering to his softer, gentler side.

The male will lie on his back on top of a towel, and make himself comfortable with pillows under his head and hips, with his legs spread apart. Shakti will sit between his legs. Together they will take a few deep breaths.

She then pours some massage oil on her palms, and begins to massage his body to get him to relax. After he begins to relax, she can massage the shaft of the *lingam* by gently squeezing it with the right hand and alternating with the left hand and gently massage the testicles and the area above the *lingam,* on the pubic bone. Next, she will move to the perineum, the area between the testicles and anus.

While the massage is taking place the couple should both be repeating the mantra, *"Om Namah Shivaya",* I honor the God who is within me, or *"Om Mane Padme Hum".*

Continuing to massage the head of the *lingam,* she places the palm over the head of the *lingam,* caressing it with the fingers. In acupressure, the many nerve endings on the *lingam* correspond to other parts of the body and massaging the *lingam* can benefit the man's overall health.

The woman giving the massage must relax, meditate, and witness herself as the Goddess, worshipping the Shiva *lingam*, while continuing to stroke it. She is creative, alternating between using one hand, to using both hands, or one finger, two fingers, three, four, five. Focus entirely on the thunderbolt.

Shakti is not to be concerned with the *lingam* getting hard or getting soft. She should be as relaxed as the man. There is no goal in a *lingam* massage other than it is a way of honoring the man. It is the woman's opportunity to set aside her ego, worship Shiva's phallus, and honor his maleness. Orgasm is not the goal of this massage, however it is a pleasant side effect. Should the man want to ejaculate, Shakti backs off and has him inhale through his nose, bringing the energy from his *Muladhar* up his spine to his third eye. There he will pause, repeat the mantra, "Ee-Ah-Oh", and release the mantra back down his spine. On the "Ee", he should visualize the energy in his third eye; on the "Ah", the energy is in his heart, and on the "Oh" it has descended to the first chakra.

To avoid premature ejaculation, during the massage or during sexual intercourse, the man closes his eyes and should concentrate on his thoughts. With his tongue in *Khechari* mudra, he bends his back and stretches his neck. He opens his nostrils wide, squares his shoulder, closes his mouth, and sucks in his breath. By delaying ejaculation, his semen will ascend.

Men can learn the art of ejaculatory mastery and control by coming close to ejaculation and then backing off on the stimulation. Deep breathing, visualization with the mantra is a method to delay ejaculation. This technique of delaying ejaculation will allow the man to make love for long periods and should be practiced.

The male sacred spot is midway between the testicles and anus, called the Million Dollar Point in Taoism. There is a small indentation about the size of a pea. Massage his *lingam* with the right hand and massage his sacred spot with the left hand. Be gentle, as it may hurt at first. Eventually, as this area is worked on and softened, he will be able to expand his orgasms and master ejaculatory control. This spot can be gently pushed when he nears ejaculation.

The other way to access the sacred spot is through the anus. Many men, especially heterosexual men, are uncomfortable about having someone touch the anus. It is a matter of preference. To access the scared spot through the anus, be sure to use lubrication. Insert a finger in his anus about an inch or so and the prostate gland can be felt. Crook the finger in a "come here" gesture. He may want stimulation of the *lingam* at the same time. As he approaches orgasm, increase the pressure on the sacred spot and let go of the *lingam.*

This can be an emotional experience for the man. He may cry and remember a traumatic event from his past. "Hold space" for him, and allow him to express his feelings without judgment.

If he chooses to let go and ejaculate, encourage him to breathe deeply during the orgasm. It will blow his mind, especially if he has come close and held back at least six times before ejaculating. Holding back six times charges up the sexual battery with tremendous energy. It is then his choice as to where he wants to send this energy--out with their ejaculate (the prevailing paradigm) or inward for other uses (men who master ejaculation are able to channel this energy into other areas of their being.)

When he feels complete with the massage, allow him to lie there quietly. Snuggle together or leave the room and let him drift off into a meditative state. Allow him to fully experience his childlike innocence and magnificent male beauty.

Worship the Yoni

Creator god Prajapati upon creating woman:
Having created her, he worshipped her sexual organ;
Therefore a woman's sexuality should be worshipped.
He stretched forth from himself a stone for pressing nectar
[i.e., causing a woman's sexual fluid to flow]
And impregnated her with that.
Her lap is the sacrificial altar;
Her hair, the sacrificial grass;
Her skin the soma press;
The depths of her sexual organ, the fire in the middle
Many mortals...go forth from this world...without merit,
Namely, those who practice sexual union without knowing this.
...Brhadaranyaka Upanishad 6.4.1-4

The *yoni*, or vagina, is regarded as a sacred temple in Sanskrit. As the source of life itself, it is revered, honored, and worshipped.

Lingam and *yoni* massage is a wonderful sexual experience, but it is so much more than that. It is a way to expand the heart that leads us to states of awareness and bliss. Without intention and knowledge, sex may still be good, but it is neither transcendental nor transforming. It is simply sex. If we want extraordinary sex, we have to work at it physically through the tantra exercises, mentally (through studies), and spiritually (through meditation).

The goal of performing *yoni* massage is not orgasm. The goal is for both parties to surrender their egos, to honor and respect Shiva and Shakti, the male and female principle.

The preparation for yoni massage is the same as the *lingam* massage or any other major sexual event. Bathing, creating an ambience, a soothing atmosphere where there are no distractions or interruptions is essential. To be focused on each other, means no phone, computer, or kids. This one-pointed attention on each other will build intimacy and draw couples closer together. Later, there should be a discussion about it. "Remember when you....", "I felt so...", "You looked so...", "You felt so...", "I did this when you did that...". Re-live every moment and talk about it openly, having a light attitude towards it. There is no reason to be shy, or afraid to express feelings, and thoughts about our body. Even after years have gone by, you can still reminisce about some special moment you shared.

Procedure for *yoni* massage: Lay Shakti on her back on a large towel. Prop her head with pillows so she can watch you sitting between her legs. Placing a pillow under her hips, she bends her knees lightly and spreads them apart.

Shiva should start by looking at her amazing form.

Constantly take refuge at my feet, my dear...
Be gracious, beloved, and
Give me pleasure with your diamond scepter.
Look at my three petalled lotus,
It is a Buddha paradise, adorned with a red Buddha,
A cosmic mother who bestows
Bliss and tranquility on the passionate.
Abandon all conceptual thought and
Unite with my reclining form;
Place my feet upon your shoulders and look me up and down.
Make the fully awakened scepter
Enter the opening in the center of the lotus.
Move a hundred, thousand, hundred thousand times
In my three-petalled lotus
Of swollen flesh.
Placing one's scepter there, offer pleasure to her mind.
Wind, inner wind-my lotus is the unexcelled!
Aroused by the tip of the diamond scepter,
It is red like a bandhuka flower.
.... Candamaharosana-tantra

Using scented oil, massage her legs, abdomen, feet, between her thighs, avoiding the area of her *yoni* till later. Gently "tease" her, talk to her, ask her how it feels, encourage her to express herself.

After a short while, massage the mound and outer lips of her *yoni*. Close both eyes and meditate on her while touching her.

Gently stroke her clitoris with clockwise and counter-clockwise circles, squeezing it between your thumb and index finger. Carefully, insert your middle finger of the right hand into her *yoni*. Very gently, explore and massage the inside of her with this finger, varying the depth, speed, and pressure.

With palm facing up, and the middle finger inside the *yoni,* move the middle finger in a "come here" gesture or crook back towards the palm. Starting at a 6 o'clock position, move gradually to the 7 o'clock position, etc. until a spongy area of tissue is felt, just under the pubic bone, behind the clitoris, around the 12 o'clock position. This is the G-spot, or in tantra, the sacred spot. Shakti may feel as if she has to urinate or it may be painful or pleasurable. Again, vary the pressure, speed, and pattern of movement, moving the middle finger from side to side, back and forth, or in circles. If it feels right, insert the ring finger insider her as well.

Trust your intuition, surrender the ego, and let the goal be to worship the god or the goddess. Become loving and available. Making love is the best meditation.

Kama Sutra

The *Kama Sutra* ("*kama*" meaning desire, *"sutras"* meaning verses) is an anthropological and historical study into the mores of an ancient society and culture in the Far East, compiled by *Vatsyayana,* a Brahmin, nearly two millennia ago. The great sage based his *sadhana* entirely on the contemplation of the Divine.

Ancient sages composed the *Kama Sastras*, based upon the *Vedas. Maharshi Nandikeshwar* was the first originator of *Kama Sutra*. Great sages like *Dattakacharya, Charayana, Suvarn-nama Ghotakmukh, Gonardiya, Gonikaputra,* and *Kuchumar* contributed to the teachings

Essentially a scholarly guide on the arts of pleasure, the *Kama Sutra* was an oral tradition, which originated around the fourth century B.C. during the *Maurya* period. Like other scriptures, the text was first memorized, and then subjected to oral explanations and commentaries by a Guru. Then, some 800 years later, during the *Gupta* period (fourth century A.D), *Vatsyayana* gathered and summarized these works in one collection, and gave the final evolution and refinement to the *Kama Sutra.*

Vatsyayana's text is a compilation and study of the art of living in society as a refined citizen, according to certain ethics and three aims of life: *artha* (prosperity), *kama* (love), and *dharma* (virtue). *Moksha* (liberation), the fourth aim of life, is a separate domain, which *Vatsyayana* did not consider in this particular treatise.

The *Kama Sutra* is not a pornographic work, but rather a study of exquisite practices that were conducive to living a gracious and satisfying life. It is the compendium of pleasure-oriented arts and sciences for the refined, prosperous citizen. *Vatsyayana's* contention was that the three aims of life (prosperity, love and virtuous conduct) had to be pursued simultaneously. Each citizen's conduct had to be inner directed to ensure the survival of the society. The great sage said that the pursuit of profit and erotic pleasure had to be controlled by individual ethics and morality.

The text was addressed to the wealthy bourgeois, living in the city, a cultured and refined lover of music, painting, theatre, dancing, and literature. The fine art of seduction required certain refinements, such as luxurious silk beddings and pillows, exotic gardens, flowers, perfumes, delicacies, and spirits, and was therefore, not a luxury afforded or available to the common person. Lovemaking was looked upon as an art that had to be learned and practiced. The text stressed cleanliness of the body, the ritual of courtship, and the mastery of the arts.

Sexual positions are a very small part of the text, yet it is the most infamous chapter. The graphic drawings of couples included in some of the later translations, are from the Muslim period, and are so completely foreign to the sacred text.

The text covered ways a man could seduce his wife and ways the wife could deceive her husband. Polygamy was widespread, particularly amongst the wealthy, but *Vatsyayana* extolled the benefits of having one wife, citing the numerous distractions and intrigues of the sovereign having to satisfy his entire harem.

The size of the male's *lingam* concerned the ancients as well, and dildos were common accessories. There were methods, probably impractical by today's standards, to increase the size of the penis. However, there was also an equal concern with the length and width of the woman's *yoni*. An emphasis was placed on the importance of matching the size of the *lingam* and *yoni*.

Vatsyayana describes three sizes of a man. The first was the hare, whose organ is six fingers width long; the bull, eight fingers width long; and the stallion, twelve fingers width long. Women were likewise categorized as being doe, mare, or cow-elephant.

The doe woman he describes as having beautiful, thick hair, thin body, golden skin, and sweetly scented secretions. The mare has strong nostrils and a *yoni* that is always hot. She has fat arms on which sweat appears, sexual secretions that smell of meat, and a bilious temperament. The cow-elephant is tall, has a massive frame, and her menses smells of an elephant's sweat.

It was not recommended that a hare mate with a cow-elephant, or a stallion with a doe. The perfect fit of the sexual organs meant a couple could make love for hours and was preferable to a mis-match of sizes for obvious reasons. However, there were positions to accommodate any mis-matched couple. Perhaps more importantly, the "perfect fit" also meant a couple should have similar attitudes and mental/spiritual compatibility.

The *Kama Sutra* is an exquisite treatise on moral eroticism, a refined and elegant art of seduction that has to be mastered. Many have taken this great piece of work by *Vatsyayana* and have distorted its original intent. It is an high art requiring many skills including no less than sixty-four arts, which include dancing, singing, playing musical instruments, preparing foods, knowledge of herbs, medicine, painting, sewing, costuming, sculpting, writing, gardening and more.

In our culture, there is an immature fascination with sexuality and the natural expression of our sexual needs seems to be an epidemic, probably because of the guilt and shame impressed upon society for centuries, primarily by religion. This denial of the senses creates an abnormal obsession with sex, just as repression is cause for perversion. There is a huge difference between vulgar explicitly and eroticism. Exploitation of sex for making money and gaining attention is not eroticism.

Vatsyayana covers petting, caresses, scratching biting, marriage, conduct of men, courtship, duties of the wife, along with other subjects for the citizen to master. Some of the practices are appropriate to today's culture; some clearly are not (for instance, using camel bones as an aphrodisiac). He shows us that eroticism is a delicate art requiring expertise in the sixty-four arts, as well as meditation and study of the sacred texts.

The Sixty-Four Arts of Saraswati

The Sixty-Four Arts are considered the Paths of Creative Energy, practical skills for the outer world, as they delight others while enriching our existence. They have been likened to flames of the inner sun, blazing brightly from the solar plexus. These skills burn up all negativity; these flames of the creative attitude purify the psyche, bringing about inner transformation. There are several variations (all basically the same) of the Sixty-Four Arts. The *Kama Sutra* describes them as:

1. Singing
2. Playing musical instruments
3. Dancing
4. Dancing, singing, playing an instrument at the same time
5. Writing and drawing
6. Henna tattooing (art of mehendi)
7. Adorning an image of a deity with rice and flowers
8. Decorating beds with flowers, or placing flowers upon the ground
9. Coloring and painting teeth, garments, hair, nails, and bodies
10. Setting stained glass onto a floor
11. The art of making beds, spreading out carpets and cushions for reclining
12. Playing music using glasses filled with water
13. Storing and collecting water in aqueducts, cisterns, and reservoirs
14. Creating pictures, trimming and decorating

15. Stringing of rosaries, necklaces, garlands, and wreaths

16. Wrapping turbans and chaplets

17. Set design, stage performance

18. Art of making earrings

19. Art of aromatherapy and making perfumes

20. Jewelry design and designing accessories of clothing

21. Magic or sorcery

22. Manual dexterity

23. Culinary arts (cooking, preparing foods)

24. Preparing flavorful and appealing drinks

25. Tailoring and sewing

26. Hand crafting out of yarn or thread

27. Ability to solve riddles and puzzles

28. Playing a game of repeating verses beginning with the same letter with which the last speaker's verse ended.

29. The art of mimicry or imitation

30. Reading, including chanting and intoning

31. Playing tricky word games

32. Swordsmanship and archery

33. Ability to draw inferences and reasoning

34. Carpentry and building skills

35. Architectural design

36. Knowledge about fine metals and gems

37. Knowledge of chemistry and mineralogy

38. Dyeing jewels, gems and beads

39. Knowledge of mines and quarries

40. Knowledge of gardening and horticulture

41. Art of cock fighting, quail fighting, and ram fighting

42. Art of teaching parrots and starlings to speak

43. Art of applying perfumed ointments to the body, and hair styling

44. Capacity to understand the written word without unnecessary letters between every syllable of a word.

46. Knowledge of language and dialects

47. Art of making flower carriages

48. Art of framing yantras and binding armlets

49. Mental exercises, such as completing lines of stanzas or verses

50. Composing poetry

51. Knowledge of dictionaries

52. Art of disguise

53. Art of changing the appearance of things, such as making cotton to appear as silk, coarse and common things to appear as fine and good

54. Skill in gambling

55. Art of spells through mantras or incantations

56. Skill in sports

57. Knowledge of etiquette and manners

58. Knowledge of the art of war, of arms, of armies

59. Knowledge of gymnastics

60. Art of reading facial features, phrenology

61. Ability to construct verses

62. Arithmetic

63. Creating artificial flowers

64. Sculpting figures and images in clay

A woman who mastered these arts held a high place in society. She was embodiment of the Goddess Saraswati. She was respected and was capable of securing her own livelihood no matter where she went.

The male who was skilled in these arts was a successful, powerful, and influential individual who lived a fulfilling life.

Sexual Asanas

A basis premise on the energy emitted and stimulated
through sexual activity of different combinations…
is that with Ki, or chi
the power lies in the subtlety,
NOT in the gross demonstration of that energy.
The male sexual energy is centered in his yang, the masculine form.
The male should embrace his maleness and feel the power of his maleness.
This yang energy initiates the flow of Shakti, or nature.
In the female's yin energy, sexual union becomes a subtle dance of opposite
energies.
The male thrusts his thunderbolt
Into his female's consciousness
This energy is then returned to Shiva from Shakti.
This cycle is repeated thru the thrusting (churning the chi)
freeing the sadhak from the bonds of this world.
This is the true nature of Tantra.
To illuminate and free the soul
with the ten-thousand suns of Shiva,
bathing it into a sea of bliss.
…J. Ram Sivananda

After religion and wealth, *kama,* or carnal pleasures is the third goal of human life. Without a proper knowledge of *kama,* one cannot experience all the other physical comforts. A married person is naturally inclined towards carnal pleasures. In other words, carnal pleasures constitute a basic reason for marriage.

Here are some basic sexual *asanas* in text and pictures.

1. *Mrigi*--Doe posture: Like a doe, a woman with a small *yoni* spreads her legs apart to facilitate the entry of the male. Thus, a horse-type *lingam* can have an easy entry.

2. *Hastini Asana*--She-elephant posture: When a woman with a large *yoni* (She –elephant) has a male partner with rabbit or bull type *lingam,* she should contract her body to the size of her partner.

3. *Samarati*--Equally matched: When both partners are of equal height, they may stretch their bodies naturally for maximum enjoyment.

4. *Badava Asan*--Cow posture: A cow-type female in union with *Ashva,* horse type male, should spread her legs as far apart as possible to facilitate the entry of a large phallus. If her partner is *Shashak,* rabbit type male, she should contract her body to the size of her partner. If he is bull type, they may spread and stretch their bodies normally to enjoy union. Shakti must allow Shiva in only when her *yoni* is well lubricated.

5. *Supine*--Lying flat on the back. In this posture, folding the knees and raising the thighs up while spreading both the legs apart facilitates an easy entry. In this posture, a doe type female can have an easy entry of even a horse-type male.

6. *Samputak*--Shiva and Shakti will both spread their legs straight during mating. This posture is useful when both the partners are about the same size.

7. *Piritak*--Hammering the *yoni* with the *lingam* can be exciting for Shiva and Shakti as long as it isn't their primary action.

8. *Vadava*--By contracting her *yoni,* a she-elephant type of female can please even a rabbit-type of male who feels an extraordinary enlargement in his organ.

9. *Bhugnak*--Female- without spreading her legs apart, shakti lays supine, bends her legs at the knees and lifts her thighs, resting her knees against the chest of her mate who then enters the her in half-sitting position.

10. *Jrimbhitak*--Shakti raises her legs and puts them on the shoulders of Shiva, who also sits with his knees up to the level of his partner's shoulders.

11. *Utpiritaka*--Shakti folds her legs and rests them against the chest of Shiva. He spreads his legs around her shoulders.

12. *Piritak*--Shakti sits in lotus posture and raises her thighs to expose her genitals

13. *Padmasana*--The female sits in *Padmasana* while lying supine and raises her thighs. Shiva mounts her by placing his hands through the folds of her legs and holding her shoulders.

14 *Imitation of Animals*--We can adopt the mannerisms of animals during their courtship and mating. We are, after all, animals, but we can approach sexuality with our human consciousness while still enjoying our union with our beloved in a healthy, natural, animalistic way.

Crow Asana

The crow *asana,* or "69" is very potent for circulating sexual energy. The sexual energy circulates between the lovers as their polarity doubles. Their mouths are both giving each other at the same time, and their *yoni* and *lingam* are receiving simultaneously. They are both in deep meditation while at the same time being completely pro-active.

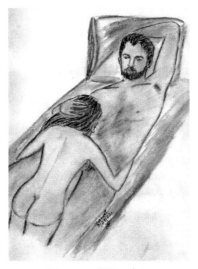

Lingam Worship

Shakti worships Shiva's *lingam*. The scriptures say that Shakti should worship Shiva's *lingam* everyday. This is an act of surrender and worship because she is honoring and revering his male essence.

[Fig.49: Yab Yum]

Classical *Yab Yum* position. Here is an excellent position for heart bonding. It is a good position for merging chakras, a very visual tactile and stimulating position. This is the lover's embrace.

....
PRACTICE
....

Challenge For Her:

1. You display your goddess prowess when you practice *Aswini Mudra* during intercourse. Begin by contracting your muscles without moving the body. Do not be afraid of your feminine power. As a goddess, you must acknowledge the power that you possess as a woman. Meditate on your femininity. You never need be in competition with the male. The thunderbolt is the initiator of life, and should be honored and treated with utmost respect.

2. Initiate sex. Your role is to get the *lingam* erect. It should not always be his "job". Remember, sex doesn't always have to end in orgasm. It can just be a brief "connection", a *play*, in the middle of the day.

Challenge For Him:

1. Allow the woman to take the lead during portions of your union. Although you will at times allow her to dominate, you are to accept your Shivahood, your manhood. Release your ego, be the yang to her yin. Honor her Shakti and accept your Shiva.

2. Practice going in soft, coming out hard. We will reiterate here, sex doesn't always have to end in orgasm, and there's no need to be concerned with the *lingam* being erect. The *connection* is what matters. Think of it like a big hug or a kiss. Think of it as a sweet way to just show your love. No pressure. Just allow love. *Connect.*

Practice For Couples:

1. Make love every day as a ritual. Take out the ego and practice. Become mindful and selfless. There is no need to have an orgasm. Sit in *yab yum*, become sensually aware, do *bandha* locks and ask your partner if they "felt that". That is how you learn what is pleasing to your other.

2. With the jewel in the lotus, Shakti, using only her internal muscles, will massage the *vajra*. There will be no outer movement. When Shiva is close to ejaculation, he will instead contract the anus; inhale through the nose bringing the energy to his third eye. He will say "ee-ah-oh" and relax the anus on the exhale. The energy in the semen will be transmuted and Shiva can ejaculate, if he chooses, without any loss of energy.

3. Practice the "thrust". Shiva is the one who primarily controls this motion outwardly. (Shakti controls the motion going on inside). He should think of the thrust as waves of the ocean and become the non-doer. He is creating a wave, an action of cosmic energy. Together with Shakti, they ride and ebb and flow of energy, pulling the energy of the *lingam* in a slow, intense motion of distinction.

4. Do not emulate and imitate the mindless hammering action that you see in porn movies. Unfortunately, many people learn their sexual technique and activity from what they see in the movies. What they see on film becomes their teacher, but it is far from ideal. In fact, it is anti-tantra. In Tantra, the partners relate to the sexual exchange as an energy dance, where they push and pull the energy back and forth through the thrust of the *lingam* and the squeeze of the *yoni*. It is a selfless act that is observed in this kinetic meditation (no mindless hammering).

//om//

Epilogue

We hope we have given you some tools to explore the practices of tantra. You may find that one or more of the practices may resonate with you better than others. The important thing is to keep your mind and your heart open to all that the Universe has in store for you. If you feel an inclination to pursue any or all these practices in more depth, by all means, please go for it. What a wonderful exploration and journey lies ahead of you.

In this book we have attempted to present the facets, the gems of light that make for a successful and orgasmic life, not just sexually, but spiritually as well. These two facets cannot be separated if you are to enjoy a completely blissful life.

These are the ancient teachings of the masters. These are their gifts to us. But certain disciplines are required on our part in order to imprint in our minds the correct behavior, attitude and conduct for living a gracious life. There are the actual practices we need to master, including the *maithun* itself.

Once you have the information, it is important to get out of your head and into your heart, for there is where the real magic and transformation takes place. This is our true center, where all the reflected light of the galaxies, the stars, and the planets affect our entire being. Nityananda said, "The heart is the hub of all places, Go there and roam."

Intellectual knowledge is not the same thing as experiential knowledge.

We can meditate, chant and do all the practices with reverence, and we can still be "light", and at ease about it. We can laugh even in the midst of a meditation, or dance, or during sex and savor the moment. Meditation doesn't have to be serious business and it should not be. Have fun with it, have fun with your partner. Laugh, love and live with passion.

Being spiritual doesn't mean you should become pious, have no sense of humor, or become rigid in body and mind.

In life, there will always be times when things seem to go wrong all at once. Don't let these rough times get to you. Remain philosophical and find solace in the profound teachings and practices of the spiritual masters. There is a Buddhist saying that when things go wrong all at once, it means something is waiting to be born.

When making love, be fully conscious and aware of every action. Never have sex unconsciously. Tantric sex can only be experienced when you have the knowledge, action and the right partner. Otherwise it becomes ordinary sex.

It is said what you get out of life is exactly what you put into it. So start living life in orgasmic bliss. Set up a daily meditation practice, do the exercises, and explore tantric sex with an honorable partner. This is the essence of tantra yoga.

May your life be blessed,
May you see only beauty
Know only peace
Hear only harmony
And feel only bliss.
May you live always in sex, love and joy.

Hari Om Tat Sat

//Om//

Biography

Chandi and J. Ram Sivananda

J. Ram Sivananda has an extensive background in psychology, martial arts, ancient philosophies and other traditions. He experienced a breakthrough in his spiritual practice over thirty years ago after a near death experience. Siva has successfully managed to weave together the tantric traditions of Taoism, Hinduism, Buddhism, and Shamanism, while developing and inventing advanced computer technology systems. Working as a scientist and engineer for many years, he trusts and believes in the metaphysical world which is much more elusive, but no less true and real.

He says, "I manifested Chandi after a series of failed relationships with women who took me away from my path. In the past I had merely 'settled' for the women I got involved with, but this time, I was very specific about what I was looking for in a partner, and set my intention on finding the Goddess I had been seeking for a lifetime. The fact that Chandi and I manifested each other is an attestation to the power of meditation and tantra practices.

"These methods of focusing clearly on what you desire are the magic of tantra yoga. It allows you to manifest your deepest desire. Through this practice you can change your life.

"This is a powerful ancient yogic practice that is still as effective today as it was thousands of years ago. It is our *sadhana* and we feel it is our *dharma* to share this knowledge with aspirants who are prepared to receive these gifts. If these words don't ring true to you, this path is probably not for you.

"The Universe contains physical energy (physics), the study of phenomenological reality, but there exists an equally powerful and concrete metaphysical reality. The practice of tantra yoga allows the aspirant to tap into this metaphysical reality".

Chandi Devi

Chandi Devi's search of a lifetime came to an end the moment she was introduced to Siddha Yoga and became a disciple of Swami Muktananda and Swami Chidvilasananda. The meditation practices of the siddhas, or enlightened ones, led her to deeply delve into the study of tantra yoga.

Chandi, a former well-known doll artist from Hawaii, completed a tantra teacher's training course with Bodhi Avinasha, and created several online businesses, including http://www.theworldoftantra.com. She is internationally known for her DVD's on tantra yoga and music CD's.

Chandi Devi has appeared on radio interviews such as "Spiritual Awakening Radio" and is a featured writer for and editor-in-chief of http://karmacaffe.com, a new interactive spiritual network that focuses on love, wealth, health for a meaningful lifestyle. She is also the co-host of radio shows "The Karmacaffe Spiritual Hour" and "Tantraworld".

Bibliography

Abhinavagupta Trident of Wisdom, by Jaideva Singh, SUNY 1989
A Golden Mind, A Golden Life, Gurumayi Chidvilasanada, SYDA
    1999
Auspicious Wisdom, by Douglas Renfrew Brooks, SUNY 1992
Chakra Workout, by Blawyn and Jones, Llewellyn Publications 1996
Chandi Path, by Swami Satyananda Saraswati, Devi Mandir 1997
Chandi Path, Study of Chapter One, by Swami Satyananda Saraswati,
    Devi Mandir 2003
Cosmic Puja, by Swami Satyananda Saraswati, Devi Mandir 2001
Devi Gita, by Swami Satyananda Saraswati, Devi Mandir 1991
Encountering the Goddess, by Thomas B. Coburn, SUNY 1991
Getting in the Gap, Wayne Dyer, Hay House 2003
Goddesses Mirror, David Kinsley, SUNY 1989
Guru Gita, Eric Baylin, SYDA 1997
Healing Mantras, by Thomas Ashley-Farrand, Ballantine 1999
How to Know God, Deepak Chopra, Harmony Books 2001
I Am That, Swami Muktananda, SYDA 1992
Jewel in the Lotus, by Bodhi Avinasha and Sunyata Saraswati, Sunstar
    1987
Jnaneshwar's Gita, Swami Kripananda, SUNY 1989
Kali Puja, by Swami Satyananda Saraswati, Devi Mandir 1996
Kama Sutra, by Alain Danielou, Inner Traditions 1993
Kashmir Shaivism, by Swami Lakshman Jee, SUNY 1985
Kundalini and the Chakras, Genevieve Lewis Paulson, Llewellyn
    Publications 1998

Kundalini, Energy of the Depths, by Lillian Silburn, SUNY 1988
Kundalini, Secret of Life, Swami Muktananda, SYDA 1979, 1994
Lakshmi, B.K. Chaturvedi, Books for All 1996
Lakshmi Puja, by Swami Satyananda Saraswati, Devi Mandir 2001
Lalitasahasranama, by R. Ananthakrishna Sastry, Adyar Library and
    Research Center 1988
Law of Success, Paramahansa Yogananda, Self Realization Foundation
    1980
Layayoga, by Shyam Sundar Goswami, Inner Traditions 1999
Life is a Gift, by Osho, Full Circle 1997
Light of the Guru, Peggy Bendet, SYDA 1994
Meditation Revolution, Douglas Renfrew Brooks, et al. SYDA
    1997
Meditations on Shiva, Constantina Rhodes Bailly, SUNY 1995
My Lord Loves a Pure Heart, by Gurumayi Chidvilasananda, SYDA
    1994
Mysticism of Sound and Music, Hazrat Inayet Khan, Shambala
    Publications 1991
Nectar of Chanting, by Swami Muktananda SYDA 1975
New Chakra Healing, by Cyndi Dale, Llewellyn Publications 1998
New Testament, Holman Bible, LifeWay Press 2000
Nothing Exists That Is Not Shiva, by Swami Muktananda, Siddha Yoga
    Publications 1997
Passionate Enlightenment, Miranda Shaw, Princeton University Press
    1994
Play of Consciousness, by Swami Muktananda, Siddha Yoga
    Publications
Sakti, the Power in Tantra, Pandit Rajmani Tigunait, PhD, Himalyan
    Institute 1998
Saraswati, B.K. Chaturvedi, Books for All 1996
Sexual Secrets, by Nik Douglas and Penny Singer, Inner Traditions
    1979
Shakti Mantras, Thomas Ashley-Farrand, Random House 2003
Shree Guru Gita, SYDA 1992
Shree Maa, the Guru and the Goddess, by Swami Satyananda Saraswati,
    Devi Mandir 1995
Shri Bhagavad Gita, by Winthrop Sargeant, SUNY 1993

Shri Lalita Sahasranamavalih, Shanti Mandir, N.Y.
Shiva, The Wild God of Ecstasy, Wolf-Dieter Storl, PhD. Inner
    Traditions 2004
Siddha Meditation, Swami Muktananda, Gurudev Siddhapeeth 1977
Tantra Bliss, by Bodhi Avinasha, Ipsalu Publishing, 2003
Tantra, the Path of Ecstasy, Georg Feuerstein, Shambala Publications
    1998
Tantric Gems Online
Tao of Sexual Massage, Stephen Russell and Jugen Kolb, GAIA 1992
Tao Te Ching, Lao Tsu, Vintage Books, 1972
Truth About Chakras, by Anodea Judith, Llewellyn 1998
Triadic Heart of Shiva, by Paul Eduardo Muller-Ortega, SUNY 1989
Tantra Unveiled, by Pandit Tigunait, Himalayan Institute 1999
There's a Spiritual Solution, Wayne Dyer, Harper Collins 2001
Upanishads, Swami Prabhavananda, the President
Virtue, Success, Pleasure, Liberation, Alain Danielou, Inner Traditions
    1993
Wheels of Life, by Judith Anodea, Llewellyn Publications 1999
Wisdom of the Ages, Wayne Dyer, Harper Collins 1998

Glossary

Abhinavagupta--the most eminent scholar and philosopher in history who authored the major texts on tantra and was a great exponent of *Kashmir Shaivism* (c.950-1015)

Abhinivesa--fear of death

Adharmic--behaving in an irresponsible manner, the opposite of *dharma*

Advaita--a philosophy in which there is no duality, only a singular state of consciousness

Agama--the Shiva Tantras, narrative between Parvati the questioner, and Shiva, who replies

Agami Karma--the actions that we perform in this lifetime that will affect our future incarnations

Ajna--the Third Eye energy center located behind the forehead, also called psychic center--one of the seven energy centers

Akrodha--non-anger

Anahat--the heart chakra energy center located in the heart region; also called pranic center-- fourth of the seven energy centers

Ananda--bliss, ecstasy

Archetypes--aspects of spirit, which is the substance of which the soul is composed. In our human life, we can say that archetypes are aspects or elements of life

Archetypal field--each archetype is surrounded by an energy field. This is analogous to the magnetic field that surrounds a magnet

Ardhakurmakasana--Half-Tortoise Pose

Artha--daily comforts, money, material wealth and prosperity

Atharva Veda--a collection of verses was used to satisfy the daily needs of the people

Asan--sitting in God's presence, sexual or sitting yogic postures, a balanced position for smooth energy flow in specific areas of the body and mind

Ashtanga Marga--the Eightfold path of Buddha

Asmita--confusing the non-*Atman* with *Atman*

Asteya--not to steal anything physically or mentally

Asuras--inner demons that besiege our minds and hearts

Asvini Mudra--an exercise contracting the anal sphincter to activate the first chakra

Atharva Veda--healing formulas and prayers from the Vedas

Atman--the Self, Divine Consciousness residing in the Self

Aum--primordial sound

Avidya--ignorance

Ayurveda--an ancient medical treatise summarizing the Hindu art of healing and prolonging life; sometimes regarded as the 5th Veda

Baba Muktananda--the saint from Maharastra who established Siddha Yoga and brought *shaktipat* to the West

Babaji--Avatar who, like Christ, was born to assist man in his spiritual evolution

Bandha--a posture in which organs and muscles are contracted to create energy lock in a specific area

Bandhuka--red hibiscus-like flower

Bhagavad Gita--Songs of the Blessed Lord, Sanskrit theosophical poems of 700 verses, regarded by Hindus as their Bible

Bhakti--spiritual love, devotion

Bhakti--yogic path of devotion

Bhava--feeling and disposition

Bhujangasana--cobra pose

Bhupura--the outer gates of three lines in the *Shri Yantra*

Bija--seed syllable

Bindu--dot in the center of the triangle in the *Shri Yantra*

Bodhisattva--spiritual warrior

Brahma--the Creator, one of the *Trimurti,* three gods in Hindu pantheon

Brahmin--aristocracy class of Hindu priests

Bubbling Spring--an acupuncture point in Chinese medicine at the cavity found in the bottom (ball) of each foot in the depression in the center of the sole

Buddha (624-544 BCE)--One who has attained the perfect state of enlightenment, also known as Siddhartha Gautam Buddha, Founder of Buddhism

Chakras--energy centers or wheels of life located along the spine in the etheric body

Champa--plumeria flower, frangipani

Chandi--the Divine Mother, consort of Shiva

Candamaharosana-tantra--tantric text on mode of worship

Chidakasa--the space behind the forehead

Chin mudra--hand gesture in which the first finger is kept at the root of the thumb, the last three fingers are unfolded

Chiti--the Universal Consciousness

Dakshina Marga--the right-hand practices of meditation

Damah--control over the inner enemies

Darshan--the vision and permanent Union with God

Deva--shining one, celestial being

Devayoni--feminine aspect of God

Devi--the Supreme Goddess, Lord Shiva's consort, *Shakti,* cosmic energy

Devi Gita--song of the Goddess, verses from the Seventh Skanda of the Shri Devi Bhagavatam

Dharana--feelings, emotions, physical sensations in body. Performing the bandhas, locks practice of concentration

Dharma--morality, ethics, religion. Our actions and morals that influence our karma

Dharmic--behaving in a virtuous, responsible manner

Dhii--benevolent intellect

Dhrti--patience

Dhyana--meditation, knowledge and understanding of what you are doing and why, application of your understanding

Diksha--spiritual awakening through initiation by a qualified guru, Divine transmission of master to disciple (see also *shaktipat*)
Doshas--constituents that govern our metabolism

Energy tones--emotions and feelings

Gandharva Tantra--an important work of the school of *Shri Vidya* having a left slant
Ganapat--another name for *Ganesh*
Ganesh--elephant-headed god, the remover of obstacles, and god of wisdom
Gayatri Mantra--This supreme mantra is called "The Mother of the Vedas"
Gita--a sacred song or poem but more usually refers to philosophical or religious doctrines in verse form
Guhya Vidya--secret knowledge
Gunas--attributes of behavior, dispositions, characteristics of all beings, viz. *tamas, rajas, sattva*
Guru--an spiritual teacher who has attained Oneness with God, is from a lineage of Masters and is learned in the scriptures
Guru Gita--sacred text, a garland of mantras extolling the greatness of the Guru
Gurumayi Chidvilasananda--current spiritual master of the Siddha Yoga path

Hari Om Tat Sat--Truth is better than religion
Homas--also *homams,* fire rituals, that can directly affect changes in this life, by making offerings with a clear intent, to the deities

Iccha--the energy of *Mahalakshmi,* desire, the basic will or impulse to create
Ida--the negative pole on left side of the vertebrae, moving upwards from the *Muladhar* to the
Indriyanigraha--controlling the five sensory organs (hearing, feeling by touch, seeing, tasting, smelling) and five motor organs (speech, grasping, locomotion, excretion, procreation) mentally and spiritually

Jalandhara--throat lock to restrict the flow of breath, done by resting the chin on the upper sternum (chest)

Japa--repetition of a certain number of highly charged words, usually counted using a mala

Jiva--individual, unit being

Jnana--the basic knowledge or awareness of creation

Jung, Carl (1875-1961)--psychiatrist who created new concepts about mind and life

Jyotish--Vedic Astrology

Kabir (1440-1518)--a great poet-saint whose followers included both Hindus and Muslins

Kailas--the abode of Shiva on the Himalayan mountaintop

Kali--She who removes the darkness, a Goddess in the Hindu pantheon

Kama--desires, love

Kamakala--the aspect of desire

Kama Sutra--treatise on erotic arts written in 400 A.D. by Vatsyayana

Kapha--bodily constitution of water and earth

Karma--cosmic law stating that our actions determine our experiences and destiny, teaching, learning

Kashmir Shaivism--philosophy of non-dualism attributed to Lord Shiva

Kaula--the most advanced form of the left-hand practice of tantra, the path of the householder, that only those who have complete control of the senses are eligible to practice

Ketaki flower--Pandanus odoratissimus, umbrella plant, magnolia flower

Khechari mudra--mudra to stimulate the kundalini shakti by touching the roof of the tongue as far back in the throat as possible

Kirtan--spiritual singing and dancing

Klesa--misery or suffering

Krishna-the eighth incarnation of Lord Vishnu

Kriyas--physical or emotional involuntary reactions that become activated when the Kundalini starts to awaken activity, dynamic yogic practice

Kriyamana karma--the result of our present actions that will take effect in this lifetime, sometimes called "Instant Karma"

Kriya Shakti--is the energy of Mahakali, the goddess in action. Action must take place in order for anything to manifest. Mahakali gives us the gift of transformation, the basic power to create

Ksama--forgiveness

Kulatattva—school or philosophy the principles of existence

Kumari--The virgin heart is the state of innocence and purity, the childlike state of Goddess

Kundalini as the microcosmic version of Shakti

Kundalini yoga--the yoga of utilizing kundalini energy for spiritual transformation

Lakshmi--Hindu goddess of prosperity, fortune and abundance

Lalita--the Goddess Supreme, she who "plays"

Lila--literally "play", "amusement" or "pastime". The idea that the apparent creation is a diversion for a creator, a means for Him to enjoy Himself

Lingam--the Divine Phallus

Lord Maheshvara--another name for Shiva

Madhya--wine, or the divine nectar

Maha--great

Mahabandha--the Triple Lock-*Mulabandha, Uddiyana, Jalandhara* done simultaneously

Mahabharatha--One of the two great epics of Hinduism, consisting of 18 voluminous chapters. The *Gita* is a small part of this epic believed to be composed about 1360 BCE.

Mahadevi--The Three Goddesses, represent the cycle of creation, preservation and transformation.

Mahakali--The Great Goddess of destruction and transformation

Mahalakshmi--The Great Goddess of wealth and preservation

Mahamudra--Put both hands forward with all the fingers entwined. The thumb and middle fingers are then joined and extended

Maharaj, Tukaram (1608-1649)--poet-saint from Maharastra, India

Mahasaraswati--The Great Goddess of creation, knowledge and the arts

Maithun--communion between man and woman or the individual and the Supreme

Makars--modes of practice

Malati--Jasmine flower

Mamsa--meat or tongue, which means one should control one's speech

Mala--a rosary, of 56 or 108 beads

Manipur--the plexus of heat, the energy center in the spinal column located behind the navel

Marga--The Truth of the Path

Matsya--fish or the two subtle nerves along the spine, the *ida* and *pingala,* that crosses and ends at the nostrils

Maya--illusion

Meditation--the means for attaining *moksha* by sitting still and emptying the mind

Mishra path--the transcendence path, dedicated to service to humanity

Moksha--higher consciousness, liberation, the goal of all religion, to be one with God

Mudra- -hand and bodily postures, literally means "gesture". *Mudra* expresses and channelizes cosmic energy within the mind and body

Mulabandha--energy lock created by the contraction of the perineum in the male and the cervix in the female

Mula--root

Muladhar--first chakra at the base of the spine where the kundalini shakti (serpent power) resides, situated in the perineal floor in men and the cervix in women

Nada yoga--the yoga of sound

Nadis--720 million principle channels that run along the spine

Nadi Shodana--Breath of Union

Nataraj--Shiva in his dancing form

Nidra--sleep

Nigama--Questions and Answers where Shiva becomes the questioner, and Parvati replies

Nirguna--unmanifest

Nishkala--released
Nityananda (d.1961)--saint of Maharastra, guru of Swami Muktananda
Niyama--internal moral/ethical strength
Nyasa--establishing the deities in the chakras within the subtle body

Ojas--primal vigor energy, vitality, basic life force
Om--the universal mantra, cosmic vibration of the universe
Osho (December 11, 1931- January 19, 1990)--controversial spiritual master

Padmasana--lotus pose, a seated meditative posture
Parabhakti--supreme love
Pashupati--another name for Shiva, Lord of the Animals
Pingala--the positive pole, running downwards alongside the right side of the spine from the *Muladhar* chakra to the Ajna chakra in the head by intersecting various chakras on the way
Pitta--bodily constitution of fire and water
Pranayam--breath retention and control, altering breath patterns
Prarabdha karma--is the portion of sanchita karma that is affecting us in the present life
Prasad--an offering usually food to and from the Guru or higher power
Pujas--ceremonies, rituals
Pundits--experts
Prakriti--nature, primary principle of force, mind and matter
Prana--vital energy force sustaining life and creation
Pranayam--technique of breathing and breath control that regulates energy flow and aims at maintaining energy balance
Pratyahar--vision, hearing, mantras, having the image/picture internally and externally, knowledge and understanding the meaning of the mantras, chanting, inscribing yantras
Puranas--Hindu spiritual teachings in question and answer form, a Smriti scripture, or that which is remembered
Purusha--self, pure consciousness, primary consciousness principle

Raga--attachment

Rajas--activity, emotions, desire, selfishness and passion, the principle of energy

Raj Vidya--princely knowledge

Ramakrishna--19th century Bengali mystic

Ramayana--one of the greatest epics of India, celebrating the life and exploits of Rama, the seventh incarnation of Vishnu

Rig Veda--one of the four Vedas, containing over 1000 hymns, derived from the Sanskrit root word "rik" meaning "to praise" is divided up into ten books

Rishis--sages who lived in the Himalayas

Rumi (1207-1273)-- one of the greatest poet-saints of Persia and Turkey

Sadashiva--the founder of Tantra and Yoga systems was the first one to introduce music, dance, medical and marriage systems to human civilization. See Shiva.

Sadhak--seeker

Sadhana--spiritual practices literally 'leading straight to a goal', refers to the spiritual disciplines followed as part of a 'path' toward Self-Realization

Sadhu--a holy being, a monk, ascetic

Saguna--manifest

Sahasrar--the thousand-petalled lotus in the crown chakra

Sakala--bound

Sakshat Param Tattva--supreme principle of thought

Sama Veda--one of the four Veda, a collection of hymns sung to beautiful melodies

Samadhi--experience of becoming One with Consciousness, the feeling of Infinite Peace

Samaya path--strictly focuses on internal meditation in the *Sahasrar* after the kundalini is awakened

Samkhya--one of the oldest orthodox philosophical systems in Hinduism

Samyak--complete thought, looking at things from all sides, and seeing that those sides are themselves positive and negative within. The opposite of right is not wrong, but not right. *Sahajo*--spontaneous bliss

Sama Veda--collection of 1,540 verses that were chanted during rituals

Samsara- the world of illusion, the eternal cycle of birth, suffering, death and rebirth

Samskara--impressions of thoughts and actions that remain in the subtle body

Samyak Ajiva--conducting honest occupation on all realms

Samyak Darsha--spiritual insight, seeing everything through the eyes of God

Samyak Karmanta--completion of actions, proper conduct

Samyak Samadhi—perfection in meditation

Samyak Sankalpa--having perfect intention and will

Samyak Smrti--perfect control of thoughts

Samyak Vak--perfect expression of organs of speech

Samyak Vyayama--taking care of body, mind and soul

Sanchita karma--the accumulated karma of this lifetime and previous lifetimes that affect us in this lifetime

Sankalpa--will, intention

Sanskrit--the language of the ancient Indian texts

Saraswati--Goddess who bestows knowledge of fine arts and power of speech

Sastras--textual studies, also spelled *shastras*

Satchitananda--existence, consciousness, bliss absolute

Satguru--a true Guru, the enlightened teacher, also spelled *sadguru.*

Satipatthana--mindfulness

Sattva--attribute of sweetness and purity of mind, steadiness, unwavering purity, principle of sentience

Satyam--love or truth

Self--the atman, divine consciousness

Self realization--is path of completeness in this lifetime so that we will not have to endure another birth in this world

Seva--selfless service

Shakta—traditon of worshipping the Goddess as the supreme Deity

Shakta sadhaks--seekers who are attentive to Goddess worship

Shakti--the feminine principle of nature and energy, potency giving birth to creation, the unlimited creative power of Supreme Consciousness, creating through the three forces of *jnana, iccha* and *kriya*

Shaktipat--the transmission of spiritual power from a Guru to the disciple. There are nine degrees of this descent of grace. *Kashimir Shaivism* further breaks down this process of awakening into twenty-seven degrees of mild, medium and intense.

Shaman--a medium between the physical and spirit worlds

Shankaracharya--the great Indian philosopher who spread the theory of non-dualism throughout India

Shaoca--external and internal cleanliness, cleanliness of the body, and environment and cleanliness of the thoughts

Shiva--the masculine energy, male principle of universal consciousness, pure, unlimited consciousness itself, the Self of all. In the trinity of Gods, *Shiva* is the destroyer of ignorance

Shiva is known by many different names according to his function. When, for example, he expresses himself through space and time, he is known as *Ishvara*. He is called *Sadashiva* when he functions through air, which incorporates the principles of both sound and touch. *Shiva* is known as *Rudra* when he operates through fire, which incorporates the principles of sound, touch and form. Also spelled *Siva*

Shavasana--corpse pose

Shree Maa--the most respected Holy Mother from the lineage of Ramakrishna

Shri--an honorific term, also spelled Shree or Sri

Shri Vidya—system of school of goddess-centered Shakta Tantrism

Shri Yantra—also *Shri Chakra*, triadic system of the Universe represented in a geometric mandala consisting of interlocking triangles and lines

Siddha--enlightened one, one who has mastery over the senses and ego

Siddhantachar--on the left hand path of tantra there are three levels of advancement. This is the middle level

Siddha Yoga--the Maha Yoga, or great yoga, includes all the other branches of yoga. Brought to the West by Swami Muktananda and now headed by Swami Chidvilasananda

Siddhasana--accomplished position

Siddhis--occult, magical or supernatural powers

Six inner enemies--desire, anger, delusion, pride, greed and envy

Sixty-four arts--special skills denoted in the Kama Sutra that are beneficial in the erotic arts

Smriti--is the Sanskrit word for "that which is remembered". Smriti scriptures are derived from the Vedas and were written to explain and clarify the Vedas

So'ham--the natural vibration of the Self, that occurs spontaneously with the inflow and outflow of the breath

Sruti--is the Sanskrit word for "revealed scripture"

Sufi Mevlevi Order--whirling dervishes

Surya--sun

Sushumna--the central pole is within the vertebral column, the main energy channel through which kundalini Shakti flows

Svadhistan--the fluidal plexus, the second chakra

Swadhyaya--chanting and recitation of ancient texts

Swami--respectful term for a monk

Swami Satyananda Saraswati--spiritual teacher from the lineage of *Adi Shankaracharya*.

Swamiji dedicates his life to the Divine Mother. A master of Sanskrit he has authored and translated many books on the Devi

Tamas--dullness, inactivity, inertia, laziness

Tantra--the mystical path extolled as the short path to self-realization, consisting of religious treatises striving for both liberation and enjoyment, the science of creation

Tantra Sastra--treatises on the practices of tantra

Tantriks--seekers on the path of tantra

Tapas, Tapasya--hardships and challenges, austerities

Tattvas--principles of life, existence

Tejas--radiance, sharpness

Traduttori--distortion

Tridosha--combination of the five elements create three major physiological functions in our body known as *Vata, Pitta* and *Kapha.*

Trikona--triangles

Trimurti--three gods in the Hindu pantheon, Brahma, Vishnu, Shiva

Tripura--Lalita, the feminine trinity of goddesses

Uddiyana--abdominal retraction lock, drawing in of the abdomen towards the backbone after exhaling

Ullman, Samuel--poet and author

Upanishad--The Upanishads are the divine revelations received by the ancient saints and seers, the sacred essence of the Vedas, dealing with metaphysical questions, lit. "sitting near"

Vajroli Mudra--thunderbolt, or *vajra* exercises, squeezing the urethral sphincter muscles

Vatsyayana--Brahmin priest who wrote the *Kama Sutra* in 400 A.D., a compendium of erotic arts

Vata--bodily constitution has the quality of wind and air

Vedanta--one of six orthodox philosophical systems or viewpoints rooted in the Upanishads as opposed to *Mimamsa*, which relies on the *Vedas* and *Brahmanas*

Vedas--sacred ancient religious scriptures of India, from the Sanskrit root word "Vid" meaning "to know", containing four major texts-*Rig, Yajur, Sama, Atharva*, which are further divided into *Samhita, Brahmana, Aranayaka and Upanishads.*

Vamakeshvari Tantra--a tantra work having a left slant

Vidya--spiritual knowledge

Vipassana—insight meditation

Vishnu--one of the trinity of gods

Visshuda--fifth chakra at the throat area

Viveka--good judgment, discrimination; the function of *buddhi*, having the ability to differentiate between the unreal and the real

Yagya--also *yagnas*, inner fire, or external ceremonial worship

Yajur Veda--scriptures that specify formulas, rituals and rules for harmonizing the functions of the Universe, a compilation of mantras and methods used by priests in performing Vedic rituals and sacrifices

Yama--external moral/ethical discipline

Yang--masculine energy

Yantras--geometric designs that are instruments and tools for contemplation, concentration and meditation, a geometric design that binds an inner connection with the Supreme Principle.

Yin--feminine energy

Yoga Nidra--sleep of the yogi

Yogasana--a balanced position for smooth energy flow in specific areas of the body and mind

Yogi or yogin--one who practices yoga and has achieved a high level of spiritual insight.

Yogini--the feminine form of yogi

Yoni--the uterus, vagina

Zen--Japanese sect of *Mahayana Buddhism* that aims at meditation by direct intuition

Index

Hari Om Tat Sat 300, 310
Hazrat Inayat Khan xxi, 124
Hill, Napoleon xxi, 160
Homas 90, 150
Honor 10, 18, 21, 26, 161, 208, 224,
    235, 242, 245, 246, 252, 265,
    269, 271, 276, 277, 279, 282,
    283, 285

I

Iccha 157, 204, 207, 282, 310
Ida 310
Inner enemies xix, 30, 32, 91, 108,
    109, 309, 317
Intellectual slavery 99, 185
intimacy xviii, xx, 56, 64, 165, 169,
    170, 171, 251, 264, 265, 277,
    282, 285
Isometrics 233

J

J. Ram Sivananda i, xxi, 226, 246, 301
Jalandhara 128, 129, 311, 312
Japa 311
Jesus Christ xxi, 4, 109, 192
Jiva 27, 45, 104, 121, 146, 205
Jnana xix, xx, 316
Joy i, 27, 33, 54, 58, 102, 105, 108,
    114, 123, 159, 160, 162, 164,
    165, 167, 193, 211, 213, 221,
    260, 275, 276, 282, 300
Jung, Carl xxi, 81, 82, 171, 197, 199

K

Kabir xxi, 19, 40, 72, 196, 311
kama xviii, 51, 235, 272, 273, 287,
    288, 293
Kama Sutra 275, 287, 288, 289, 290,
    303, 311, 318, 319
Karma xviii, 7, 13, 17, 31, 70, 81, 82,
    83, 84, 85, 86, 87, 88, 89, 90,
    91, 104, 117, 147, 148, 149,
    151, 188, 202, 207, 252, 253,
    260, 274, 279, 309, 312, 314,

316
Kaula, kula 30
Kirtan 122, 311
Kriyamana Karma 90
Kriyas 311
Kriya Shakti 312
Kumari xxi, 196, 312
Kundalini 5, 12, 13, 14, 27, 44, 45,
    46, 47, 48, 49, 72, 74, 103, 127,
    129, 221, 279, 303, 304, 311,
    312

L

Lalita 30, 125, 126, 305, 312, 318
Lawrence, D.H. xxi, 180
Lingam 5, 25, 61, 126, 170, 171, 203,
    209, 242, 246, 247, 258, 259,
    263, 264, 276, 278, 281, 282,
    283, 284, 285, 288, 293, 294,
    295, 296, 297, 298
Lord Maheshvara 312
Love i, xviii, xx, 4, 6, 12, 20, 30, 33,
    36, 37, 44, 45, 59, 61, 62, 63,
    64, 74, 83, 84, 87, 88, 89, 90,
    91, 100, 102, 111, 112, 113,
    124, 148, 149, 154, 157, 159,
    160, 162, 164, 165, 166, 167,
    168, 169, 170, 172, 174, 175,
    178, 179, 188, 189, 190, 191,
    192, 193, 194, 195, 196, 197,
    202, 208, 211, 218, 223, 225,
    226, 227, 229, 231, 235, 239,
    245, 248, 249, 251, 252, 254,
    255, 262, 265, 269, 270, 272,
    275, 276, 277, 278, 279, 283,
    287, 288, 289, 297, 298, 300,
    308, 311, 314, 316

M

Mahabandha 131, 141, 247, 312
Mahadevi 30, 312
Mahakali 30, 31, 312
Mahalakshmi 29, 30, 31, 310, 312
Maharaj, Jnaneshwar xxi, 18

Z

Zimmer, Heinrich xvii, xxi

Recommended Sites:
http://www.theworldoftantra.com
http://www.karmacaffe.com

For inquiries or to be added to our mailing list, please send your
email address to:
info@theworldoftantra.com or
chandi@karmacaffe.com

Printed in the United Kingdom by
Lightning Source UK Ltd., Milton Keynes
136545UK00001B/214/P